About Island Press

Since 1984, the nonprofit organization Island Press has been stimulating, shaping, and communicating ideas that are essential for solving environmental problems worldwide. With more than 1,000 titles in print and some 30 new releases each year, we are the nation's leading publisher on environmental issues. We identify innovative thinkers and emerging trends in the environmental field. We work with world-renowned experts and authors to develop cross-disciplinary solutions to environmental challenges.

Island Press designs and executes educational campaigns, in conjunction with our authors, to communicate their critical messages in print, in person, and online using the latest technologies, innovative programs, and the media. Our goal is to reach targeted audiences—scientists, policy makers, environmental advocates, urban planners, the media, and concerned citizens—with information that can be used to create the framework for long-term ecological health and human well-being.

Island Press gratefully acknowledges major support from The Bobolink Foundation, Caldera Foundation, The Curtis and Edith Munson Foundation, The Forrest C. and Frances H. Lattner Foundation, The JPB Foundation, The Kresge Foundation, The Summit Charitable Foundation, Inc., and many other generous organizations and individuals.

The opinions expressed in this book are those of the author(s) and do not necessarily reflect the views of our supporters.

Build Beyond Zero

New Ideas for Carbon-Smart Architecture

Build Beyond Zero

New Ideas for Carbon-Smart Architecture

Bruce King and Chris Magwood

ISLANDPRESS | Washington | Covelo

Library of Congress Control Number: 2021952307

All Island Press books are printed on environmentally responsible materials.

Manufactured in the United States of America
10 9 8 7 6 5 4 3 2 1

Research and writing for this book was supported by the non-profit Ecological Building Network (EBNet) and Builders for Climate Action.

All illustrations by Bruce King except as noted

Keywords: agricultural byproducts; architecture and engineering education; biological architecture; carbon capture, utilization, and storage (CCUS); carbon-smart; circular economy; climate justice; concrete; construction emissions; embodied carbon; embodied energy; green building; lab-grown materials; life cycle assessment (LCA); modular or prefab construction; plastics; purpose-grown crops; waste stream fibers; wood and mass timber; whole-building footprint

Contents

Acknowledgments   ix

Dedication   xi

Acronyms and Definitions   xiii

Foreword by Kathrina Simonen   xix

Introduction   1

1   The Story of Carbon: The Birth of the Universe, of Carbon, and of Life   9

2   A Brief History of Green Building: Waking Up to Climate Emergency   19

    Box 2.1: The Existing Building Solution by Larry Strain   27

3   Life Cycle Analysis: Tracking Carbon's Stocks and Flows   33

4   Metals and Minerals: Steeling Ourselves   53

5   Concrete: Many Ways to Make a Rock   65

    Box 5.4: The Case for Modern Earthen Building by Lola Ben-Alon   89

    Box 5.5: More than a Floor by Gayatri Datar   92

    Box 5.6: Entering the North American Market as an Earth Block

           Producer by Lisa Morey   95

    Box 5.7: Can We Grow Carbon-Storing Buildings? by

           Wil V. Srubar III   97

6   Biological Architecture: Wood and Mass Timber, Agricultural
     Byproducts, Purpose-Grown Crops, Waste Stream Fibers, and
     Lab-Grown Materials   105
     Box 6.2: Landscape Architecture: Connecting to the Carbon
                Conversation by Pamela Conrad   140

7   Witches' Brew: Plastics, Chemistry, and Carbon   151

8   Construction: On Site and Under Zero   163

9   Education: We All Need Schooling to Make This Possible   173

10   Circular Economy: Extending the Lifespan of Captured Carbon   185

11   Policy and Governance: Twenty-First-Century Cat Herding   195

12   A Just Transition: Building a Better Society Means More than
     Capturing Carbon   215
     Box 12.3: A Manifesto for the Pivotal Decade by Ann Edminster   226

13   The Next Three Decades: Where Do We Go from Here?   231

14   What's Next? *Wow. Just Wow.*   243

     Endnotes   247
     Contributors   253
     Authors   257

Acknowledgments

As is usually the case with books like this, we owe an enormous debt to a lot of people: dear friends and family who suffered our extended absences (or our babbling and moaning presences) and the fast-growing global hive mind that is working out carbon emissions from the built environment. Thank you each and all, be ye held forever blameless for any errors and oversights in the pages that follow.

Contributing authors
Lola Ben-Alon, Pamela Conrad, Gayatri Datar, Ann Edminster, Lisa Morey, Kate Simonen, Wil V. Srubar III, and Larry Strain

Contributing family
Sarah Weller King and Jen Feigin

And for the support, teaching, good work, and encouragement
Javaria Ahmed, Jane Anderson, Jay Arehart, David Arkin, Maurice and Joy Bennett, Erik Bowden, Massey Burke, Stephanie Carlisle, Ty Cashman, Brent Constanz, Anthony Dente, Michael Dosier, David and Pat Eisenberg, Pliny Fisk, Juan (Johnny) Gonzalez, Jason Grant, Geoffrey Guest, Alana Guzzetta, Anthony Hickling, Andrew Himes, Hal Hinkle, Bjørn Kierulf, Lucy King, Peter Kloepfer, Tim Krahn, Julie Kriegh, Patric Langevin, Meghan Lewis, Shane MacInnes, Ladi March-Goldwire, Fernando Martirena, Ed Mazria, Ace McArleton, Gavin McIntyre,

Anthony Pak, Liebe Patterson, Jacob Deva Racusin, Richard Riman, Kirsten Ritchie, Brad Roberts, Karen Scrivener, Henry Siegel, Stacy Smedley, Nehemiah Stone, David and Nancy Thacher, John and Carry Thacher, Anni Tilt, David Warner, Margery Weller, Elizabeth Whalen, Craig White, Frances Yang, Everyday Zen Sangha, and Ryan Zizzo

To all of you who choose compassion—
kindness is more fun.

Hafiz said:

Even after all this time
the Sun never says to the Earth
"You owe me."
Look at what happens to a love like that.
It lights the whole world.

Acronyms and Definitions

Note to reader: We offer this list at the outset to clarify a few commonly used terms but not to be a comprehensive glossary. We also hope it will be helpful to provide a bit of explication for some of the acronyms in this fast-developing world of carbon and buildings. Speaking of which, let's start by defining, for our purposes here anyway, *carbon* and *buildings*.

Building: A building is a device for protecting human beings: from sun and rain, from wind and snow, from heat and cold, and all too often from each other. Many see buildings as art forms, and by design or not they do always express artistry (whether good art or bad art is always food for lively conversation), cultural values, and often social and economic status. But to the extent that they fail to protect from sun and snow and mean people, they fail to be buildings and are just landscape art. You can never really separate pure functionality from aesthetics, economics, or social context, but in the end a building is a device for protecting human beings. Buckminster Fuller, one of the greatest engineers and inventors ever, remarked that he never thought about beauty while he was designing. But if he finished his design and it was not beautiful, he knew it wasn't right and would start over. That's about as good a guide as any, echoing the way life makes things (ever notice bad or ugly design in Nature?). In this book we advocate for adding another functional use of buildings, and more broadly the entire built environment: a great place to durably store large amounts of carbon that we've retrieved from the air.

While we're at it, a *green* building is one that seeks to limit the harm its existence causes to those inside or outside its walls, typically by limiting its use of fossil fuels and harmful chemicals. A *deep green* building is one that goes further and seeks to foster, heal, or restore the life both inside and outside its walls; this book is about deep green building, beyond zero.

Carbon: *Carbon* **is bandied around a lot when often people often mean slightly different things, so let's clarify the terms we will be using.**
Carbon and *carbon dioxide* (CO_2), for example, are two different things, although they get interchanged quite a lot in climate conversations. The fraction of carbon in carbon dioxide is the ratio of weights: The atomic weight of carbon is 12 atomic mass units, and the weight of carbon dioxide is 44 because it includes two oxygen atoms that each weigh 16. To switch from one to the other, use this formula: 1 ton of carbon is, you might say, equivalent to 44/12 = 3.67 tons of carbon dioxide. Plants such as straw (about 35–50 percent carbon) or softwoods (about 50 percent carbon) *sequester* (i.e., durably store) carbon by absorbing carbon dioxide and releasing the oxygen. They feed us oxygen with their respiration, and we oxygen-breathing creatures feed them CO_2 with our respiration. A lovely relationship, no? A ton of carbon in the forest or field—or as part of a building—represents or simply is 3.67 tons of carbon dioxide absorbed and removed from the air.

Here we must also address a semantic question that recurs among the growing community of carbon-wise builders: When a building is truly absorbing more carbon in its lifetime than it ever causes to be emitted, is that carbon *negative* or carbon *positive*? Arguments have been made both ways, and both terms are used in various writings, but we will go with our peers and use *carbon smart* to denote the goal to which we point: more carbon absorbed than emitted (or, at least, the smallest possible lifetime footprint).

Finally: *embodied energy* and *embodied carbon*. Be warned that terms such as *zero energy* (ZE), *net zero energy* (NZE), and *zero net energy* (ZNE) are increasingly tossed about in loosely interchangeable ways in conversation about building energy efficiency. Even more confusing, their close cousins *zero carbon* and *zero net carbon* are also appearing. This is a complex matter in itself, because terms change meaning with scale (product, building, community, nation, or globe?), with grid efficiency (coal, hydro, nuclear, solar, wind?), time frame (daily, annualized, or lifetime?), and other factors. You will sometimes hear *embodied energy* and *embodied carbon* used interchangeably, as if synonymous. They emphatically are not. The units for measurement are different, and although they often rise or fall roughly in parallel, there are many exceptions. Plastic foam insulation, for example, has low embodied energy but extremely high embodied carbon because of the particular chemicals used to make it, and anything manufactured with hydroelectricity can have very high embodied energy but very low embodied carbon.

CCUS: carbon capture, utilization, and storage

CO_2e: carbon dioxide equivalent

CO_2e denotes *carbon-equivalent* emissions from gases such as methane, nitrous oxide, or the hydrofluorocarbons used for heat pumps and foam insulation, calibrated according to their *global warming potential* (GWP) because some gases have ten or a hundred or even thousands of times the heat-trapping effect of carbon dioxide. From here on out we'll use *embodied carbon* or *carbon footprint* to connote embodied carbon equivalents, or *eCO_2e*. We might also sometimes be lazy and just say "carbon" when we mean CO_2e emissions, but we trust you'll get the drift without confusion. Globally, carbon dioxide accounts for about three quarters of human-generated warming, the rest being from the various other heat-trapping gases.

EC3: Embodied Carbon in Construction Calculator

EC3 is a free and open-source database of construction EPDs and a matching building impact calculator for use in design and material procurement (see end of chapter 3).

EPD: Environmental Product Declaration

A "nutrition label" based on a life cycle assessment that declares the various environmental impacts of a product. We're interested mainly in climate disruption as stated in GWP, but an EPD will also report other effects such as ozone depletion and eutrophication of waterways. (More on EPDs in chapter 3.)

GHG: greenhouse gas

In much-simplified atmospheric physics, a greenhouse gas allows the abundant energy of the sun to pass through as visible and ultraviolet light but then absorbs the infrared energy that a warmed Earth tries to send back to space; it is essentially a blanket around Earth.

GWP: global warming potential

GWP is a measure of the heat absorbed by any greenhouse gas in the atmosphere, adjusted as a multiple of the heat that would be absorbed by the same mass of carbon dioxide (see CO_2e).

Infrastructure

All the durable things we build that *aren't* buildings (although people often occupy them), such as power and water treatment plants, water and sewer lines, roads and highways, curbs and gutters, power lines and switching stations, docks, and airports.

ISO: International Standards Organization (or International Organization for Standards).

LCA: life cycle assessment

LCA (sometimes also called life cycle analysis) is a multistep procedure for calculating the lifetime environmental impact of a product or service. (Much more on LCA in chapters 2 and 3.)

LCC: life cycle costing

LCC is a life cycle approach that looks at the direct monetary costs involved with a product or service but not its environmental impact.

LCI: life cycle inventory

LCI is the data collection portion of, or basis for, an LCA.

LCIA: life cycle impact assessment

LCIA is the reply to "What does this LCA mean?"

LEED: Leadership in Energy and Environmental Design

LEED is a green building certification program used worldwide in many forms that is developed, maintained, and published by the U.S. Green Building Council (USGBC, and also the World Green Building Council and other national green building councils).

Tons and tonnes of trouble

Bruce is from the United States and uses tons (imperial system), Chris is from Canada and uses tonnes (metric system). When we're quoting a source, it is generally in metric tonnes, because that's the common language of climate science, but either way we stay true to the source (likewise with other units such as temperature and length). A metric tonne is 1,000 kilograms or 2,205 pounds, and a short (imperial) ton is 2,000 pounds or 0.91 metric tonnes. For many of the values we state, the difference is less than the fuzz factor (degree of precision), so it doesn't very much matter. As an engineer, Bruce is obsessive about precision where it matters but also obsessive about *not* being obsessive where it doesn't, or when precision is implied but not justified. Anyone can punch numbers on a calculator, but that doesn't mean you know an answer to seven decimal places. We can be accurate without necessarily being very precise—as is often the case in the nascent science of carbon accounting.

WBLCA: whole-building life cycle assessment

WBLCA is a multicriteria method for the transparent evaluation of the goods and services that make up a building project. The comparison of WBLCA results can guide teams in achieving the goal of sustainable design in one or several categories.

Foreword

What if instead of emitting carbon, factories drew down carbon from the atmosphere and stored it in building materials? What if instead of shipping materials around the world we developed regional supply chains connecting rural and urban economies? What if building was a major solution to climate change?

Less than a decade ago, I would have smiled and told you these were fanciful dreams and returned to my work to reduce material impacts—in essence, to make buildings less bad. Today this vision—buildings as solutions to climate change—inspires and motivates my work as founding director of the Carbon Leadership Forum.

We can and must eliminate industrial emissions, and the building sector can be a powerful market driver for low-carbon material production. Given the staggering mass of building materials used globally and the relatively long life of building products, developing and scaling carbon-storing material solutions holds great global potential.

No matter your role, from curious student to leading industry professional, you all have a part to play in shifting the paradigm in which buildings can be a major solution to climate change. We must halve emissions in the next decade, and thus we must approach decarbonization holistically and systematically. For the building industry that means radically decreasing energy use of new and existing buildings, eliminating the combustion of fossil fuels on site (electrification), integrating buildings into decarbonized electrical grids, eliminating embodied carbon (what this book is about), and doing all this work to advance a more healthy and just society.

Bruce King and Chris Magwood bring decades of experience designing and building, using both conventional and novel carbon-storing building materials. Their deep knowledge and optimistic tenacity have inspired me to be bolder in aspiration and more confident in execution. If you are curious about building materials, their impact and opportunities for action, this is the book for you. I encourage you to dive in to learn more. Dive in to understand what is possible today and what will be possible tomorrow. Dive in to ensure you are doing your part in the needed transformation of how we build and what we build with.

Kathrina Simonen, AIA SE
Professor and chair, Department of Architecture, University of Washington
Founding director, Carbon Leadership Forum

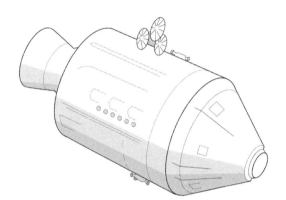

Houston, we have a problem . . .

Introduction

Human beings can be very cool. When we laugh and sing, other creatures draw in to listen. Or, when put into difficult or impossible situations, we often rise up in ways no one could have predicted, even us. Look at Mohandas Gandhi, who endured repeated harassment, imprisonment, and torture on the way to successfully uniting and leading his country to independence. Consider the Shackleton Expedition of more than a hundred years ago, surviving and traveling under extraordinary circumstances out of Antarctica. Or Susan B. Anthony and the suffragettes, enduring ridicule and stigmatization to achieve the women's vote that we now take for granted. Or Ella Fitzgerald, Miles Davis, and several generations of Black jazz musicians who lived in a nation of systemic racism and often brutal oppression—and brought forth a rich, fabulous, joyful body of music the likes of which had never before been heard on Earth. Or just mothers everywhere, without whose difficulties there would never have been your or my passage into this world.

Here's another example: consider the Apollo 13 moon mission of 1970, an epic story memorialized by the quote at the beginning of this introduction and depicted in a film of the same name, a hopeful parable for our times. The space capsule was well on its way to the moon when the astronauts realized that their precious oxygen supply was leaking into space, and they would have to turn back. The frantic ensuing calculations by engineers equipped with pencils and slide rules led to a successful turnaround using the moon's gravity as a sort of lacrosse stick to catch and then "throw" the capsule back toward Earth.

But then things got worse. Although there was just enough oxygen to keep the astronauts alive for the return journey, a new problem came up: carbon dioxide. The astronauts' own exhalations were causing a buildup of CO_2 in the capsule that would become lethal before they could get home. Thus came the second frantic challenge: Using only the limited supply of tubes, tape, and fabric available in the command module, design a CO_2 filter. The engineers on the ground did so in the few hours they had available. But then came the third act of our parable, perhaps the most telling.

A buildup of CO_2 will cause any mammal to grow sleepy and confused on the way to asphyxiating, so the clever CO_2 solution devised on Earth had to be communicated to three men with fast-diminishing mental capacity so that they could replicate and activate the CO_2 filter—their only way to stay alive. (Anyone starting to see a metaphor here?) They did it and made it home, a triumph not just for slide rule–packing geeks but for all of humanity.

There they were, and here we are: in dire circumstances while so many of us, including political leaders, are in belligerent denial that there even *is* a problem, much less that we should do anything about it. Will human beings survive this massive tragedy? Will we pull a rabbit out of our global hat and live to see another chapter of *Homo sapiens* on Earth? What a time to be alive, and we make bold to think that we might play some role in fostering a happy outcome. So, we wrote this book that starts with a simple assertion:

Zero is not enough.

Let us give you the takeaway right at the start: We're going to argue for, provide a map toward, and show you examples of a built environment that absorbs more greenhouse gases than it emits, acting as a CO_2 filter in the space capsule that is Earth. As fast as possible. This is a time of climate emergency, and the building industry must do everything it can (along with agriculture, transportation, energy, food, and every other human industry) to retrieve carbon that we've put in the air and store it effectively and durably on Earth. As Paul Hawken and his many colleagues articulated in *Drawdown*, the climate disruption humanity has initiated wouldn't be resolved even if we could completely and instantly stop our burning of fossil fuels with their resulting warming emissions.[1]

We have to draw the carbon back down as fast as we can, and buildings have a huge role to play in that effort. The construction industry uses far more physical material than any other and so is strategically poised to act as receiver for the carbon we retrieve and collect. "Buildings made of sky" is more than a poetic metaphor; it is an effective pointer to an architecture to cool the planet.

"Net Zero" has been an effective rallying cry for the green building movement, signaling a goal of having every building "need nothing," generating at least as much energy as it uses. Enormous strides have been made in improving the performance of every type of new building as well as, even more importantly, renovating the vast and energy-inefficient collection of existing buildings in every country. We offer an enthusiastic tip of the hat here to Architecture 2030, the International Living Futures Institute, the New Buildings Institute, the U.S. and World Green Building Councils, and many people (some of whom contributed to this book) and organizations who have labored so hard and so long to turn the built environment into a nonpolluting network living lightly and gracefully on the land. If we can get every building to net zero energy use in the next few decades, it will be a huge success.

And not enough.

While we pursue net zero—with better insulation, air sealing, windows, air conditioners, solar photovoltaics, and other components of an efficient building—we need to look at what we make all those things *with,* and at the supply chains that deliver all those products and materials to a jobsite. By various estimates, production of building materials accounts for 10 to 15 percent of global warming emissions; buildings are a culprit but at the same time stand poised to act as climate healers. The construction industry with its exuberant consumption of materials can become a huge repository for the carbon we retrieve from the sky in the form of trees and plants we already grow (chapter 6), in the form of emissions we capture at the smokestacks of industrial plants (chapter 5), and as a result of our nascent but growing partnership with the fungi, bacteria, and microbes that can help us deal with pollutants and "grow" buildings without fossil fuels (chapter 6).

More broadly, we can look to Nature for a few clues to effective and sustainable ways to go about our business. Nature—the entire, mysterious, fabulously complex system of life on Earth—runs entirely on solar and geothermal power. She makes mistakes and then corrects. She is not efficient, she is *effective*; most if not all living things produce far more seeds, eggs, and offspring than are needed to maintain their species. The rest is food for the others: inefficient but effective. Of particular interest to an engineer is her tendency toward *resilience*. A complex system with many interacting parts is more robust than one with only a few, and likewise we engineers consistently find that, in building a system, you are almost always better off relying on many small, connected parts rather than one or two big ones. Forty small columns under a building rather than ten big ones; twenty routes in and out of a building or city rather than just a few; five microgrids or ten thousand rooftops powering a town rather than one distant power plant; twenty-seven small, regional suppliers rather than one national one. And so on. Let's take these clues and build resilience. We can get to net zero and then must get farther.

Any intelligent fool can make things bigger, more complex, and more violent. It takes a touch of genius—and a lot of courage—to move in the opposite direction.
    —E. F. Schumacher

A building is a device for protecting human beings, but it also bears noting that our individual and collective notions of what constitutes "protecting human beings" has evolved quite a bit. You who are reading this probably take for granted that the building you're in will keep you dry, warm in winter and cool in summer, will provide a steady supply of electrical power, hot and cold running water, efficient and sanitary waste management, not collapse in an earthquake and not trap you in a fire, and of course provide internet access. These are all pretty basic services that, increasingly, much of the world takes for granted, yet only dry and warm were available to even the wealthiest people on Earth up to the past century. Now we all expect all the good stuff, and our building codes require it. (More on the value and maddening complexity of building regulation in chapter 11.) Thanks to fossil fuels, we all live in a world of vastly greater comfort and security—though not yet for everyone—and vastly greater expectations of our buildings, not to mention cars, grocery stores, and Netflix. Much of the trick in a post–fossil fuel world will be to provide these services, or at least the really crucial ones, using renewable energy and much more clever design.

In the pages to follow we provide a snapshot of a beginning of and map toward a carbon-smart built environment that acts as a CO_2 filter in our space capsule called Earth. We will try to peer into the future, but inevitably we will be bound by our moment in time (2020–2021) and by our perspective as Bruce and Chris, two old white dads in North America. We have enlisted help from several colleagues to widen the perspective, but we're all stuck in our particular moment in the growing carbon-smart movement, by our moments in our lives, and by our place in history. We can't do much about time, but it's always useful to try and step back for a longer view. A look in the rear-view mirror can be illuminating.

Bruce writes from a narrow little valley in the coastal hills of California, 20 miles north of San Francisco, squarely in the middle of a climate crisis, the social upheaval of MeToo, Black Lives Matter, and related movements, raging wildfires, the U.S. election of 2020, and the first truly global experience, the COVID-19 pandemic. But it certainly hasn't always been this way.

Three hundred years ago in this spot, and for many thousands of years before that, the Aguasto tribe of the Coast Miwok Indians lived their lives among a great many related tribes. The climate was and still is mild, and the hills, bay, and ocean are full of food; some believe that this, the San Francisco Bay Area, hosted the densest human population in  pre-Columbian North America. The indigenous architecture was about as simple as it gets: massive slabs of redwood bark leaned against each other to keep off the sun and rain.

Two hundred years ago in this spot, Spanish invaders were completing a series of Catholic missions along the coast of California. (The history books Bruce grew up with called them "explorers," somehow failing to notice that the Americas were fully populated and spiritually just fine when Columbus and then the missionaries arrived on these shores with crosses held high and guns pointed forward.) With those missions a building technology completed its journey across the globe from its origins on the Nubian upper Nile—*aṭ-ṭawbu*, *al daub*, *adobe*, the mud brick—across Arabian North Africa to Moorish Spain, then across the Atlantic and across America as the Spanish missions, built by the newly converted and conscripted native slaves. Those massive mission buildings must have awed the Indians up and down America's west coast (which was the main idea, of course) but didn't prove to be very well adapted to a land that violently shakes from time to time. They wouldn't still be here today but for the largesse of well-heeled lovers of historic and earthen architecture, and we'll have more on new and seismically safer technologies for clay (earthen) construction in chapter 6.

One hundred years ago in this spot, in the wake of the Gold Rush and then the devastating earthquake and fire of 1906, everybody was busy rebuilding almost everything in the San Francisco Bay Area. To do this, they accelerated what they had already started: the near complete cutting of the ancient redwood forests of the north coast. And how could they not? There were an awful lot of people to house and whole city blocks to rebuild. So our hard-nosed ancestors with the handlebar mustaches and their can-do spirit developed 30-foot-long crosscut saws and the other technologies needed to turn those majestic groves into 2×4s and roof shingles.

Today in this spot we build with pretty much anything and everything, simply because we can. San Francisco is booming with new high rises made of steel from China, the housing expands with softwoods from the north forests, we pour our foundations with concrete made of sand and gravel retrieved from distant river-beds, and we fill every building with finishes, electronics, and furniture made with hundreds of chemical compounds that never existed on Earth until the past few decades. We touch and breathe those chemicals every day and then have to clean up the toxic ash they leave after the big fires come through. The modern global infrastructure, so very well-oiled both literally and figuratively, enables us to make new chemical compounds that we don't actually understand and to cheaply ship anything we want between any two points on Earth. (More on green and not-so-green chemistry in chapter 7.) That's how things stand today in this little valley, and on this Earth.

Four snapshots in time of architecture and building in just this one spot. It will be similar yet also completely different wherever you sit, reader, but the underlying theme will be the same. Just like our predecessors, we make eager use of all the material resources we can get our hands on, be they lumber, rocks, or polyvinyl chloride, and all the energy we can afford, be it slaves, firewood, or West Texas Intermediate Crude.

The astute reader will notice a hint of disdain in the preceding paragraphs, because we hold seemingly different values than our ancestors and predecessors. But what, if given the chance, might you or I have done differently if plopped down in another moment of history? There were a number of Franciscan friars who tried valiantly to protect and preserve indigenous culture, or at least see that the Indians were well treated. But the arrival of gun- and disease-bearing Europeans in the Americas was inevitably a brutal steamroller. Likewise, there were many who fought to protect the ancient redwoods. To some extent they succeeded because, fortunately for us, they had the financial and political resources to acquire and set aside a few tracts, now designated as national monuments.

Chris writes from Treaty 20 Michi Saagiig territory, in the traditional territory of the Michi Saagiig and Chippewa nations, collectively known as the Williams Treaties First Nations, which include Curve Lake, Hiawatha, Alderville, Scugog Island, Rama, Beausoleil, and Georgina Island First Nations, where he respectfully acknowledges that the Williams Treaties First Nations are the stewards and caretakers of these lands and waters in perpetuity and that they continue to maintain this responsibility to ensure their health and integrity for generations to come. And on these lands, in the mid-1990s, he undertook building a straw bale house in the woods for his family.

He is one of a number of "alternative" builders who have been building carbon smart (intentionally or unintentionally) for a few decades. These innovators have been making climate-positive buildings in the pursuit of making the healthiest, most ecologically sound and regionally appropriate buildings they could. They have been using a lot of plant-based materials—straw, hemp, bamboo, cork, and "good wood" among them—along with earthen materials to replace high-impact materials such as concrete, steel, and petrochemicals. In doing so, they were making buildings that had lots of benefits for the occupants and the ecosystem. Oh, and they were unwittingly reversing climate change in a very small, but very significant, way.

The buildings Chris has made are small. They also store a lot of carbon: Net storage results of 150 kilograms of CO_2 per square meter (150 kg CO_2/m^2) are not unusual, and they can be double or triple that amount. On an individual basis, everything he has built in his career is a drop in the net emissions bucket that is our atmosphere. But it is exciting to recognize that a global group of "alternative builders" have made these carbon-storing buildings with no R&D budgets, no institutional support, no incentives, and against the full weight of a regulatory system that does not smile on innovation. However, the buildings have been made affordably, and they have reliably withstood the test of time over the past quarter century. If this is possible, imagine what our sector can do if we actually apply some resources, intent, and institutional support to this notion!

It is time for all our buildings to intentionally reverse climate change, not just those being made by alternative builders. In this book, you'll meet a whole bunch of smart, experienced, and committed people who are helping to make this happen. If we can apply a good dose of collective will and intent, the notion that the world's buildings could become the planet's sixth major carbon sink is not a naive, fanciful dream. It is an achievable criterion that we can and should use as we design, regulate, and construct buildings.

Reversing and healing climate disruption is no more an ethical matter than assembling a CO_2 filter was for the astronauts of Apollo 13. This is survival: of our own species and of the many others who are put at risk by our actions. (And we must offer a solemn goodbye to the species already lost due to our presence.)

Wherever we're going, we're going faster and faster, and the world 100 or 500 years from now is sure to be at least as shocking to us as ours would be to time travelers from 1492, 1776, or 1939. What the table of life will look like then is anybody's guess, and there is plenty of great science fiction out there depicting wildly different scenarios for humanity. Some believe we will extend lifespans far beyond the dreary 80 years or so available today and move ourselves (whatever "self" is) into silicon-based or enhanced artificial bodies. We're already well on our way, after all, with our hearing aids, titanium joints, enhancements, and artificial organs. Maybe someday we won't need buildings or any sort of shelter from sun and rain, from heat and cold. Maybe that will be great, maybe not so much, but for now we've got many billions of organic carbon-based people to house, more billions on the way, and a buildup of CO_2 that looks to prove lethal to most of us, one way or another, if we don't get to work putting the emissions engine into reverse.

Human beings can be very cool, and ready, we dare to think, to grow out of this troubled and vicious adolescence. Our job now is to halt the emissions and to bring as many of them back home to Earth as we can—with our buildings and cities, with our farms and landscapes, with technology, heart, and urgency. Bring ourselves back to Earth, while we're at it. The odds are heavily stacked against us, but that's okay. They were stacked against the revolutionaries of 1776, against Harriet Tubman, Mohandas Gandhi, and Nelson Mandela, against the suffragettes, against Apollo 13. So? We're human beings; we eat bad odds for breakfast.

In this book, we invite you to imagine the very real potential for our built environment to be a site of net carbon storage, a massive drawdown pool that—along with intentional climate-positive efforts in every other sector of human endeavor—could heal our climate.

Welcome to *Build Beyond Zero*.

1. The Story of Carbon: The Birth of the Universe, of Carbon, and of Life

We drink from wells we did not dig,
we are warmed by fires we did not build.

—Deuteronomy

With this book we present a solution, one among many that can start to reverse climate disruption and begin climate healing. First, however, we need to take a careful look at the problem we hope to solve, which starts with a look in the rearview mirror: How did we get here?

In the introduction we portrayed a short history of culture and architecture near San Francisco and Toronto, for just the past few hundred years. Now we vastly expand our time and spatial scales, starting with a whirlwind tour of the story of the Universe, within which is the story of carbon, within which is the story of us, the human beings, as science gets it so far.

13.7 Billion Years Ago

The Big Bang (BB) banged and is still banging, right here, right now, right where you're sitting. Modern physicists devote their careers to trying to puzzle out just what that "bang" was, in which the entire known universe began from one point in space and time. What happened in the first second? The first microsecond, or nanosecond? What was there before that? Has this happened before? When reading modern cosmology, it can seem like this Big Thing happened, like *Star Wars*, long ago and far away. It certainly did begin a long time ago—14 billion years is a bit

9

beyond most people's comprehension— yet you are in and part of it. Everything you can see or love or hate or build or build with is part of the Big Bang, even if it's not quite so loud and bright anymore.

BB + 380,000 or So Years

Things have finally cooled and depressurized enough for the first physical matter, the elements hydrogen and helium, to appear and begin coalescing into ever-denser clouds of gas until—

BB +200 or So Million Years

The first stars appear, beginning to forge the heavier elements in their cores via nuclear fusion, eventually to go supernova (explode), scattering those heavier elements into space to then set to work coalescing into more clouds until—

BB + 2 Billion Years (12 or So Billion Years Ago)

The next generations of stars start to appear (everything still exploding outward in every direction from the Big Bang), in many cases those new stars form with orbiting planets and moons, leading in at least one case to—

4.5 Billion Years Ago

Our Earth, Sun, and solar system are formed. After a half billion or so formative years of grinding, sloshing, and fuss, the Earth settles down a bit with a more or less stable world of continents, oceans, and atmosphere. And then the fun begins with the first appearance of—

About 4 Billion Years Ago

Life! Wow, life! As inexplicable to us as the original Big Bang itself, life started with very, very simple anaerobic microorganisms, developing and evolving over eons to fabulous complexity recurring several times over as six mass extinctions reset the stage (for various reasons, though none until now due to the effects of any single species). Climate changes, endless tectonic rearrangement of land masses, the wobbling of the poles, and many other effects keep things moving and changing while the impetus to live and evolve hums unceasingly in every living thing.

About a Quarter of a Billion Years Ago

Before we get to the emergence of human beings, let's note a few among so many interesting periods in the geologic record, the ones that stand out in this Story of

Carbon: the ones that gave us fossil fuels. The Carboniferous was a geologic period from the end of the Devonian, 360 million years ago (mya) to the beginning of the Permian 300 mya. The name *Carboniferous* means "coal-bearing," and that's what it became: a lush, thickly forested Earth that over time became beds of coal whose use would change the world. Oil, or more properly petroleum, has a more varied geologic provenance: decayed algae and plant life coming a bit from the Paleozoic (541 to 252 mya) and the Cenozoic (65 mya), but mostly from the Mesozoic (252 to 66 mya). So hundreds of millions of years ago the stage was set for a goofy band of primates to come along and discover these reservoirs of superconcentrated energy—and immediately complete their takeover of the planet.

About 3 Million Years Ago

The seminal genus *Homo* appears in Africa (we are all African!), moving and evolving north up the Nile River valley and the Arabian Sea to scatter, eventually, all over the world into multiple predecessors and versions of early *Homo sapiens*.

About 300,000 Years Ago

Anatomically modern *Homo sapiens* appear in many forms and places, as we can infer from the fossil record. Hard evidence of our arrival comes from as much as forty thousand years ago, most famously the cave paintings such as those of Chauvet and Lascaux in France that solidly announce people like us in their social organization and cognitive ability. This was the emergence of a particular version of *Homo sapiens* (sometimes but not always called *Homo sapiens sapiens*) who were both fruitful and dominant, spreading all over the world and eliminating competing versions of *Homo sapiens*. These were human beings who, if given the chance, could learn to successfully fit into your world, or vice versa. They could think, they could feel, they could reason, they could imagine. More about that imagination thing in a moment.

10,000 or So Years Ago

The Agricultural Revolution: We learned to grow and manage plants and animals for food. Generally thought to have first started in the Fertile Crescent of southwest Asia (modern Egypt, Palestine, Syria, and Iraq), agriculture also had other beginnings in Asia and the Americas. The Agricultural Revolution arguably spawned many, many other things that changed us, such as political states, mass religion, and the beginning of architecture: durable buildings, cities, and infrastructure.

250 Years Ago

The British, like many others around the world who had found coal, had been burning it (or its undercooked cousin, peat) for centuries to warm their homes and schools. But they could only mine the coal down to the water table, not far below the surface, because going deeper meant flooded mines. Steam-powered pumps were already around, but Scottish inventor James Watt (from whom we get the eponymous unit of electrical power) devised in 1776 a dramatic improvement that could not only pump water more effectively but also be put to use driving all sorts of other mechanisms such as trains, tractors, and looms. That moment is generally credited with launching the Industrial Revolution and also accelerated humanity up a hockey stick population surge that still roars on today (figure 1.1).

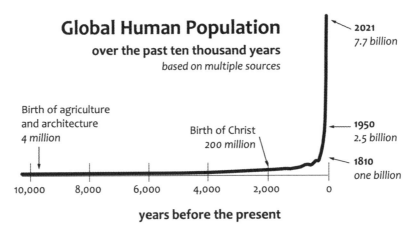

FIGURE 1.1. Global population since the dawn of agriculture.

Today

Here you are, the stardust kid! Here we all are, and our kin: giraffes, turtles, kelp forests, red winter wheat, the mold on the cheese, and every other living thing. We who live are a carbon family, tied by our common ancestry. Our bodies are 18 percent carbon, most of the rest being hydrogen and oxygen (as water) sprinkled with a number of trace elements. We are the carbon-based human beings in the billions who, like the sorcerer's apprentice, have discovered a magic that now runs out of control, threatening to destroy us and so much around us.

But Wait! There's More!

In our rough and simplified version, this is the Story of Carbon to the present moment—the creation story as given by science and the scientific method.

Here we can note fun correlations between scientific fact (or, anyway, agreed-upon inference) and the creation myths that permeate human culture and history. Hydrogen and carbon, for example, can be imagined as Adam and Eve, progenitors of the family of life (and fundamental to a circular economy; more on those two crucial elements in chapter 11, "Policy and Governance"). Or the Big Bang as Vimalakirti's one small room of emptiness that easily holds tens of thousands of Buddhas and radiant beings, all on resplendent thrones, or the Hindu cycle of *yugas*, immense cycles of time far, far beyond human comprehension. Or old Coyote—dirty, tricky, stinky Coyote—who grabbed a nice, neat blanket full of stars and shook it, making the Milky Way.

And so on. We note the correlations and invite you to draw your own connections as you like. But don't think, dear reader, that this is an idle sidebar exercise; it is foundational to this book and to the future of humanity. If you—if we—don't look at and recognize the beliefs and myths that we hold, that we swim in like a fish in the sea, then we're running blind, and that can be quite dangerous.

> *Legends, myths, gods and religions appeared for the first time with the Cognitive Revolution. . . . None of these things exists outside the stories that people invent and tell one another. There are no gods in the universe, no nations, no money, no human rights, no laws, and no justice outside the common imagination of human beings. . . . Fiction has enabled us not merely to imagine things, but to do so collectively. We can weave common myths such as the biblical creation story, the Dreamtime myths of Aboriginal Australians, and the nationalist myths of modern states. Such myths give Sapiens the unprecedented ability to cooperate flexibly in large numbers. . . .*
>
> *Wolves and chimpanzees cooperate far more flexibly than ants, but they can do so only with small numbers of other individuals that they know intimately. Sapiens can cooperate in extremely flexible ways with countless numbers of strangers. That's why Sapiens rule the world.*
>
> —Yuval Noah Harari, *Sapiens*

When we share the same myth, the same creation stories and world narratives, we thrive and conquer the world. When we don't, we often fight. Not always, but often enough, and our tendency to be vicious and combative is usually rooted in differing myths. Consider, just for a few examples, the Crusades of the Middle Ages, the rape of Nanjing, the attack on the World Trade Center on 9/11, or the attack on the U.S. Capitol by QAnon adherents on January 6, 2021. All made by fervent believers more than certain that they were doing the Right Thing, usually for "God" in one way or another. We act out our creation stories and cover the land with misery and blood. We started this book with the assertion that human beings can be very cool, but must also solemnly note that all too often we are emphatically not.

Even worse, many of our mythic narratives don't jibe well with science and amount to an ongoing argument with reality. There is a very old cartoon depicting two South Pacific Islanders standing on a beach and looking out across the ocean at the smoking volcano on the distant horizon. One of them says, "Well, either the fire god Kam'aah'aa is angry because we haven't sacrificed a virgin after the last eclipse, or else a mass of nonviscous and superheated magma has forced its way through a tectonic fracture in the crustal plate." A funny joke, yes, but not so funny, if they go with the first theory, for some young village girl and her family. That's the trouble with arguing with reality: Someone always gets hurt.

We've been acting out wacky mythic things for a very long time, of course, but at this particular moment in the Story of Carbon, that tendency is hugely amplified for several reasons.

We Are Many

In a very, very short time we have exploded in population: Just in my lifetime, the global population has more than tripled. We're driving a mass extinction by our commandeering of territory and consumption of resources, and our presence on Earth is felt by every creature. From the deepest ocean to the highest peaks, from the poles to deep in the Amazon rainforest, we can be felt, even if not seen, smelled, and heard outright.

We Are Connected

Technology links us together, for both better and worse. Jet travel quickly spread the COVID pandemic all over the world, and phone and video connections, just a science fiction dream until a generation ago, are now common.

We Have a New Kind of Problem

COVID appears to have been the first truly global experience, the first global problem. But of course it's not: Our cumulative effect on each other and the rest of life (tragically externalized as "the environment"), especially as disruption to the climate, has been a visible and growing global problem for decades.

And We Most Definitely Do Not Share the Same Creation Myth

This is much more than subscribing to different religions, problematic as that so often is. My creation myth tells me who I am, who my tribe or community is, and likewise defines my nation and the world. It tells me who are the Good Guys and who are the Bad Guys (you can't have one without the other). I couldn't possibly fathom the mindset of my own great, great, great, great grandfather, about whom I know almost nothing, and neither does my worldview much correlate with his, or that of a North Korean farmer, a Nepali government bureaucrat, an Amazon tribeswoman, or plenty of people in my own country. Add a few dozen examples of your own; we all occupy different worlds, almost but not quite literally, with completely different Good Guys and Bad Guys.

What could possibly go wrong?

In today's politics, I find that a lot of transient and trivial issues of the moment dominate the political imagination through the media, and in doing so, they diminish and marginalize these bigger issues we should be thinking about. . . . Nothing I see today indicates that people are taking these problems as seriously as we need to. We need leaders who, informed by science, adopt a common-sense practicality. Let's understand our stories, but let's look at the facts. There's the story that China tells about itself—that it has been humiliated by the West and it's going to do something about that. And there's the story that America, and I suppose the West, tells about itself— that it's the dominant power and should be because it's the custodian of democracy and human rights. So, we have colliding stories. And then we have the facts: The tech risk doesn't know any borders; the virus risk doesn't know any borders. That's why we need people around us with different stories to challenge us, especially with science: What's our hypothesis? What's the evidence? How can we change as we get new information? What we need instead is a vision of reality rooted in the facts, as best we can discern them with our limited imaginations.

—Jerry Brown[1]

We're all made of carbon, we breathe the same air in and out all day, and our appearance on Earth is intimately tied to the stable, even if minute, presence of carbon dioxide in the atmosphere (figure 1.2).

We're all in grave danger together, yet we look at each other with distrust and carry on or amplify our old animosities and hostilities. Things are made even more challenging by the fact that the first warning cries about climate change, such as

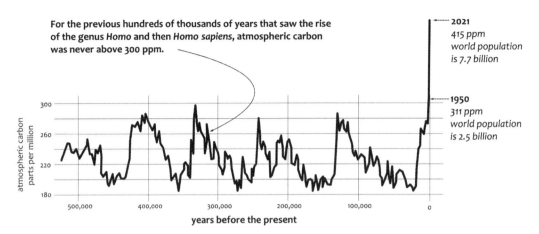

For the previous hundreds of thousands of years that saw the rise of the genus *Homo* and then *Homo sapiens*, atmospheric carbon was never above 300 ppm.

2021
415 ppm
world population is 7.7 billion

1950
311 ppm
world population is 2.5 billion

atmospheric carbon parts per million

years before the present

FIGURE 1.2. Atmospheric carbon over the past half million years.

Jim Hansen's 1988 testimony before Congress, or Al Gore's 2006 release of *An Inconvenient Truth*, or even this book, are often made by those who have benefited most from the Industrial Revolution and suffered least from the ensuing climate disruption. We who live in our comfortable, secure homes are not well positioned to lecture the rest of the world about climate-harming emissions.

All of which adds up to slim odds for a species that needs to quickly come together to face and deal realistically with the unprecedented problem we've created. The climate doesn't care about our myths: Physics is physics, and the warming continues while we quibble. Fortunately the solution, not to be too simplistic, is fairly straightforward: Reverse the emissions engine with a fast, massive carbon drawdown (figure 1.3).

Accomplishing that drawdown will involve plenty of infrastructural work, technological innovation, and political will. But not much of that can happen while we're all reading from different playbooks—while we're living different mythic narratives. The flip side of that, of course, is that once we *do* get aligned in recognition of this grave threat, we can rise quickly and effectively to the challenge, because human beings can be very cool (box 1.1).

The Story of Carbon goes on, as does our book. In writing this we have very much in mind where the Story of Carbon is going—what sort of world we are leaving for future generations both of human beings and of all the other species we travel with on Spaceship Earth. They have almost no voice in our town councils and congresses, yet they are just starting to be heard through the mouths of the youngest among us. One of them is poet Amanda Gorman, who stole the show at President

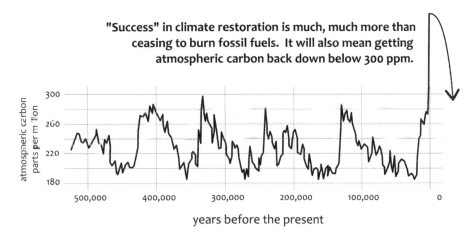

"Success" in climate restoration is much, much more than ceasing to burn fossil fuels. It will also mean getting atmospheric carbon back down below 300 ppm.

FIGURE 1.3. Drawdown time.

Box 1.1   The Curious Case of the Conscious Carbon

It's worth examining your myths, and it's also worth examining the examiner.

As you face any task, it's good to know your tools. Ask any chef or carpenter or surgeon. Yet most of us get up and start our day without checking the one tool that we all use. It goes by many names; let's just call it awareness. You've always had it (if "had" is the right word), but have you ever examined it? Just in case you never have before, give it a shot: Take a moment and let awareness look at awareness. There's nothing stopping you, and you don't need any tools or training—although there are rich and lovely traditions for just this purpose all over the world going back to before recorded history. You're already fully equipped for the task, because what you are looking at is what you are looking with.

To be clear, we're not talking about studying the most complex of all known objects, the brain. There are plenty of exciting developments in neuroscience, but you and I and most people probably can't fully appreciate them. We can appreciate advances in cognitive science that bring to light the many biases that all humans have, which deeply affect how we see and act in the world. Indeed, we live in an exhilarating time of scientific inquiry in which we're discovering astonishing things every day about distant galaxies, deep history, and the microcommunities of life in ocean, soil, and our bodies. We're getting new insight into such everyday things as space, time, thinking, and breathing—how the movement of air in and out of our bodies is so crucial not just to survival but to health. Your body, like the Earth, depends on a healthy flow of various gases in ways much more complex than it might seem and on maintaining just the right level of our old friend carbon dioxide. Everything is very much connected.

But we're not here inviting you to study science as much as we're inviting you to look at looking. It's not a question to be answered—there is no "answer"—it's more like an invitation to an inquiry to take up anytime, anywhere, regardless of circumstances. You might be happy or sad, man or woman, rich or poor, Black or White, doesn't matter at all. But you are aware, so let awareness look at awareness, see where it takes you. A host of questions can arise: How much awareness do I have? What are the boundaries? Are there any? Where does my awareness end and yours begin? And so on.

continued

Box 1.1 *continued*

This has nothing to do with concrete or buildings or climate, yet it has everything to do with everything. We offer this invitation not as a minor aside but as another fundament to this book (and many other things), as we live in an age when awareness, or more specifically attention, is the currency of the realm. Tech giants such as Apple, Google, and Facebook make their fortunes mainly by capturing and holding your attention, then selling it along with the data that accompany it. The better I am at grabbing and holding your attention, the more money I can make. Most of the time you're online, especially if you're availing yourself of "free" stuff, you're not the customer, you're the product. If only for that reason—though there are plenty of others—it seems worth a bit of, well, attention.

Let awareness settle on awareness, see what happens. The great physicist Richard Feynman remarked, "I'd rather have a question that can't be answered than an answer that can't be questioned." Or, as Einstein said, the mindset that got us into the troubles we're in today is not the mindset that will get us out, so it behooves us to take a look—a look at looking.

Joseph Biden's inauguration ceremony. She spoke for America in a singular political moment but might just as well have been speaking for humanity—the goofy, world-dominating primates who eat bad odds for breakfast—in our singular moment in the Story of Carbon.

> *We did not feel prepared to be the heirs*
> *of such a terrifying hour*
> *but within it we found the power*
> *to author a new chapter*
> *To offer hope and laughter to ourselves*
> *So while once we asked,*
> *how could we possibly prevail over catastrophe?*
> *Now we assert*
> *How could catastrophe possibly prevail over us?*
> *We will not march back to what was*
> *but move to what shall be.*

> —Amanda Gorman, January 20, 2021 at the U.S. Presidential Inauguration

2. A Brief History of Green Building: Waking Up to Climate Emergency

This is a book about how buildings can help heal the climate, so it naturally focuses on carbon: carbon flows, carbon stocks, the rate of flow, storage, and emission, and so on. Building beyond zero depends on having a robust means of accounting for these stocks and flows, so we have duly spent a bit of time unpacking the still nascent state of life cycle analysis (LCA); much more on that in the next chapter. You can't improve what you can't count, and although most of us aren't LCA specialists and probably will never have more than basic facility in that skill, we do need to have a sense of how it works, what it has told us so far, and what changes need to happen to support climate triage. So we developed an illustrated history to help us all see what's happening and how we got here.

In the Days of Yore: The Early Days of Green Building

By the late 1970s, the first green building pioneers had worked out that the amount of energy needed to operate most buildings was huge, and unnecessarily so. Until recently, most buildings everywhere were so energy *inefficient* that a visiting alien might have assumed that we were building devices for the purpose of turning fossil carbon into a warmer atmosphere, which only incidentally provided light and temperature control to the humans living inside them; the Earth's cities looked and functioned very much like the cooling fins on a motorcycle engine. Very early analyses showed that the operating energy for just about any building, over the course of a few decades of expected service, would dwarf the embodied energy needed to make the building. Thus, our marching orders were clear: The green building movement of the subsequent few decades focused almost exclusively on reducing operating energy (very few were talking yet about *carbon* emissions; it was all about operating and embodied *energy*). For all building types we have now worked out how to drastically reduce those operating emissions, in many cases down to "zero" (by its various definitions). For buildings and for human economy writ large, the goal coalesced around "getting to zero" (figure 2.1). It very much bears adding that green building has always included *healthy* building—a parallel and variously related effort to rid buildings of harmful chemicals. That effort has been fruitful against daunting challenges and has its many pioneers and heroes (see chapter 7). But for our purpose here, we focus on energy and its deeply related carbon emissions.

An Inconvenient Truth: It's the Climate, Stupid!

Reducing operating energy in buildings has a certain market appeal because things like insulation are the gift that keeps on giving: There's money in energy efficiency, and green building appealed directly to people's pocketbooks. And after the Organization of the Petroleum Exporting Countries (OPEC) oil embargo of 1973, when gas and oil prices shot up threefold, people and businesses were spooked and keen to invest in technology that would shield them from further disruptions. Solar panels and rolls of batt insulation were hot! Green building catered to everyone's self-interest and so began to get traction in the marketplace and in the halls of government. Moreover, we were saving energy, which lessened our dependence on unreliable foreign oil sources; efficient homes increased national energy security.

Then, ever so slowly, climate disruption entered our awareness. First labeled *global warming*, it spawned jokes in the 1980s like "Won't nuclear winter cancel global warming?" That actually could get a laugh in the Reagan–Bush years in the United States and obscured the gravity of a threat that has since worsened and correctly been renamed *climate emergency*. We might have more easily dealt with climate disruption had we jumped right on it (as we did for ozone depletion), but we didn't. We continued to cling to energy consumption as the central metric for green buildings. But not all energy comes with the same climate impacts; saving energy does not directly translate to reducing emissions. Saving on fossil fuel energy does indeed reduce emissions, but developing renewable electricity—an ever-increasing share of the global energy supply—has a drastically reduced impact on the climate. And not all energy and emissions come from building operations. The green building world has begun to add up all the emissions that come from making materials and assembling them into buildings, and everybody's been surprised at their scale and climate impact.

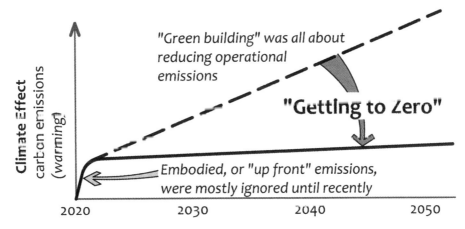

FIGURE 2.1. **Early days.** It was all about operational energy, not carbon emissions, and bending the dotted line down to flat—to a "net zero" building. The up-front or embodied energy of construction seemed noticeable but not worth fussing over very much.

Our inaction as a society has resulted in climate emergency, and emergency requires triage: Under imminent threat, you prioritize actions to save life. In the case of buildings, this means that we need to eliminate all the emissions associated with the next two decades of construction and building operation. We in the green building movement assumed for a long time that we were already doing the right thing because reducing energy demand in new buildings meant less global warming. Only recently have we started looking more closely and noticing that over the next few decades the emissions arising from manufacturing materials and making buildings dominates the emissions profile of virtually all buildings. Whether you were building a super-efficient building or not, embodied emissions suddenly were a priority.

Double Whoops! The Time Value of Emissions

With a collective slap on our foreheads, we then realized that the climate *effect* was much more than the *amount* of the emissions; when they went into the air mattered too. With various adjustment factors that make the climate math interesting (more on that later), the climate effect is still basically the amount of emissions multiplied by the time they are in the air. This is easy to see in figure 2.2 because the climate effect is not the *height* of the line (amount of emissions), it's the area extending right of the line (emissions × time).

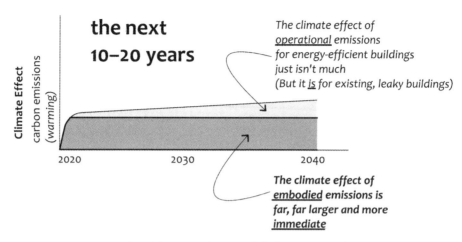

FIGURE 2.2. **Perspective.** This is no longer global warming; this is climate emergency, and our focus must narrow to these next crucial decades. The shaded areas depict climate impact and show how much embodied emissions matter.

Considering this time value of emissions, our colleagues from Architecture 2030 calculate that, averaged over multiple building types and climate zones, three quarters of the climate impact from a project built today, over the next two decades, will be from the materials chosen for its construction.

Let's Get Granular: Material Emissions Versus Whole-Building Footprint

As we start to pay more attention to embodied carbon, and in particular write policy to drive improvements, there is widespread consensus that policy should use the so-called whole-building life cycle analysis (WBLCA), sometimes called the building carbon footprint. Very much akin to the way we analyze and govern the operational energy performance of a whole building, WBLCA provides both designers and regulators with flexibility for working with each unique project; give a little here, take a little there, but in total make the whole building's embodied carbon meet some defined metric such as (typically) a limit of so many kilograms of carbon dioxide equivalent (CO_2e) per square meter of floor space.

Unfortunately, as we said, current LCA practice doesn't generally account for time value or for carbon storage. At present, common practice is to take a detailed look at the assumed life of a building and make assumptions about what happens at the end of its service life, which gives us something like the life stages shown in figure 2.3.

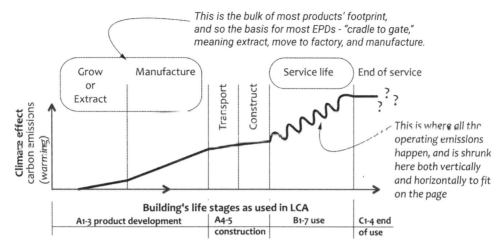

FIGURE 2.3. **Cradle to grave.** Life cycle assessment (LCA) breaks down emissions into the many life stages that every building passes through, each in its own unique way. Many Environmental Product Declarations (EPDs) expressly limit themselves to counting emissions from all processes that occur before products leave the factory ("cradle-to-gate," stages A1–A3 in LCA), because this can be most precisely known and generally constitutes most of a product's embodied carbon.

This is fine as a first approximation, but it misses the time factor. If we compare a conventional building to a low embodied carbon one, assume that the lifetime operating emissions for each are about the same, use a common static WBLCA, and put things more in proportion, we see a modest reduction in end-of-life footprint (figure 2.4).

However, if we shift our focus from the final carbon footprint at the end of the building's lifespan to the ongoing, dynamic climate impact based on the timing of emissions, it becomes clear that the low embodied carbon building has a dramatically lower climate impact, despite only a modest improvement at end of life (figure 2.5). Fewer emissions have been resident in the atmosphere over the building's life, resulting in reduced climate impact.

If we stay on our current green building trajectory and can flatten the operational emissions of our buildings through efficiency improvements and clean energy supply, the low embodied carbon building will have even less area under the line compared with the conventional building. The time to address emissions is now, and the place to address them is up front, where the burst of embodied emissions goes into the atmosphere, where they can no longer be reduced.

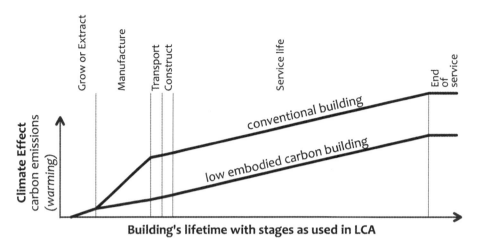

FIGURE 2.4. **A misleading picture**. Nice, but not such a big deal, right? A standard (static) life cycle assessment shows us a modest but not particularly exciting improvement when we use materials with low carbon emissions.

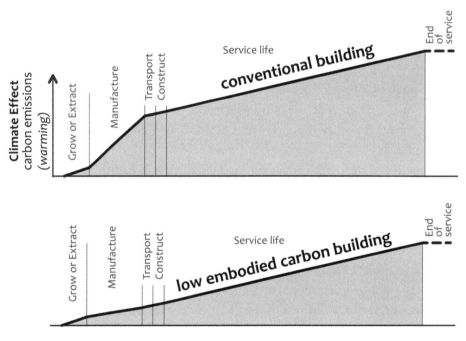

FIGURE 2.5. **The truth comes out** when we look at the area under those lines, which reports climate *impact*; the effect of using low-carbon materials is much bigger. Both at the start and over its useful lifetime, the low-carbon building has dramatically less harmful climate effects.

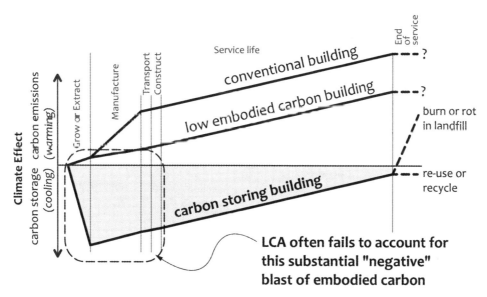

FIGURE 2.6. **Below the surface.** Here is where stored carbon can help us. But life cycle assessment can let us down, because it often doesn't know how to account for that "good" (stored) carbon in the up-front stages.

Build Beyond Zero: Materials as Carbon Repositories

Now, let's introduce the carbon-storing materials that are at the heart of this book: materials that are quite literally made out of carbon that has been drawn out of the atmosphere, either by photosynthesis (plant-based materials) or carbonation (mineralization of atmospheric carbon). The carbon that they have absorbed from the air is removed in order to become building materials. In a static LCA view, we see this as "negative emissions" at the beginning of the life cycle. The time period of this carbon drawdown can be as short as a few weeks for fast-growing algae or more than 80 years for northern boreal softwood trees. Regardless, our carbon LCA line now begins its journey on a downward slope before it goes up again as emissions occur during harvest, transport, manufacture, and construction. In many cases, these manufacturing emissions are substantially less than the amount of carbon stored in the material, and the use of enough of these materials can enable our building to start its operational phase below the zero-carbon line (figure 2.6).

If the net stored carbon is enough and the building's operations clean enough, this building can reach the end of its lifespan and have a net negative carbon footprint. Just as important, note that even if our carbon-storing material, such as wood, straw, or hemp, were to burn or rot after some service life, *it still gave us a period of carbon drawdown* when we needed it most. That burn/rot scenario is

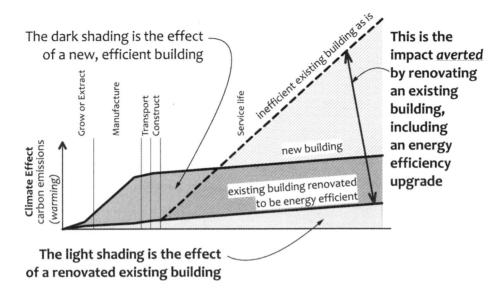

The dark shading is the effect of a new, efficient building

This is the impact *averted* by renovating an existing building, including an energy efficiency upgrade

The light shading is the effect of a renovated existing building

FIGURE 2.7. **Don't tear it down!** We can reduce this complex graphic to a simple takeaway: **If you are choosing between building a new building (no matter how green and efficient) and renovating an existing one that has decent bones (structure and enclosure), the climate will thank you for taking the latter option.** It will probably cost less, too. But to be clear, "renovating" may or may not include rearranging the walls and finishes, but it should definitely include a deep energy efficiency upgrade including more insulation, reduced air leakage, more efficient mechanical systems, and all other components of a tailored upgrade.

obviously to be avoided, as is easily done with good design, good construction, and maintenance.

The dotted lines on the right of the graphs denote the end of service life (C1–C4 in LCA accounting). Most LCA methods require that we make some assumptions about the final fate of a building, product, or material. Will it be recycled? Landfilled? Burned? There's a lot of uncertainty here, but everyone agrees that we at least have to try to make reasonable predictions about the end stage, and doing so pushes designers, builders, and manufacturers to think in terms of a circular economy, not just throwing things away when we don't want them anymore.

Don't Tear It Down! Notice Those Existing Buildings Everywhere?

Most of this book addresses ways to build new buildings as carbon repositories. But we just can't say enough: Most of the positive climate effect we can have for the next few decades will come from renovating, with a deep energy upgrade, the buildings we already have so that the world's cities do not act like the cooling fins on a motorcycle engine (figure 2.7).

This is a good place to hand the microphone over to our old friend, Larry Strain, FAIA (box 2.1). For many decades Larry and his partner, Henry Siegel, have been leading voices in green building while managing Siegel & Strain Architects in Berkeley, California. Whereas many in the burgeoning new carbon architecture, such as Chris and me, have been focused on identifying the best materials for climate-friendly construction, Larry has been working to facilitate reuse and upgrade of the buildings, worldwide, that we already have. As you can read for yourself, Larry constantly points out that best solutions for the planet can also be the best solutions for the poorest among us, for whom that energy bill is no trivial expense.

With all that as introduction, let's take a closer look at how we account for carbon: life cycle assessment.

Box 2.1 The Existing Building Solution
By Larry Strain

This book is about building true zero carbon buildings; here we point to the importance of fixing the buildings we already have to be zero carbon. The embodied carbon savings from reusing buildings is essential but only part of the story.

New buildings can't solve the climate crisis. The widely held gold standard for reducing emissions from the built environment is to build new, zero net energy (ZNE) buildings. Given that we keep making new buildings, they do need to be ZNE. But there are a couple problems with this strategy: The first is that building all those new structures will (usually) generate a lot of embodied emissions, and the second is that it doesn't reduce the operating emissions from all the buildings we already have, which are almost three times greater than annual embodied emissions of new construction. This book, like its predecessor *The New Carbon Architecture*, offers a way to address the first problem: Make buildings out of low-carbon and carbon-storing materials, in essence turning the built environment into a giant carbon sink. This chapter considers the embodied carbon savings from reusing buildings compared with building new ones, but we also look at how to reduce operating carbon to zero.

Reuse: A Complete Strategy
Reuse as a strategy depends on having a supply of buildings to reuse. We have a lot of them in the more built-out Northern Hemisphere. In the less built-out Southern Hemisphere, where new construction will be more prevalent, adoption of the low-carbon approaches outlined in the following chapters will be all the more critical. In the United States, existing building floor area—97 billion square feet of commercial space and 244 billion square feet of residential space—is roughly eighty-five times the

continued

Box 2.1 *continued*

magnitude of annual new construction. Operating those buildings accounts for about 27 percent of U.S. emissions: 12 percent from commercial and 15 percent from residential buildings. Existing buildings offer immediate opportunities to achieve an environmentally responsible and socially equitable future because:

- Renovating an existing structure has a much lower carbon footprint than building a new one because it uses fewer materials, and it avoids most of the *future* embodied emissions from new construction;
- When the renovation includes deep efficiency upgrades it also reduces *current* operating emissions from the buildings we already have.

Before we dive into the carbon benefits of reuse, it's worth mentioning another reason to reuse and upgrade buildings: the human and social benefits we get from investing in and caring for the places we live and work.

People: Community Benefits

Buildings are where we live, work, and play; they make up our streets, communities, and cities. Reusing and improving them is first and foremost an investment in people. Saving, reusing, and improving buildings maintains and strengthens existing neighborhoods, builds financial equity, creates local jobs, strengthens community control, and increases neighborhood resilience. Existing diverse neighborhoods that have not been gentrified offer more opportunities and typically have a higher percentage of businesses owned by people of color than areas that have been "developed."[a] This doesn't mean we don't need to maintain and improve what we have, and it doesn't mean we don't need new buildings. But taking care of what we already have and improving efficiency not only saves money and operating emissions, it also improves thermal comfort, indoor air quality, and health. Renovating and upgrading buildings also generates more jobs per dollar invested than new construction, and the jobs tend to be local and favor small businesses.[b] Investing in buildings that are in communities that have been subjected to historic discrimination, racism, and economic redlining has the potential to bring sustainable and equitable climate solutions and meaningful economic outcomes to the communities that have been most affected by climate change and racism. In the words of Hop Hopkins, director of strategic partnerships for the Sierra Club, "You can't have climate change without sacrifice zones, and you can't have sacrifice zones without disposable people, and you can't have disposable people without racism."[c] It's not just a question of equity; the people directly affected by racism and climate change are the ones who know what solutions are needed. Decisions must be made by, and benefits accrued to, those affected by those investments.

Reducing Embodied Carbon: Reusing What We Have

Reusing buildings reduces carbon emissions compared with new construction, not because of the embodied carbon in the building you are saving—that's a done deal—but because of the avoided carbon that doesn't go into making a new building. Most of the embodied emissions in buildings are from the foundation and the structure, which are typically saved when you renovate a building.

It helps to understand how materials and their emissions are distributed for different building types (figure 2.8). On a per square foot basis, tall heavy buildings have a much larger carbon footprint than

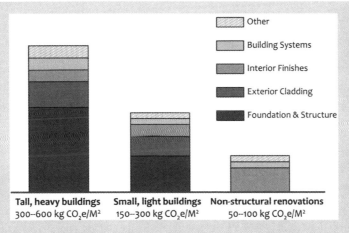

Other

Building Systems

Interior Finishes

Exterior Cladding

Foundation & Structure

Tall, heavy buildings
300–600 kg CO$_2$e/M^2

Small, light buildings
150–300 kg CO$_2$e/M^2

Non-structural renovations
50–100 kg CO$_2$e/M^2

FIGURE 2.8. Carbon emissions by building type and materials.

small, light buildings, partly because they weigh more but mostly because of what they are made from. Beyond a certain size and height, buildings have steel and concrete or masonry structural systems, although cross-laminated timber is becoming a viable way to build tall buildings (chapter 6). Small light buildings, in North America and parts of northern Europe, typically have wood structures, which have a much lower carbon footprint than steel and concrete. So, generally, the structures we want to avoid building more of are large, heavy steel and concrete structures; these are the structures we should be reusing and renovating.

Renovations that reuse most of the structure and the exterior cladding have embodied emissions that are 50 to 75 percent lower than those of a comparable new building. But they still have embodied emissions, and it is possible to reduce these remaining emissions even further. Instead of replacing interior finish materials such as acoustic ceilings and carpet, we can expose and use the structure as the interior finish; we can use low-carbon and carbon sequestering materials such as natural fiber instead of synthetic fiber carpets, or biobased insulation products such as cellulose instead of fiberglass and foam. When we do need a new building, we can design it to accommodate change—higher floor-to-floor heights to allow for different uses, structural elements that can be deconstructed and reused, and building components that are removable and easy to maintain. When we are able to adapt our buildings more easily, we may not be as likely to replace them.

Even when we can't reuse a building, we can still salvage and reuse the materials in it. Demolition generates a lot of waste. If we deconstruct buildings, we can reuse their materials instead of discarding them, avoiding new manufacturing emissions and keeping biobased materials out of landfills where they will eventually decompose and release methane, a potent greenhouse gas.

Reducing Operating Carbon: Upgrading What We Have
Reducing operating emissions with energy upgrades is what really sets reuse apart as a strategy for reducing total carbon emissions, because operating emissions from existing buildings account for the majority of building emissions. We have been doing efficiency upgrades since the 1970s, so we know

continued

Box 2.1 *continued*

how, and although it has helped keep our national energy use (in the United States and other countries) and emissions relatively flat—helping offset the buildings, appliances, computers, and air conditioners that we add each year—we need to do much better than flat. Our efficiency programs have been driven by economic returns rather than the urgency of the climate crisis, typically achieving only 25–35 percent improvements when they need to be at 75 percent now and zero by 2050.[d]

Upgrading to Zero

So how do we make existing buildings net zero?

Since the 1970s, the order of efficiency measures, driven by cost and long-term savings, have been

- Improve building efficiency: insulation, windows, shading, air sealing, daylighting;
- Improve systems efficiency: lighting, HVAC systems, water heating, appliances, controls, and so on;
- Power buildings with renewable energy.

With the decarbonization of the grid, the advent of high-efficiency electric heat pumps, and the increasingly short window we have to solve the crisis we are in, a new strategy has risen to the top of the list:

- Eliminate on-site combustion of fossil fuels and power the building with clean electricity.

Our approach to efficiency upgrades must be driven by the urgency of the climate crisis. We need big reductions, and we need them fast. Reducing operating emissions is something we know how to do and has the potential to reduce global emissions by 25 to 30 percent. We also we need to make sure the carbon invested in energy upgrades doesn't exceed the carbon saved. Adding blown-in cellulose insulation and recommissioning and replacing inefficient HVAC with high-efficiency heat pumps have a good return on carbon invested; reskinning a building with a high-performance aluminum–glass curtain wall or wrapping a building in foam insulation does not. We should focus on carbon reduction strategies that have a positive payback within 10–15 years, or we should be looking for other strategies.

Finding Opportunities

Upgrading our existing building stock is a massive undertaking. We need to inventory what we have and identify the buildings that have the highest potential for both reuse and carbon savings. We need to develop strategies that can achieve the level of upgrades needed at a scale that makes a difference. As for reuse opportunities, as has already been pointed out, the pandemic changed everything. Although the dust hasn't settled yet, it's clear that we have, and will continue to have, a surplus of commercial floor space. We also have families facing foreclosures and many people already living on the streets. We have an opportunity to house people by repurposing what we already have.

Reuse Opportunities: Embodied Carbon Savings

- Vacant or underused buildings
- Large, structurally sound buildings that don't need significant structural or envelope upgrades
- Structures that can accommodate new uses without major alterations

Upgrade Opportunities: Operational Carbon Savings
- Start with the buildings that use the most energy. Large commercial buildings typically make up about 10 percent of a city's total square footage but consume 50 percent of the energy.
- Eliminate on-site combustion of fossil fuels: Power buildings with electricity from clean energy sources.
- Poor-performing buildings have more potential to reduce carbon emissions—more room for improvement—than efficient buildings because of their
  - Old, inefficient HVAC and lighting systems and controls
  - Leaky, inefficient building envelopes with little or no insulation, single-glazed and unshaded windows.

Net Zero Opportunities: On- and Off-Site Renewable
- One- to three-story buildings with unshaded roofs and west- or east-facing facades.
- Buildings with adjacent unshaded land. Parking lots with photovoltaic canopies produce power and have the added benefit of shading the cars and pavement and reducing the heat island effect around the building.
- Purchase clean power.

Efficiency strategies will vary depending on many things. Commercial buildings typically have higher internal loads, with heating, cooling, and ventilation loads driven more by the lighting, equipment, and people in the building than by outside conditions, so lighting and equipment upgrades are a good place to start. For low-rise residential buildings, with nighttime use, envelope upgrades will have more impact, although appliances, water heating, and equipment upgrades will also yield large savings. Converting underused commercial buildings into high-performance, net zero residential buildings will require efficiency strategies for improving building envelopes and building systems that weren't designed for residential, nighttime occupancy.

3. Life Cycle Analysis: Tracking Carbon's Stocks and Flows

We see carbon-storing buildings as an unprecedented opportunity to help heal the climate. But to understand whether and how we can build beyond zero, we need to account for all of those material-related emissions and all of our proposed carbon storage in materials. In the previous chapters we made the case for "Why"; now we must look at "How." There's a fair bit of truth to the adage that what we don't measure, we can't fix. The time is now to get serious about counting carbon in buildings.

In a short time, we've achieved an impressive degree of cooperation and agreement on measuring material emissions with life cycle assessment (LCA) and reporting those results in Environmental Product Declarations (EPDs) (see box 3.1). This is the good news.

But, as explained in the previous chapter, the current state of LCA is sorely lacking in two crucial areas: valuing carbon storage in materials, and the time value of emissions. Without these factors properly recognized, we will be lacking the robust accounting strategy that will enable us to turn buildings from drivers of climate change to climate healers. We need to get this right, and quickly.

This chapter is an overview of current LCA practice for materials, products, and buildings and a rallying call for why we need LCA to start making storage and time key factors in our carbon accounting.

LCA Accounting for Emissions: The Basics

When we make building products, we produce greenhouse gas (GHG) emissions. These emissions arise from many sources: fuel use in machinery that harvests and

Box 3.1   What Is an Environmental Product Declaration (EPD)?

Wouldn't it be great if building products had a "nutrition label," just as food products do? Environmental Product Declarations may not be quite as comparable and easy to understand, but they are the closest thing we have, and they contain all the information one needs to compare Global Warming Potential (GWP) between products that fulfill the same purpose in a building.

In an EPD, the reader will find the methods and results of an analysis of all the energy and impact flows into and out of the manufacturing of a building product. These documents are voluntarily produced by a manufacturer or an alliance of manufacturers according to a set of rules and are verified by an independent third party.

In 2006, International Standards Organization (ISO) standard 14025:2006 established the principles and specified the procedures for developing Type III environmental declaration programs and Type III environmental declarations, known as EPDs, to "present quantified environmental information on the life cycle of a product to enable comparisons between products fulfilling the same function." Based on Product Category Rules (PCRs) and derived from independently verified life cycle assessment (LCA) data, life cycle inventory analysis data, or information modules in accordance with the ISO 14040 series of standards,[a] EPDs have become the standard for comparison of building products. The consistent parameters and reporting format make LCA data more accessible to a wider audience. Hundreds of building product manufacturers around the world have voluntarily produced EPDs, and this growing bank of data has been invaluable for researchers and building professionals.

A researcher wanting to compare GWP results from EPDs of competing building materials has a few more questions to answer to get meaningful results:

- Product uses must be the same. Only materials that can be used for the same purpose can be directly compared. It's not meaningful to compare a roofing material to a window, but two roofing materials and two windows can be compared.
- Product stages must be aligned. If one LCA is "cradle-to-gate" (stages A1–A3) and another is "cradle-to-grave" (stages A1–C4), then it would be useful only to compare stages A1–A3 of both products.
- Material use must be quantified. The functional unit of an LCA study is not directly comparable for most materials. To compare wood framing to steel framing, we would need to know how much wood is needed to frame a wall of a certain size and how much metal framing it would take to make a wall with the same structural and functional properties and then convert the GWP results per functional unit to a GWP result per quantity of material needed for the building.

EPDs are the most consistent and reliable source of information about emissions from building materials, although we still need to methodically account for various levels of fuzziness in results. For example, is your product EPD a national average (very fuzzy), a company average (better), a factory average (even better), or product specific (precise)? The pool of EPDs continues to grow rapidly, and as more manufacturers produce these documents, the easier it will be for designers and builders to make accurate and informed decisions about material selection.

Note

a. See the ISO Browsing Platform, "Environmental management—Life cycle assessment—Principles and framework," https://www.iso.org/obp/ui/#iso:std:iso:14040:ed-2:v1:en

transports raw materials; land use changes from mining, forestry, and agriculture; energy to run factories; chemical process emissions; and so on. Every step of every procedure for every material typically results in some amount of GHG being released. LCA attempts to quantify all those emissions and attribute them to a specific quantity of a particular building product. (It is sometimes useful to note that we rarely use plain materials in a construction project; even such common "materials" as concrete and steel are *products* with at least a few constituent materials or processes, each with at least a few nodes on their upstream supply chains. That said, we will often use the terms interchangeably, just as the industry does.) Once we know the emissions caused by a certain product, we can multiply that emission factor by the amount of the product we will use, and we'll know—to a reasonable degree of certainty—our impact on the climate.

Simply put, LCA works like this:

1. **Draw an appropriate boundary.** All impacts within this boundary, defined by Product Category Rules (PCRs), are counted and attributed to the building material being studied. All impacts outside the boundary are excluded. Common boundaries include cradle-to-gate, cradle-to-grave, and cradle-to-cradle. If we know the boundaries of the LCA study, we can compare results with those of other studies with the same boundaries.

2. **Measure inputs and outputs at each stage within the boundary.** Using data from manufacturers and from regional, state, or national life cycle inventories (LCIs), we can assess and calculate the types and quantities of energy and resources that go into the material and all the outputs, including GHG emissions, arising from all activities needed to produce the material that occur within the boundary conditions.

3. **Report emissions in a useful way.** GHG emissions are expressed in relation to a "declared unit" of material (for example, 1 kilogram or 1 cubic meter). All GHGs are measured and then converted to kilograms of CO_2 equivalent (kg CO_2e) as a common factor for expressing global warming potential (GWP) attributed to the material, usually over a hundred-year time span. The standard means of reporting this information is via EPDs.

4. **Calculate the emission profile for a specific quantity of material.** From the GWP factor for a material, a user (or an LCA software program) can figure out how much of this particular material will be needed in a building and multiply the GWP factor by the necessary quantity of material to estimate the emissions caused by the use of the material in a particular building scenario. We can

examine the emission profile of the material and compare it with potential replacements. We can also add the GWP of all the materials in a building together to examine the emission profile of whole buildings.

In this book, we are discussing mainly LCA studies of building products, but it is important to note that LCA studies exist at many scales. An LCA can be performed on a single ingredient of a material, on all the components of a material or product, or on an entire building composed of hundreds of materials or products. In this hierarchy of LCAs, it is common for one LCA to reference results from other LCAs: A product-level study may embed results from individual ingredient LCAs, and a whole-building LCA (WBLCA) will certainly assemble results from a large number of product-level studies.

Climate concerns are focused on the measurement of GWP within LCA studies, but this is only one of seven impact categories that are reported:

- Global warming potential (GWP)
- Ozone depletion potential (ODP)
- Acidification potential (AP)
- Eutrophication potential (EP)
- Photochemical ozone creation potential (POCP)
- Abiotic depletion potential–elements (ADPE)
- Abiotic depletion potential–fossil fuels (ADPF)

We focus here on GWP, not just because it's central to the book but also because it represents by far the most grave and long-lasting danger to life on Earth. Many have calculated that those other abuses to the environment, such as eutrophication or ozone depletion, can be repaired or self-repair in a matter of decades or at most centuries, whereas global climate disruption is hitting us hard now and may persist for millennia. Still, none of these are impacts we want to ignore, and wherever possible we want to find options that positively address climate change and other criteria.

It's fairly easy to sketch the bare bones of LCA, just as it's easy to explain the concept of taxes. But as with taxes, there are a lot of accounting protocols, conventions, and rules. A suite of standards within the ISO 14000, *Environmental Management Standards*, helps to define LCA practice, including ISO 14040 and 14044, *Life Cycle Assessment Framework*; ISO 14067, *Quantifying Carbon Footprint*; and *Life Cycle Accounting and Reporting Standard*. LCA is a field of study and practice that has its own academic journals, professional organizations, consultants, training programs, and specialists. Performing a WBLCA is a complex task usually undertaken by trained professionals, and as with taxes, there are loopholes and gray zones that can cause anything from raised eyebrows to legal action.

What Does LCA Really Show Us?

Conducting an LCA is an ambitious and fraught undertaking; with so many factors and variables at play, there is a lot of room for arguing and questioning results. Each phase of LCA offers particular issues that create varying degrees of uncertainty. In fact, the analysis of uncertainty within LCA practice is a body of literature unto itself, with much thoughtful commentary on offer.

If we want to make informed decisions from our reading of LCA results, we need to explore the structure of an LCA study in a bit more detail. In LCA, analyses of inputs and outputs are related to each distinct stage in the life cycle of a product. These stages are given alphanumeric codes (figure 3.1).

Emission results are tabulated for each distinct stage of a product's life. They can be considered by individual stage, grouped together by category, or summed for a total. Each life cycle stage represents a portion of the total and carries its own degree of uncertainty. If we understand the proportion of the emission impact and the uncertainty, this can help inform our reading of an LCA and guide the choices we make.

Material Life Cycle Stages				
A1-3 product development	**A4-5** construction process	**B1-7** use (B6 and B7 are used in whole building LCA for energy and water use-- not applicable here)	**C1-4** end of use	**D** new life
A1 raw material acquisition / A2 raw material transport / A3 material/product manufacture	A4 material/product transport / A5 construction	B1 use in building / B2 maintenance / B3 repair / B4 replace / B5 refurbish	C1 deconstruction/demolition / C2 transport / C3 waste processing	D reuse, recycle, repurpose

FIGURE 3.1. **Life cycle phases.** Life cycle assessment divides the life cycles of products and buildings into distinct phases and attributes global warming potential values to each unique stage.

1. **A1–A3, Product Stage: 65–80 percent of full life cycle impact.** These are typically the most reliable data in LCA because at this stage it is possible to directly measure input and output flows. The best A1–A3 data come from factory-specific flows and include detailed measurements throughout the supply chain to capture real-world information for all material and energy inputs. The worst data are based on high-level averages (e.g., statewide electrical grid data) and averages for inputs from the supply chain. Specific data have a high degree of certainty, but low-quality data can create an uncertainty factor up to ±35 percent. The LCA study will declare the data sources, allowing us to attribute a reasonable uncertainty factor.

2. **A4, Transportation to Site: 5-15 percent of full life cycle impact.** In a typical LCA, an average transportation distance for a particular material is determined based on distribution patterns, and generalized assumptions are made about modes of transportation and resulting fuel use. Some LCA software programs will adjust this factor based on a specific project location, but given the nature of modern logistics the actual distance from factory to construction site may not be representative of the path a material has taken. Because of these vague calculations, uncertainty can be over 100 percent.

3. **A5, Construction: 5–10 percent of full life cycle impact.** LCA studies assume average factors for the equipment, time, and energy used for construction processes. Variability in construction methods and energy systems in these averages can result in uncertainty over 100 percent.

4. **B1–B3, Use, Maintenance, and Repair: 5–10 percent of full life cycle impact.** Assumptions are made about the frequency of cleaning, maintenance, and repair—based on recommendations from manufacturers—as well as the products and energy used for these tasks. Uncertainty can be over 100 percent.

5. **B4, Replacement: 100 percent of the A1–A5 impacts.** This is the end of life for a product, but for a whole building a product may be replaced multiple times over the life of the building. Assumptions are made here about time frames for replacement, based on manufacturer recommendations. Actual replacement schedules will depend on installation quality, wear, maintenance, and capitalization. An assumption is made that the replacement product will be the same type and have the same emission profile of the original. Uncertainty can be over 100 percent.

6. **C1–C4, End of Life: 5–25 percent of full life cycle impacts.** Two types of uncertainty exist at this stage: gauging the length of time to be assigned to the lifespan of a building material and determining what happens to the material at the end

of its life. Product lifespans are typically based on manufacturer recommendations, but these figures don't necessarily reflect actual serviceable lifespan as much as warranties and legal concerns. The needs and whims of building owners may dramatically shorten or lengthen the actual lifespan of many materials. Once a material has reached the actual end of its life, LCA studies make assumptions about the inputs needed to dismantle, transport, and dispose of materials. Another set of assumptions is used to calculate disposal emissions from options that include incineration, landfilling, or recycling. Percentages of materials that go to each of these disposal streams are broad averages, and the emissions resulting from each type of disposal are likewise averages. Landfill emissions, in particular, can vary widely depending on landfill practices and climate. End-of-life scenarios make assumptions about what will happen many decades in the future based on today's behavior. Our societies do not have a stellar track record when it comes to dealing with "waste" in an appropriate way, but end-of-life impacts are assumed to be the same decades or even a century into the future as they are today. Uncertainty for this stage can be over 100 percent.

If you are now rolling your eyes and wondering about the point of this whole LCA exercise, take heart. All this uncertainty doesn't mean we can't use LCA results. Instead, it means we should be clear about the value of all the information presented in an LCA study and understand whether or how it may influence our decision making.

The information we learn from stages A1–A3 is very important and quite reliable. Because these stages represent most emissions from materials (and therefore the buildings made from them), it is well worth looking closely at A1–A3 results. Making decisions about material choices from these data is prudent, impactful, and increasingly common. We know that the emissions estimated at this stage are relatively accurate and that they happen *now*. If we make choices that dramatically lower A1–A3 emissions, we have made a measurable difference on our climate impact, and we've done it today, the most important time to do so.

Although the uncertainty and overall emission impact get fuzzier as we look at results from stages B and C, we shouldn't ignore them. Questioning B- and C-stage LCA results may spur us to undertake our own more rigorous and specific studies of certain aspects of a project rather than rely on assumptions and averages built into the underlying calculations. We can explore options that will outperform LCA assumptions through improved practice, creativity, and holistic systems thinking. We should not see B- and C-stage results as definitive conclusions but as benchmarks to be surpassed.

The practice of LCA must include a robust practice of interpretation rather than the simple reporting of aggregated results. Used to base impactful decisions today, LCA can drive deep emission reductions. Used as a tool to inform and develop best practices, LCA is a rich resource. Used as a singular, flat data point based on a cumulative end-of-life total, it is at best barely sufficient and at worst misleading.

LCA Accounting for Carbon Storage: The Basics

Building beyond zero is going to require us to durably store vast amounts of carbon in buildings, and this can happen in two possible ways:

- **Biogenic carbon storage.** Biogenic materials begin their life cycle as plants, doing the thing that plants do so well: photosynthesizing CO_2 from the atmosphere and using the carbon atoms to build their bodies while expelling the oxygen atoms (and providing us with a breathable atmosphere). Plants are doing the thing that the Intergovernmental Panel on Climate Change says we need to do: draw carbon out of the atmosphere and take it out of circulation. Every year, the growth of plant biomass on Earth removes between 119 and 169 gigatons of carbon from the atmosphere. Most of this carbon is returned to the atmosphere in fairly short order, as annual crops, leaves, and foliage grow, die, and break down or are eaten, releasing methane, or sometimes by burning. Some of this carbon stays out of the atmosphere for a longer period of time in the form of trees and other perennial biomass. This biomass, too, eventually dies, breaks down, and returns to the atmosphere. The cycle of carbon absorption into biomass and release back to the atmosphere has been in close balance for thousands of years.

  A large portion of the carbon we advocate storing in buildings comes from interrupting this cycle: We let biogenic materials draw down CO_2 as they have always done, but we don't let all that carbon go back to the atmosphere. Instead, we put it away—bank it somewhere safe until we get our fossil fuel emissions under control. Buildings offer just such a durable place for biogenic carbon to remain out of the atmosphere.

  The natural growth cycle of a particular biogenic material and the length of time this biogenic carbon resides in a building determine the value of this storage on repairing the climate (more on this in the previous chapter). When materials are used as long-lasting building elements in the structure, enclosure, and foundation, the carbon they store is locked up for the duration of the building's useful life. The same cannot be said for short-lived products. Consider an engineered wood product, such as plywood. If used for concrete formwork it will probably be discarded within a few weeks; depending on the disposal method (e.g., landfill, incineration), the biogenic carbon could be released back into the atmosphere within a short period of time. Contrastingly, an identical plywood product could be used in the structural elements of a building with a 60-year lifespan, as floor sheathing, for example. In this case, the carbon would be sequestered for decades before it is discarded or, in a best-case scenario, recycled and directly reused at the end of its first useful life.

- **Mineral carbonation.** Biological, geological, and industrial or chemical processes can turn atmospheric carbon into carbonate mineral forms. The shells of oysters and the structure of coral are examples of biological carbonation. CO_2 can also react with metal oxides in and on Earth's surface to form stable carbonates. Both forms of mineral sequestration are long lasting. Currently, very few building products make use of short-cycle carbonates, but this is an area that is beginning to be explored and shows great potential (see chapter 6).

    It is important to differentiate mineral sequestration that has happened quite recently (within a few years) from what has happened historically. There is no positive impact on the climate if we put a kilogram of limestone into a building that is made with million-year-old atmospheric carbon. But there can be a very positive impact on the climate if we put a kilogram of algae-grown carbonate in a building because that CO_2 was drawn out of the atmosphere recently, helping to reduce the current load of GHGs that are driving climate change.

Measuring carbon storage in materials was not central in the development of LCA methods; the practice was developed to measure emissions, not storage. Mineral sequestration, in the rare occurrences where it shows up in building material LCA, makes for easy accounting: A kilogram of recently withdrawn atmospheric carbon sequestered in a material is valued at a 1:1 ratio, offering a kilogram of carbon storage because the carbon will reliably remain in mineral form for many centuries.

Because it is very likely to return to the atmosphere as CO_2 (by burning) or methane (by decomposing) within a geologically short period of time, biogenic carbon is a thornier issue. The notion of biogenic carbon storage was formally introduced into LCA practice in 2017, in the second edition of ISO 21930, *Sustainability in Buildings and Civil Engineering Works—Core Rules for Environmental Product Declarations of Construction Products and Services.* Section 7.2.7, "Accounting of biogenic carbon uptake and emissions during the life cycle," and states,

> *Bio-based materials originating from renewable resources (such as wood, linseed oil, cork or bio-based polymers) contain biogenic carbon. The mass flows to and from nature and biogenic carbon removal(s) and emissions throughout the product system shall be reported as a flow of biogenic carbon expressed in CO_2 in the LCI. When entering the product system (i.e., a flow to the technosphere from nature), this biogenic carbon flow shall be characterized in the LCI with −1kg CO_2e/kg of biogenic carbon in the calculation of the GWP, since it represents a removal of carbon that is part of the carbon cycle of bio-based materials.*

This "clarification" of the rules for biogenic carbon accounting hasn't actually brought clarity and consistency to the practice. The identification and valuation of biogenic carbon in LCAs and EPDs is handled in several different ways:

- **Ignore biogenic carbon.** Many LCA studies and EPDs do not identify biogenic carbon in materials or attribute any storage value. In such cases, a biogenic material is treated like any other material, and only emissions are counted.
- **Assume carbon neutrality.** Biogenic carbon is "canceled out" on the assumption that the amount of carbon removed from the atmosphere during plant growth is fully returned to the atmosphere at the end of the product's lifespan. In practice this approach results in the same zero value as ignoring the biogenic carbon.
- **Account for biogenic carbon storage in the harvesting stage (Stage A1 in LCA) as a "negative emission," with every kilogram of atmospheric CO_2 in the biogenic material subtracting 1 kilogram of CO_2 emissions.** Although this approach begins to actually value stored carbon, some LCA studies do this subtraction of storage from emissions behind the scenes and only report the net result in A1. Others report the emissions and the storage as distinct figures to provide maximum transparency. This type of separated reporting is becoming more widely accepted and mandated and will become the norm in coming years.

  After showing up as a negative number in A1, biogenic carbon is then recounted in the form of anticipated carbon release in the end-of-life stage (Stage C-4). Here, the LCA report makes certain assumptions about how the biogenic material will be disposed, and, depending on these assumptions, some or all of the CO_2 contained in the material is calculated to go back to the atmosphere, becoming a "positive emission" and fully or partially erasing the storage value attributed to the material at the beginning of its lifespan. The norm is to report the GWP of a product as the sum total of storage and emissions at end-of-life.

Until we get to the point where we can see the "negative" and "positive" emissions of biogenic carbon in every LCA (and be transparent about the underlying methods to justify these figures), we are stuck with four different kinds of reporting that we must recognize and understand if we want to make comparisons between the GWP of materials.

Researchers and LCA practitioners who are interested in accurate accounting for biogenic carbon storage often choose to do their own biogenic carbon assessments so that storage can be reported separately from emissions in a consistent manner.

Dynamic LCA: The All-Important Time Value of Emissions
Climate scientists agree that reducing emissions *now*—whether by emitting less or storing more—is a more impactful mitigation than the same actions taken later in the future. Yet work on the carbon storage side of LCA has lagged because it requires some different methodological considerations and because, until very recently, it has not been considered important enough to receive the attention it deserves. The time values of emissions and of carbon storage are not inherently recognized in conventional LCA practice, which tends to focus on a singular, static total life cycle emission figure for comparisons between building materials and whole buildings. The use of this single end-of-life data point for comparison does not account for the dynamic impact of timing of emissions or storage (more explanation of this in chapter 2). Climate change compels us to take a more comprehensive view of LCA results because a ton of emissions released today has far more climate impact than a ton of emissions released a decade from now. Because we measure the lifespan of building materials and buildings in decades, this dynamic is critically important to the case for carbon storing buildings and LCA that truly expresses their climate impacts.

Two main time-related factors inform a dynamic LCA:

• **The front end matters, a lot.** Most emissions from building materials arise at the product stage (A1–A3), and because these emissions are also the most reliably assessed, we can be confident that our quantities for them are relatively accurate. These bulk emissions are committed to the atmosphere before a building is built, and nothing that occurs over the lifespan of the building alters them. The timing of these emissions is now; the climate impacts last for centuries. If we are going to intervene to reduce emissions and commit to storage, this is the most impactful time to do so. Evaluations between materials (and whole building designs) should include an A1–A3 comparison that is heavily weighted in the decision-making process because changes at this stage will have the biggest climate impacts.

• **The future is fuzzy.** The movement toward low-carbon and zero-carbon economies could change many of our assumptions about B- and C-stage emissions. Although LCA uses the best available data to estimate these emissions, the actual GHG intensity in some or all of these stages could be dramatically different when they occur in the future. The further away from today, the more likely our current assumptions are to be wrong. From cleaning products to emissions from maintenance energy use to actual replacement of a material, there is a strong likelihood that emissions for these activities and materials will be much lower than today and are therefore overcounted in LCA. This is particularly true when we consider C-stage end-of-life assumptions. There is a growing consensus that landfill is not an appropriate resting place for billions of tons of materials that cost us valuable resources, time, and emissions to create, and current patterns of landfill, incineration, and recycling are likely to change over the next decades. This is particularly true for biogenic materials, for which incineration and landfill are the most common end-of-life assumptions made in LCA. As we move to placing a higher value on averting emissions, we are very likely to discourage both of these options and favor recycling (see chapter 10) or creating biochar (pyrolysis, or burning of biomass in the absence of oxygen; see chapter 6), which will permanently sequester the bulk of biogenic carbon while creating useful heat and energy. Either of these end-of-life scenarios, plus others we may not even know are coming, will completely change the C-stage outcomes and further improve the results for biogenic materials. With so much uncertainty about today's LCA end-of-life figures, it is prudent to use them as indicators of what could be, not what will be.

There is obviously a balance to be walked here, because we don't want to make decisions today with an unduly optimistic assumption that tomorrow will truly be the lower-emission future we need it to be. Nor do we want to see decisions made that drive today's emissions higher based on B- and C-stage LCA assumptions that may prove quite wrong, incomplete, or misleading. Choosing a material with very high

A-stage emissions based on its potentially long lifespan or lack of emissions in the C-stage will drive climate change faster and put the future in danger.

Beyond assisting us to make good decisions for emission reductions, a dynamic view of LCA stages builds the case for the crucial climate benefit from carbon storage in building materials.

As was discussed in chapter 2, the climate responds to emissions and storage from the time they happen onward, not stuck at any singular moment. The drawdown of atmospheric carbon happens as the carbon-storing material is made, whether by natural photosynthesis or in a factory: There is less carbon in the atmosphere from that moment onward, and this is good for slowing climate change. As the carbon-storing material is converted into a building material there will be emissions that put some GHGs back into the atmosphere, but if these emissions are less than what was absorbed in the formation of the material, there is a net drawdown. This "negative" balance (which is positive for the climate but expressed as a negative number in LCA accounting) endures for the lifespan of the material. The amount of carbon that returns to the atmosphere depends a lot on what we decide to do with it many decades later. If we're smart about it, most of that carbon can stay out of the atmosphere. But even if we're not smart about it and it is fully released to the atmosphere, this dynamic profile is dramatically different from that of the nonstoring material (see figure 2.6 in the previous chapter). Nonstoring materials only generate emissions. It may be a little or it may be a lot, but either way there are more GHGs in the atmosphere the day they are made than the day before, and the climate warms up a bit more and continues to warm the entire time those emissions are in the atmosphere.

In the dynamic view, the impact of the emitting material is what we need to consider. This isn't just a matter of a wee difference in total life cycle emissions, as current LCA usually intimates; it's the dramatic difference between the emissions or storage multiplied by the time they're in (or taken out of) the air. It's the difference between buildings that can heal the climate and buildings that will make it worse.

One of the reasons that LCA has not, until recently, addressed dynamic issues surrounding biogenic carbon is that biogenic materials have had only a small presence in mainstream construction. Timber products have long been the only biogenic material with a prominent role in architecture, and they were used most widely in the often-ignored low-rise building sector until the recent development of mass timber structures for large or tall buildings. The carbon-storing capacity of mass timber buildings has been much celebrated in recent years and has been both the central focus of the movement to acknowledge dynamic biogenic carbon storage in LCA and a source of the arguments against it. Figuring out the dynamics of carbon storage in timber products requires a very wide lens to see clearly, because we need to consider the dynamics of forest ecosystems to get the accounting right; we'll explore this in chapter 6.

However, timber is not the only option for carbon storage in buildings, and most of the other materials we'll explore in that chapter offer simpler accounting, can show up in more parts of a building, and are available in more parts of the world.

Tools for Measuring Emissions

The past decade has seen an explosion of LCA software tools intended to help building designers understand and ideally lower the carbon footprint of buildings. This is exciting, but, as discussed, none of these tools currently accounts for dynamic carbon storage in a systematic and robust way. This is something we need to change—and we can see it beginning to change already.

Currently, LCA tools take two distinct forms: Some focus on a full life cycle assessment and others focus only on the A1–A3 product stage.

WBLCA Tools

The market for tools that can be used to assess the emission profile of whole buildings has expanded rapidly over the past decade. Existing tools have become more accessible and powerful, and new entries join the market regularly. Many of these tools can now be connected with, or are embedded directly into, popular design software. This allows users to get quick feedback on design decisions and to rapidly examine iterations of a building design to maximize emission reductions or storage potential. Most WBLCA tools incorporate robust reporting and visualizations to help design teams and clients understand complex LCA results and to make decisions changing the GHG footprint of a building.

The data inside LCA software tend to skew toward the country or region of origin for the software, making some options more or less attractive depending on the user's location. The best LCA software is transparent about the data sources being used to generate results. The inclusion of references to the underlying LCA studies or EPDs is valuable for users who want to be able to understand and verify the results they are seeing. Best to avoid LCA software programs that are a "black box" from which results emerge with no indication of data sources.

The field of LCA software will continue to expand as building certification programs and government incentives and policies start to require the submission of a WBLCA as part of compliance packages. As LCA data and methods become more standardized, this information will become ubiquitous in building design. And as design practitioners get more familiar with the results and what those results mean, the use of LCA will be absorbed into typical practice, much as energy modeling software has become a central decision-making tool.

Procurement Tools

WBLCA tools tend to provide industry average data, allowing design teams to compare categories of materials. When it comes to procurement, however, a builder needs product-specific data in order to make decisions with the best emission outcome. Within a single product category, it is possible for two products of essentially the same material to have very different emission profiles.

Procurement tools allow comparisons at this product-specific level. These tools focus on comparisons of product-stage (A1–A3) EPDs which, as noted above, represent the bulk of overall emissions from products. The granular nature of the data allows users to anticipate transportation impacts by understanding where competing products are manufactured and the approximate distance to the specific construction site.

Procurement tools can have an interesting and positive competitive effect in the marketplace. By revealing differences in emissions between competing products, they offer a compelling sales case; the more important emission reduction and carbon storage become, the more of a differentiator is the EPD. For example, we've seen product transparency change the food industry in the past decade, and side-by-side comparisons of EPD results in procurement tools—in combination with strong incentive and policy signals from governments (see chapter 11)—are likely to have a similar impact in driving down emissions across entire industries as procurement decisions are ever more guided by climate goals. Concrete, to take a prominent example, is coming under increasing regulation to drive down its enormous footprint (see chapter 6), because producers can make concrete meeting project requirements that nonetheless varies enormously in its emissions. (See box 3.2.)

Show Me the Money! What Is Storage Really Worth?

We have asserted that the climate impact of a GHG is the amount of the emissions multiplied by the time it is in the air. That's roughly true—more precision on that in a moment—and essential to recognize as we try to deal effectively with GHGs through all of human economy. What happens *now*, whether emissions or storage, matters more than what happens in the future.

But it's worth looking at this a little more carefully for a more accurate picture of what's happening. The time value of emissions or storage of carbon is somewhat, though not exactly, like the time value of money in an economy with interest rates.

Box 3.2   Building Transparency and the EC3 Tool

The nonprofit Building Transparency is a result of nearly fifty industry partners coming together to develop the Embodied Carbon in Construction Calculator (EC3). EC3 was initially created by Stacy Smedley of Skanksa and Phil Northcott of C Change Labs, and initial funding came from Microsoft, MKA Foundation, Charles Pankow Foundation, Interface, and Skanska USA. The Carbon Leadership Forum incubated the tool up to the public beta launch in November 2019.

In early 2020, Building Transparency was established as a new Washington State nonprofit to continue the management and development of the EC3 tool and to provide the resources and education necessary to ensure its adoption. Building Transparency has continued to develop EC3 in collaboration with manufacturing as well as architectural, engineering, and construction (AEC) professional partners and has expanded its offerings to cover other essential gaps needed to address embodied carbon's role in climate change.

The EC3 tool is free and easy to use, allowing benchmarking, assessment, and reductions in embodied carbon focused on the up-front supply chain emissions of construction materials. It uses building material quantities from construction estimates and building information modeling models and a robust database of digital, third-party verified EPDs. Powered by these data, the EC3 tool can be implemented in both the design and procurement phases to look at a project's overall embodied carbon emissions, enabling the specification and procurement of the lower-carbon options.

The EC3 tool also allows owners, green building certification programs, and policymakers to assess supply chain data to create EPD requirements and set embodied carbon limits and reductions at the construction material and project scale.

The tool and its subsequent effects on the industry are driving demand for low-carbon solutions and incentivizing product manufacturers and suppliers to provide disclosure and transparency and to foster innovation that reduces the GWP of their products.

Building Transparency is developing Open EPD, an open data format for sharing digital third-party verified EPDs between program operators, EPD databases, LCA tools, design tools, reporting, and procurement.

In a remarkably short time, Building Transparency has changed the landscape for the measurement and reporting of embodied carbon. Next in their sights is a comprehensive method for assessing the value of biogenic carbon storage in building materials, a critical step in getting the industry to build beyond zero.

Source: https://www.buildingtransparency.org/

A ton emitted today has more climate impact than a ton emitted in 10 or 30 or 100 years (100 being the time frame typically used by the Intergovernmental Panel on Climate Change). Conversely, you could say there is a *discount value* to future emissions (or carbon stored) when compared with the present value. What that discount rate should be is already a topic of both research and debate, although it is based on physics, not the quarterly decisions of a board of governors or any other human beings. The physics, basically, describes the decay of GHGs in the atmosphere. If

I add a ton of CO_2 to the air, I increase the partial pressure of CO_2 relative to all the other gases that make up what you and I are breathing right now. That increase will more forcefully push the CO_2 into places like plants that photosynthesize it or the rocks, lakes, and oceans that absorb it. If poetically inclined, you might say that the resulting decay is the carbon trying to come home to Earth. In the long view of history, CO_2 levels in the atmosphere varied but stayed within boundaries through natural cycling. But in the past 200 years we have pushed carbon in the form of fossil fuel emissions up into the air far faster than natural processes can bring it home. Hence climate warming and disruption.

The exact rate of decay will vary with different GHGs, be they carbon dioxide, methane, nitrous oxide, or the highly potent hydrofluorocarbons that we use for refrigerants. The rate will also vary with the (starting) partial pressure of the gas, seasonal temperature, and other factors. All that said, for all GHGs you get, over 100 years, a curve that looks like the one in figure 3.2.

Now comes the interesting part: Emissions decay, but carbon stored in a building does not. Except when it does, and so here things get contentious. Many events, such as fire and rot of anything cellulosic, will lessen the storage life of a building material, but we can't predict those events. As we said, we can greatly decrease their likelihood with good design, construction, and maintenance, but we can't reduce the chances to zero. We have to allow for the fact that, to use a technical engineering expression, shit happens, and the decay curve gives us a mathematical basis for answering the question, How long does it need to last in order to have been worthwhile? (figure 3.3).

How long, indeed. The answer to this question is still very much being debated; it might be 55 years, it might be 46 years, it might be something else. It will also be different for different gases, but some averaged value, as well as time frame if other than 100 years, will be needed for policy purposes. That value will probably be debated for a while yet, for there's already money on the table. (See "The Time Value of Carbon and Carbon Storage: Clarifying the Terms and the Policy Implications of the Debate"[1] from the World Resources Institute.) As we start to put a price on carbon in the various possible ways we have of penalizing emissions and rewarding storage, the profits (or costs) to everybody in every value chain keep going up. Businesses care, and they increasingly care a lot. The trick for companies, investors, and policymakers is not just to determine the appropriate discount rate by which to value carbon storage but to craft rules and price signals that will as quickly as possible foster a virtuous cycle toward a regenerative, beyond-zero economy.

The length of time needed to achieve equivalence between a ton of present storage and 100 years of a ton of today's emissions has been called the *equivalence time*,

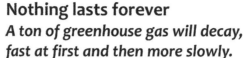

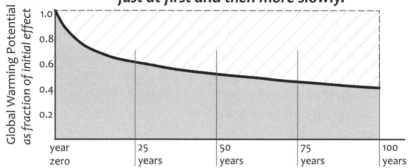

FIGURE 3.2. **Not the gas it used to be.** If we describe climate impact in ton-years (as people increasingly do), then a ton of CO_2 emitted today would have the impact of 100 ton-years after 100 years—if there were no decay. But there is decay, so the century impact of today's ton of emissions is not the area of the rectangle but more like 60 or 70 ton-years (i.e., the shaded area under this decay curve).

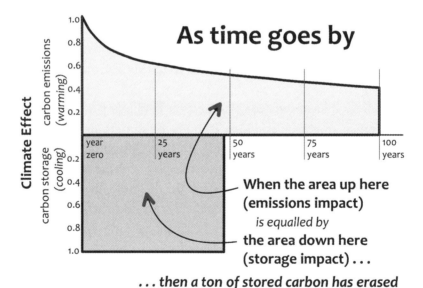

FIGURE 3.3. **Compared to what?** How long does carbon stored in a building material need to endure undecayed in order to have offset 100 (or 60, or 50) ton-years of emissions?

Table 3.1. The Time Value of Stored Biogenic Carbon

Biogenic Carbon Stored	Duration of Storage	Equivalent Offset of Present-Day Emissions
100 tons	1 year × 2.17%	2.17 tons
100 tons	20 years × 2.17%	43.4 tons
100 tons	46 years × 2.17%	**100** tons
100 tons	80 years × 2.17%	174 tons

T_e. The discount rate for carbon accounting purposes is its inverse: $100/T_e$. For a 46-year duration, T_e is $100/46 = 2.17$ percent for a 100-year time frame. Then you get some simple math, as shown in table 3.1.

The math can get more complex, of course, and it depends on setting a duration and equivalence time and discount rate. But the point here stands: Carbon stored today, even if we can't be sure of its longevity, does offset present emissions; it does assist climate restoration. It buys us some time, slows the buildup of emissions, and holds promise to last longer than expected through social and technological developments. And companies such as Aureus Earth are bringing much-needed financial instruments to incentivize the decarbonization of the construction industry and store biogenic carbon for generations. Carbon is already becoming a physical asset that can be monetized in new building and infrastructure projects.

A related issue that we see rising in prominence is a *carbon return on investment* (CROI), by which we can evaluate when a carbon expenditure (emission) today will pay back. CROI is used in many ways, such as for carbon capture, utilization, and storage (CCUS) systems, but conceptually it always has the same basis in LCA. For buildings and building products, we will increasingly use CROI as a means of finding, for example, how long it takes a particular solar array to pay back the carbon emitted in its manufacture.

We've Seen This Movie Before

The proliferation of LCA and EPDs and their growing influence and use in building design and procurement follow an arc that has appeared in many industries.

In transportation, fuel economy was not a concern for a long time, until the oil embargo of the 1970s put it squarely on the table for governments and citizens; within a short time, fuel mileage figures became important for car sales. Industry resisted, arguing about methodology but eventually accepting the need to provide this information to buyers. Governments enacted requirements and tightened standards over time. Corporations made fleet-wide requirements and buying decisions based on fuel economy. Many who buy a car today factor fuel mileage into their decision, and for many it is a tipping point in an otherwise close decision between two competing models.

The analogy doesn't end there. The introduction of electric vehicles (EVs) introduced a twist into the standard measurement of fuel economy that has much in common with the introduction of carbon-storing building materials. Both raise a similar fundamental question: What do we do when the very means of comparison is no longer pertinent? We can be certain that EVs have a very different kind of fuel use and emission profile because they don't use the liquid fossil fuel by which fuel economy is measured. For EVs, new standards have started to emerge—as have controversies about metrics and methods—and both industry and buyers are becoming literate with them as the climate crisis compels us to figure this out.

Carbon-storing building materials have the same transformative potential as EVs and are likely to follow a similar pathway to widespread valuation and adoption. Both EVs and carbon-storing materials were early competitors with fossil fuel–based options until the growth of the fossil fuel economy obscured them. Both EVs and carbon-storing materials returned to small-scale use in the hands of ecologically minded tinkerers in the late 1960s and 1970s but were not seen as credible options or real threats to the dominant paradigm as they reemerged. EVs are now widely viewed as necessary for curbing emissions and mitigating climate change, and their presence in the marketplace has grown faster than almost anyone predicted. Now most governments are wholeheartedly incorporating EVs into their low-carbon strategies. This book makes the case that carbon-storing building materials offer not just a theoretical comparison but a similarly transformative part of our climate response.

LCA and EPDs can show us which building materials are the emission-heavy V-8 engines in their material category, which are the slightly better V-6s, and which are the fuel-sipping 4-cylinder or transformative EV options.

Carbon-Storing Materials Are the EVs of Building Materials

And, as with fuel economy, the number listed on the sales sheet "may not reflect actual real-world mileage," but that shouldn't stop us from identifying their remarkable value even while working out the details of how to measure and value their impact.

We humans can always figure out how to count things properly. We need to count emissions *and* storage and to do so in full acknowledgment of the time value of both, so we maximize our positive climate impact in the shortest time possible.

4. Metals and Minerals: Steeling Ourselves

In human history the discovery of metals, and the subsequent and ongoing developments in how to use, blend, and reuse them, has been one of the more transformative byproducts of the Agricultural Revolution. First we made simple jewelry, ploughs, and swords, but soon enough we were electrifying nations and flying to the moon. Along with concrete in its many forms, metals are the main fundaments of mineral architecture. We'll look at concrete in the next chapter, but first a broader look at minerals.

Minerals are what you can dig out of the Earth, somewhere on the planet; the word literally means "substances obtained by mining." *Mineral* can also mean different things to different people, but is generally taken to mean a solid, inorganic, naturally occurring element or compound. It bears noting that *all* human modifications to the landscape start with minerals—earth—because everything we build with originated in the Earth's crust and has its present form as a result of some combination of geological, biological, or industrial processes. For example, wood is the result of solar energy and biological growth using nutrients pulled from the soil and carbon from the air (which itself came from the Earth). Structural steel—and all other metals—are the distillation of certain ore-bearing rocks. Portland cement is made by heating and grinding limestone along with various other trace earthen materials. Glass is melted sand. Even oil-based plastics are the product of processing ancient beds of plants and algae that have been transformed into oil by complex geological processes over tens of millions of years. All buildings are earthen buildings because every building material we see around us today came, one way or another, from the Earth. Most of the trick with low-carbon building amounts to minimizing the amount of transport and processing between harvesting something and placing it into your building. A short, simple supply chain is the key to low-carbon construction.

For our purposes in this book, *mineral* means "abiotic"—not harvested or derived from biological (organic) sources such as trees, straw, hemp, or bamboo. So far, so somewhat clear. However, like biologists with their ever-shifting categories and definitions for life, we have our gray areas, too, so we address plastics and the fast-expanding world of biologically grown materials wherever they best fit in coming chapters; they are both mineral and plant based.

Furthermore, although we seem to use nearly everything we find on the Earth—for instance, a typical smartphone draws on more than two thirds of the elements in the periodic table—the greenhouse gas emissions of building materials are very much concentrated in two things: steel and concrete. In the spirit of bank robber Willie Sutton, who famously responded, when asked why he robbed banks, "Because that's where the money is!," we will focus a lot on steel and concrete because that's where the emissions are. Our aim is to target the low-hanging (or anyway outsized) fruit, not to assemble a comprehensive, academic assessment that anyway would be obsolete before the ink dried. To illustrate: Read through the fast-expanding field of research (see https://carbonleadershipforum.org/), where you will see various versions of a pie chart that looks something like figure 4.1, depicting the relative emissions of building materials.

Figure 4.1 is a simplification, of course, and needs a few comments and clarifications. The size of the pie and its slices will vary depending on whether you're looking at a renovation, a new building, a region, a building type (high rise? single-family home? warehouse?), a country (Peru? USA? China?), or the world. A concrete block warehouse will be almost all concrete and steel, but a typical office renovation will have almost none. Plastic foam insulation, because of the high global warming potential (GWP) of the gases used to make it, can make up a surprisingly large part of a project footprint, especially on retrofits; the same is true for HVAC units and heat pumps, which usually run on similar high-GWP hydrofluorocarbon gases.

But the general proportions stay pretty much as shown for new construction: Most of the emissions are in structure and enclosure. That is a main reason why it is almost always better to retrofit an existing structure rather than generate the emissions for a new structure and enclosure (see chapter 2, box 2.1). Globally, concrete is responsible for about 8 percent of total emissions, almost all of which goes to buildings and infrastructure, and steel contributes 7 percent, just over half of

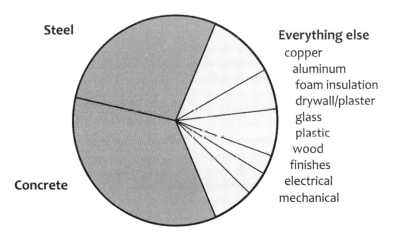

FIGURE 4.1. Comparative size of embodied emissions.

which goes to buildings and infrastructure. Those two alone more than make up the aggregate 11 percent of emissions commonly attributed to the sum of building materials. "Everything else" comprises more than an afterthought and would seemingly bring the total contribution of building materials to something more like 15 percent of the global total. But this fuzziness in the numbers only reflects the youth of life cycle assessment science, where we have good accuracy but not yet as much precision, in both data and accounting systems, as we'd like (see chapter 3). For example, if you emit a thousand tons of CO_2 in building a power plant, is that attributed to the building industry or to the power industry? If I build a mass timber office building rather than using reinforced concrete, but I don't source the wood from a well-managed forest, did I really do the right thing for the climate? (Spoiler alert: Probably not.) While we work out how to account for emissions along the many and complex value chains, everyone should pull on their oars. If you make doorknobs, do everything you can to make great, lowest-carbon-possible doorknobs. If you make flooring, find a way to make net carbon-absorbing flooring, as has been pioneered by Interface. Find a way, and ask your suppliers to find ways. Drive demand by demanding.

And now to metal.

Metals

We love metal. We use massive amounts of it, in buildings and everywhere else. We love copper and tin, silver and gold, zinc, iron and chromium, magnesium and molybdenum and many you've never heard of. Sometimes we have a conflicted love, as with poisonous lead, arsenic, uranium, and plutonium. Metals make up a big part of humanity's carbon footprint, one not so easily reduced. With present technology, and looking at trends, we can envision getting metal production to or near to a zero-carbon footprint but not *beyond* zero for several reasons.

- **Metals are elemental.** Iron, copper, tin, silicon, zinc, aluminum, magnesium, and the rest are right up there on the periodic table of the elements. We can mix them into different alloys (combinations), but, except for physicists with very expensive equipment making miniscule quantities, only God, via nuclear fusion, can make a metal.

- **There's only so much.** We have to make do with what we can find in the Earth's crust, and that is getting harder and harder to do because we long ago found and used the high-assay stuff. Copper, for example, may have been the first metal put to use by humans because it could be found in almost pure metal condition (no smelting required) on the island of Cyprus in the Mediterranean, thousands of years ago. We have gone from mining almost pure assay copper to, a century ago, mining rock that was just 2 or 3 percent copper, to ripping up entire mountainsides today—much to the dismay of local peoples, plants, and animals—for rock that is less than 1 percent copper. The story is similar for many other metals, and it takes on geopolitical overtones, as when the so-called rare earths essential to modern electronics are disproportionately found in China. Fortunately, our favorite metal, iron, which becomes steel when mixed with manganese, nickel, chromium, or other trace elements, is still plentiful on Earth and relatively easy to access in rock that is more than half iron. Even so, most steel going into buildings has a very high recycled content because, increasingly, the easiest place to harvest steel, copper, and other metals is from the industrial ecosystem rather than raw land in some distant locale. Based entirely on economics, the global metal industry is developing a higher and higher degree of circularity; the broken rake you throw away was once an axle in Boston and will become an I-beam in Guangzhou.

- **Production is energy intensive.** You don't make steel with your everyday solar oven. The production of raw metal from ore and the recycling of scrap are the poster children for heavy industry: huge, scary buckets hanging in cavernous buildings, pouring red-hot molten steel to unseen receptacles below. Great for annual reports and James Bond movies but not so much for a disrupted climate. Steel and most other heavy industries have made much progress in the past few decades on energy efficiency, driven more by rising energy costs than by climate concerns. But energy efficiency can only get us so far, especially when ever-rising demand means the industry as a whole is using more energy—with the attendant emissions—than ever.

- **There are few if any substitutes.** Metals are generally irreplaceable: But for some dazzling materials being produced in laboratories (i.e., not much at scale), there's nothing like metal to carry high structural loads, resist weathering, or conduct electricity and deliver power. Yes, certain bamboos can act like steel in very limited ways, but they have too many drawbacks to ever scale (at least as steel replacement; see more about what we *can* do with bamboo in chapter 6). There are nonmetallic concrete reinforcing bars made from melting basalt or sand (i.e., fiberglass), but again, many constraints and high carbon emission intensity make these technologies unattractive at scale. Carbon fiber, or more properly carbon fiber reinforced polymer (CFRP), has a spectacular strength-to-weight ratio and so is especially useful for transportation: bicycles, boats, cars, trucks, and especially aircraft that use less fuel because they are substantially lighter. But CFRP is also extremely energy and emission intensive and, unlike metal, is very hard to recycle. With present and foreseeable technology CFRP probably has a place in aviation, but from a climate emergency perspective, not much more. A growing family of strong ceramics show promise to supplant metals for various structural uses, but few have evolved much past NASA and the laboratory, and they have similarly large energy and emission footprints as CFRP. Fiber optic cable is changing the world with its ability to transmit stunning amounts of information at near-light speed, but it is not showing any promise as a courier of electrical power. Carbon nanotubes can conduct electricity (and carry intense weight, insulate, and, it seems, do almost anything) but are generally far from commercialization. To date, we move power from one place, such as a generating station or solar array, to another, such as where you're sitting, with copper wire.

Metal, mainly steel, aluminum, and copper, makes modern architecture and our modern lives possible. That doesn't look to change much any time soon.

Getting to Zero

Now that we've established that metals are mostly irreplaceable, limited in supply, and extremely energy-intensive to produce, what can we do?

We'll start with a pointer to two very useful works on decarbonizing steel. The International Energy Agency published the "Iron and Steel Technology Roadmap,"[1] and Global Energy Monitor published "Pedal to the Metal."[2] Those looking for more detail than we can provide here are urged to read those resources.

Regarding steel, we have good news and bad news. The good news is that we are technologically within a generation of making and recycling steel (and all metals) with clean, green hydrogen (more on that in a moment). The bad news is that the industry isn't trying very hard to move that way, because until very recently they haven't received many signals from the market or policymakers that anyone very much cared. In most developed countries there has been much improvement, mainly in improved efficiencies and conversion to electric arc furnaces, the cleanest option for making both virgin and recycled steel. But most of the steel, as with cement, is being made in China and India where the strong preference is for the simpler, cheaper, and far dirtier (in carbon emissions as well as particulates) blast oxygen furnace technology.

Hydrogen and CO2-Free Steel

Hydrogen, the first and simplest element, is what you see when you look at stars, including our sun, which is hydrogen and helium in a long, essentially constant state of nuclear fusion reaction. Solar energy is nuclear energy! Hydrogen loves to combine with carbon, and that's how we get all the life forms we know of. It's much of what you are. We eat carbohydrates for food, we burn hydrocarbons for energy.

Hydrogen is also the future, at least in the sense that it will enable steel, cement, and every other energy-intensive industry to carry on without burden to the climate. You hear more and more of a "hydrogen economy" because making hydrogen gas by electrolysis provides a means of storing and transporting concentrated energy, potentially using pipes and infrastructure we've already built, supplanting a role of fossil fuels in the Industrial Revolution. It is *not* an energy *source,* like oil and gas; it is a medium for storing and transporting energy. Harvest a boatload of solar and wind energy in west Texas and transport it to cold, cloudy Chicago in the form of compressed hydrogen gas. Hydrogen will be our batteries, or at least part of our energy management strategy. Many believe that solid batteries (such as lithium-ion) are the better bet, but most agree that some combination of the two will fully enable a renewable energy future. Hydrogen will fill the gaps left by renewable wind and solar energy, which are abundant but intermittent, diffuse, and not uniformly accessible.

So far, all good news. The most abundant element in the universe comes to our rescue as the key to a sustainable, climate-friendly human economy. Except for a teensy problem: Very few are (yet) making hydrogen gas in the quantities we need, and so few of the players in heavy industries such as electricity, metals, cement, or transport want to commit the gargantuan investments needed for hydrogen fueling without robust, reliable suppliers and supply chains. But at least a few hard-nosed business leaders and investors are betting big on the hydrogen economy.[3] Many more will be needed.

Rapidly scaling hydrogen production up may look at present like a daunting task, but remember: We've done this many times before. Someone had to build the first gas station, the first airport, or the first electric vehicle charging station, each of which probably seemed lonely and foolish for a while. The extensive worldwide infrastructure we've already built for oil and methane (natural) gas is already starting to be adapted to store and convey hydrogen, so the ramp-up is not quite as formidable as it first seems.

A primary means of fostering and hastening the transition to a hydrogen economy would of course be through enlightened policymaking, such as establishing a price on carbon (see chapter 11).

The opportunity for CO_2-free steel is riding on multiple compound cost-reduction pathways: renewable energy, where solar and wind costs are still dropping fast year-on-year, hydrogen electrolyzers, still in early stages of cost compression, and hydrogen direct reduction, a quite nascent technology. Since the energy supply components are already performing at the levels required for competitiveness, what is really holding back the opportunity is the pace at which this new steelmaking technology can be commercially rolled out and scaled into the market.[4]

To date, almost all raw steel is made by heating and reducing (removing oxygen from) iron ore in a furnace intermixed with pulverized coal, or coke (coal that has been baked without oxygen at about 2,000°F) as fuel. This highly emission-intensive process is much of what makes for steel's big footprint—and also why improvement has been so difficult.

Enter the new technology of *hydrogen direct reduction,* in which hydrogen (ideally produced with renewable energy, as just discussed) supplants the coke in heating the ore. But this is not a trivial technology, unfortunately, and shifting from coal/coke to hydrogen is a very capital-intensive proposition. Still, the industry has begun, or anyway it has pioneers.

Steel maker SSAB, in a joint venture with iron ore producer LKAB and utility Vattenfall, opened a whole-building demonstration plant in Luleå, Sweden, the HYBRIT project, which includes an iron ore direct reduction unit fed with hydrogen by a water electrolysis plant using fossil-free electricity. SSAB is a small player in the steel industry, but recently one of the giants, ArcelorMittal, announced the start of hydrogen-based ironmaking in its MIDREX direct reduction plant in Hamburg. Unfortunately, the industry as a whole is taking only small, tentative steps.

Got Them Stranded-Assets Blues Again

Steel, like other heavy industries, faces some enormous capital expenditures in shifting from coal and other fossil fuels to hydrogen-based operations, or more generally in (truly) reducing its footprint. Worse, the industry is making the switch even harder because both India and China are building more blast oxygen furnace capacity; the Global Energy Monitor report mentioned earlier estimates that they may soon have "stranded assets"—obsolete factories and equipment—worth $3–4 and $43–65 billion, respectively.[5]

ResponsibleSteel, the industry's global, multistakeholder standard and certification program, is developing a standard to identify and reward companies that are committed to creating a "responsible" steel value chain. This will cover everything from the sourcing of raw materials through the sale of their final products. Many opt for the easy route of buying carbon offsets, using alternative fuels such as wood pellets rather than coal (even while lacking any evidence that that is better for the climate), and other strategies to "atone for the sin" of continuing business as usual. It makes for good press, showing all the executives smiling and planting saplings, but isn't addressing the fundamental problem.

The technology is there, the financial reasons are growing, and customers are asking steel makers to step up. In a world that needs their product but is growing uninhabitable, steel makers will need to reach to zero, the sooner the better.

More Metals and Minerals: Those Other Pie Slices

"Everything else" includes quite a lot: hundreds of metal alloys, types of glass, plastic polymers, grouts, coatings, and so on that in aggregate produce a lot of emissions (figure 4.2). They are distinguished further by presenting a more complex and nuanced challenge.

For one thing, they are rarely simple. Steel and concrete show up in buildings almost entirely unvarnished: Rebar and wide flange beams are nothing but steel, and but for a few squirts of chemical admixtures (as are and should be increasingly common), concrete really is just sand and gravel rearranged to have the shape and strength we want. Almost everything else shows up in a product assembly, such as insulated copper wiring, window walls with glass, aluminum, sealants, insulation,

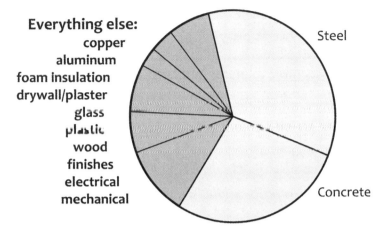

Everything else:
copper
aluminum
foam insulation
drywall/plaster
glass
plastic
wood
finishes
electrical
mechanical

Steel

Concrete

FIGURE 4.2. Comparative size of embodied emissions.

and carpeting with dozens of polymer components. This complicates a discussion of carbon emissions and certainly hinders recycling and the overarching movement toward a circular economy.

Furthermore, a carbon emission assessment is made more complex by health, longevity, and durability factors. If I must choose between two steel suppliers offering essentially the same commodity but with different carbon footprints, my choice is fairly easy. But if I must choose between, say, vinyl-coated wood and anodized aluminum windows, I have to assess not only the usual factors of cost, availability, and constructability but also longevity, thermal performance, volatile organic compounds to which the makers and users will be subjected, and embodied carbon. I can't know much about health effects or global warming emissions until I and other customers start asking window manufacturers for Environmental Product Declarations (EPDs) and Health Product Declarations by which I can make an informed comparison. I might want the window with the higher carbon footprint because it will insulate much better throughout its useful life. But probably not: Some studies have already shown that going the extra mile for operational energy performance (such as by using triple- rather than double-pane windows or adding a layer of rigid foam insulation all around a building) may improve energy performance by a few percent over the next few decades but bring an up-front cost to the climate that won't be paid back for 10 or 20 years. In a climate emergency, when we need to reverse the emission engine hard and fast, that often doesn't make sense.

Like steel, most if not all of these materials require factories that can handle and process large volumes of heavy stuff, usually with a lot of heat added along the way. This is heavy industry using expensive machinery needing a lot of power, and it doesn't change overnight. As the price of energy has generally risen and proven volatile, they have plenty of motivation to increase their energy efficiency, and have done so. There is plenty more room for improvement, but there is also plenty of impulse for just buying dubious carbon offsets or outright greenwashing. The World Green Building Council adds,

> *Encouragingly, for these and other heavy industries, significant emissions reduction opportunities already exist, both in their production and in how they are specified and used. In some parts of the world, sectoral decarbonisation roadmaps have already been established. In developed markets, manufacturers have typically already invested in maximizing plant efficiencies and in many cases have started to switch to alternative energy sources such as biofuels, energy-from-waste or other renewable sources. Further significant emissions reductions will require more fundamental changes, such as switching raw material feedstocks, investing in new production methods, or applying carbon capture technologies. In the global south where many countries are newly industrialised or still becoming industrialised, manufacturing plants may use older, less efficient technology and production techniques. It is critical that manufacturers operating in these regions have the technology and the finance available to "leapfrog" directly to low- and zero-carbon manufacturing approaches with their next investment cycles.*[6]

Just as with steel, we cannot get to net zero in materials supply and management with just incremental efficiency improvements, and certainly not with shell games such as substituting wood pellets for coal as fuel or buying carbon offsets. Also, as with steel, our endgame may require a wholesale shift to renewable energy made available in the necessary concentrated form as hydrogen. Customers will be asking for improvements of every sort, and ideally we will soon have a virtuous cycle of industry racing to optimal performance—racing to zero, if not, in some cases, to carbon sequestration. That's the carrot. The stick, so urgently needed, is a price on carbon emissions.

What Can You Do?

Plenty. You owners, developers, architects, engineers, and builders can't make a hydrogen economy appear overnight, but you can add your voice to calling for it. In the meantime, ask. Ask your supplier for EPDs, ask about the footprint of the steel you're using, and write specifications and make purchases that favor the lowest-carbon options. Be thrifty in the use of steel (and all metals); use them only where you need them. As with pretty much every other material we address in this book, you can reduce emissions a lot just by paying attention, asking, and making informed choices with the least climate impact.

And now to the big boy, concrete.

5. Concrete: Many Ways to Make a Rock

Concrete is artificial rock: You mix up some sand and gravel with some kind of glue and then pour it or spray it or pack it into whatever form you want to get the desired shape and functionality when it hardens. Sometimes you don't even need glue, as when you stabilize soil and rock by containment in gabions, bags, tubes, rock walls, or even old tires. But mostly you use glue to combine a lot of little rocks into a bigger rock. That's about it. That's how you make a concrete block, an adobe brick, a sheet of gypsum board, a city sidewalk, the Sydney Opera House, or the Pantheon—to name just a few among thousands of examples. That's how you build most of the buildings that human beings have ever built—with sand and gravel bound together. There might also be some fibers or chemical additives or other interesting ingredients, and it gets much, much more complicated than you might think, but that's the gist of it: gravel and a binder, be it chemical, biological, or by containment. Pretty simple, and pound for pound concrete is one of the lowest-carbon building materials around. Yet somehow it accounts for 8 percent of global emissions.

How? Because we make so much, that's how (figures 5.1 and 5.2).

Modern Concrete
The first reinforced concrete structures appeared in the middle of nineteenth-century England, accelerating both the birth of composite building technology and engineering as "applied science" and a formal profession. The Ingalls Building, built

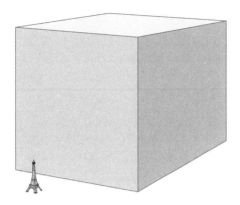

FIGURE 5.1. **Global concrete production** next to Eiffel Tower. Ten billion tons a year makes a cube almost a mile (1,600 meters) on a side, most of it sand and gravel.

FIGURE 5.2. **This much oil.** As long as we're looking at these things, the global annual consumption of petroleum is slightly larger—a cube about 5,800 feet (1,700 meters) on a side (36 billion barrels per year, from multiple sources).

in 1903 in Cincinnati, Ohio, is the world's first reinforced concrete skyscraper. The first hundred years or so of concrete architecture fostered the birth of modernism but also saw the unfortunate spread of "Brutalism" and soul-deadening housing in many parts of the world. Bureaucrats everywhere still keep that tradition alive in the name of affordable housing, but at the same time architects and engineers have created soaring bridges, delightful forms, and endless new spaces for working, worshipping, living, and learning. These were the first examples of engineers and material scientists creating new materials or technology and then watching the artists and architects take them to new heights, both aesthetic and literal. Great fun, and the tradition then expanded (for both better and worse) with the introduction of hot-rolled steel shapes, plastic compounds of uncountable number, plywood, glued-laminated wood, and, of late, mass timber. We invent new stuff and then explore ways to effectively use it as structure, skin, insulation, or many other functions in our ever more complex buildings. That dynamic continues apace, ever faster, and will surely lead to reimagining concrete in ways not yet visible to us.

Concrete as most people think of it—and as modern building codes require—is sand and gravel glued together with *portland cement,* which is basically made by heating and grinding limestone mixed with a bit of clay and gypsum. When it was

Box 5.1   Asphalt: The Other Concrete

You have probably spent a fair bit of your life riding in cars, trucks, and buses on roads paved with portland cement concrete or, more likely, asphalt concrete or *tarmac*. Sometimes called *bitumen* when it occurs in nature (as it does in many places), or *asphalt* when it is a distilled product of certain crude oils, asphalt (to use the generic term for asphalt concrete) is the preferred binder for roadways because it can remain hard and durable, yet also a bit flexible, through wide ranges of use, heat, and weather.

Where it occurs naturally around the world, bitumen was typically put to good use by the local peoples. The tar oozing from beach bluffs in southern California was used by the native Chumash Indians to seal their oceangoing canoes. Thus, the occupying Spanish dubbed that location *Carpinteria*, the carpenter's shop. Two centuries later the occupying oil companies figured out that there was petroleum deeper down and built the oil drilling rigs in the Santa Barbara Channel. Bruce was a high school student in the area in 1969 when one of those rigs blew a pipe and spilled about 90,000 barrels of crude into the channel, decimating sea and shore life over a huge area. Though only a modest incident compared with later oil spill disasters around the United States and the world, that one sparked the first Earth Day and energized the nascent environmental movement. Still, it bears noting that petroleum is a natural substance and that our use of it goes back to before the dawn of cities and architecture.

Like portland cement, asphalt has many uses besides as roadways, especially as mastic, tar, self-sealing flashing tape, and impregnated roll paper for wall and roof water barriers. Pretty handy stuff when you want to stay dry. And so, between supporting our cars and trucks and keeping our buildings dry, we use a lot of asphalt—enough to make a cube about 1,200 feet (365 m) high, also much bigger than the Eiffel Tower (figures 5.3 and 5.4).

FIGURE 5.3. **This much asphalt** (bitumen) gets used on Earth every year.

FIGURE 5.4. **A Texas-sized parking lot!** We have covered a total area on the surface of the Earth—roads, sidewalks, and buildings, by various estimates, with the equivalent of a 330-mile-diameter circle—about the size of the state of Texas, or of France, Myanmar, or Afghanistan. We expect that area to double in the next few decades.

invented in England 200 years ago, portland cement was a technological leap forward from the lime plasters that had been around in many forms all over the world for millennia. Inventor Joseph Aspdin found by trial and error that by burning the limestone a bit hotter (over 1,400°C or 2,600°F) and intermixing ground clay, he could get a vastly better product. It set up faster, was stronger sooner, could be used underwater, and in many ways was just better than anything we'd had before.[1] Portland cement quickly took over and is now the most used building material in the world after water, sand, and gravel (notably, the other main ingredients of concrete). It was a truly great and game-changing technology, now required by law to be present in anything called "concrete." It is embedded in our standards and codes and therefore intimately part of almost all building projects. *Cement* and *concrete* are even embedded in everyday culture, as many people use the terms as if they were synonymous; even Google search gets confused about that.

We love portland cement, and for good reason: It is a fantastic building material. Cheap, easy to make anywhere there's limestone (which is almost everywhere), and easy to use.

What's not to like?

Global climate disruption is what. Baking rock to 2,600°F (1,400°C) takes a lot of energy, which is typically provided by burning fossil fuels (and sometimes also waste materials such as tires, generating a lot of additional unpleasant emissions). Also, the resulting chemical reaction that converts limestone ($CaCO_3$) to lime (CaO) and carbon dioxide (CO_2) means you get about a ton of emissions for every ton of cement. That is why concrete, which is otherwise just sand, gravel, and water, generates 8 percent of global warming emissions. That is why if concrete were a country, it would be the third largest emitter after the United States and China. We need all that concrete, and we will need even more in the years and decades to come.

Bringing Down the Footprint: Efforts to Decarbonize Concrete

Can we make good concrete that does everything we want it to without all the emissions?

Of course we can. We can have all that concrete without all the emissions by rethinking "rock"—by opening up the definition of "concrete" and making effective use of our global body of knowledge applied to whatever human and mineral resources are available at any particular location on Earth. We're moving in that direction in a number of ways, some of them available now, some of them a few years out.

Our Climate Ambition is our member companies' commitment to drive down the CO_2 footprint of their operations and products, and aspire to deliver society with carbon neutral concrete by 2050.

—The Global Cement and Concrete Association[2]

For an industry as conservative and entrenched as concrete, a remarkable amount of work and innovation is happening worldwide to reduce its carbon footprint. (See *Eco-Efficient Cements* for an excellent, comprehensive and highly recommended resource.[3]) It won't be easy, and it will surely be the result, at least for the foreseeable future, of engaging many different efforts and developments in tandem: for the industry as a whole, for the surrounding industrial ecosystem, and for individual concrete suppliers.

Start with basics: The way we make concrete—artificial rock—is by gluing together a bunch of little rocks to get a bigger rock. It's been this way since the walls of Jericho, but we've learned a bit since Jericho, such as about granularity (box 5.2).

The mechanics and rheology (the behavior and physics of liquids or liquid–solid mixes) of all this can seem quite complex in academic articles, yet in essence it's pretty simple, and every child playing in wet sand or soil figures all this out. They don't know about surface tension and the capillary force that binds the sand particles to each other, but they quickly find that too wet or too dry doesn't work. They don't know about the mechanics of grading particles and reducing void spaces, thus reducing the distance that the binding water has to "stretch," as in box 5.2. They just work out that packing the damp sand makes it stronger. That's all they need, and with that they build their castles to the sky.

Even with very well-graded aggregate particles, you still need a binder, and there are a great many ways that the industry is working to improve on cement.

Cement plant efficiencies have been improving for decades, mainly by switching from wet process to dry process kilns; it's not hard to see that you can save a lot of energy if you don't have to heat a lot of water along with the limestone. Along with other energy improvements, the efficiencies of plants worldwide now vary quite a lot. The newest plants, mainly in China—the world's biggest producer and arguably the world's biggest innovator—have about half the emissions of the older plants in the United States.

Alternative Fuels
Concrete and cement have a long history with fossil fuels and emissions. The first portland cement kilns used coal, but cement kilns are indifferent to their fuel

Box 5.2   Nitty Gritty: The Better You Pack Those Particles, the Stronger the Concrete

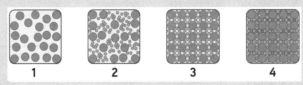

Basic

Mix some rocks with some glue. Not terribly strong, but it worked for most people for most of history. Note that we're showing round rocks to illustrate a few points, but of course most rocks are angular and irregular, be they sand particles, gravel, or larger cobbles. Rounder rocks make it easier to work a wet mass of concrete before the glue hardens, but they will make for a weaker product (no big deal for most concrete, but sometimes a very big deal; see figure 5.6 on the Burj Khalifa). Usually, the glue isn't as strong as the rocks, so the less glue you use—the pale gray area in these illustrations—the stronger your resulting concrete. When you've figured that out, you get to:

Mix It Up

By using different particle sizes, such as sand and gravel, you can reduce the void space—the part that must be filled with glue. This also shortens the distance that the glue has to stretch to connect any two adjacent pieces of aggregate. The problems here are twofold: The more you fill the voids with smaller particles, the harder it is to work or pour or pump the wet mix. Also, many small (silt size and smaller) particles tend to flocculate (clump together), making weak lumps of larger quasi-aggregate. The same is true of clay and portland cement particles: They tend to gum things up (weaken the mass) at the microscopic level.

Squeeze Play

By compacting a damp (but not wet) mass of concrete, you can force the little rocks into the voids between the bigger rocks. Welcome to rammed earth and modern roller-compacted concrete. This is how we built the Great Wall of China, the Pantheon, the Interstate Highway system, and every rammed earth structure everywhere. You can get roughly the same effect with wet concrete by vibrating it while still fresh, but that is an art as well as a science; most engineers' specifications proscribe overvibrating, because that can lead to problems. Both systems work very well but don't deflocculate the clumps, so you start to yearn for modern tech.

Modern Tech

There is now a large array of chemical admixtures available to concrete builders that act like grease: They reduce the amount of water you need without sacrificing flow or workability. (There are also admixtures for all sorts of other things, such as accelerating or delaying set time, or entraining air bubbles.) Reducing water content is always a good thing, because the less water you use, the less void space you have as the water dries, thus the stronger your concrete, especially clay concrete. So-called *mid*-range and high-range water-reducing admixtures, commonly called superplasticizers, are stunningly effective at turning a clump of wet concrete into a puddle by deflocculating all those little clumps. That opens up the possibility of using even better-graded rock (aggregate) sizes, as pictured, to the point of having vanishingly little void space that the glue needs to fill. Your artificial particle rock is getting to be almost as strong as solid rock.

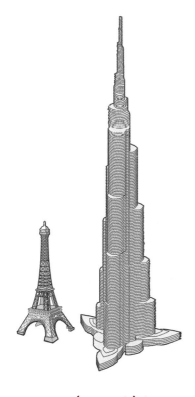

FIGURE 5.6. **Castles made of sand.** The tallest building in the world is the Burj Khalifa in Dubai, 2,716 feet (828 meters) or half a mile high in the middle of the desert—almost three times as high as the Eiffel Tower. But it was built, in part, with sand imported from Australia, because the desert sands surrounding it have been rounded by rolling together in the wind, and they wouldn't give its concrete the strength it needs. Believe it or not, sand is in short supply in many places, and so we hear increasingly of "sand mafias" in India and elsewhere who will hurt and kill to gain access to a resource that is no longer as plentiful as grains in the Sahara.

source, as long as it's intense. Today the industry uses coal, coke, fuel oil, and natural gas—fossil fuels. In many places, especially Europe and the United Kingdom, fossil fuels are partially replaced by municipal and agricultural wastes. This is surely a good idea for easing the solid waste management problem faced by every city, but it's not so good for our climate. Plenty of global warming emissions still go into the air, along with a number of gases and particulates that may or may not be trapped by pollution equipment.

Of particular concern is the widespread and growing use in Europe and the United Kingdom of burning wood pellets manufactured in the United States and Russia.

Although most renewable energy policy frameworks treat biomass as though it is carbon-neutral at the point of combustion, in reality this cannot be assumed, as biomass emits more carbon per unit of energy than most fossil fuels. . . . One reason for the perception of biomass as carbon-neutral is the fact that, under IPCC greenhouse gas accounting rules, its associated emissions are recorded in the land use rather than the energy sector. However, the different ways in which land use emissions are accounted for means that a proportion of the emissions from biomass may never be accounted for.[4]

Burning wood in efficient stoves to heat homes in thickly forested landscapes makes plenty of sense, but manufactured pellets shipped across the ocean for industrial energy supply do not. More generally, we haven't seen alternative fuels in use to date that show much promise for improving the climate. At the same time, and just as with the steel industry, a solution is emerging for a low-carbon fuel to make cement: hydrogen. (Hydrogen is discussed in chapter 4 and chapter 11.)

Blended Cements and Supplementary Cementitious Materials
The largest and most promising near-term decarbonization of concrete is by clinker substitution. *Clinker* is what you get when you calcine (bake) limestone and then intergrind it with clay and gypsum. Yes, it gets more complicated, but that's the basic process, and much portland cement is nothing but clinker. Portland cement is sometimes pure clinker, but increasingly it is clinker mixed or interground with supplementary cementitious materials (SCMs). SCMs are not inert filler; each in slightly different ways supplants and augments clinker in cement, usually yielding concrete that is superior in most respects to pure clinker concrete. That, and the attendant reduction in carbon footprint, is why many in the industry are now saying that concrete without SCMs belongs in a museum and nowhere else. (SCMs are also called *pozzolans,* named for the volcanic soils the ancient Romans mined near Pozzuoli, Italy, for their concrete.) The percentage of clinker in any portland cement is called the *clinker factor.* When SCMs are mixed at a cement plant for sale in bags or bulk, they are called *blended cements* and fall under special standards and requirements in most countries. Larger ready-mix concrete plants may also have separate silos of pure cement and SCMs (e.g., slag) with which they can site blend to whatever mix proportions they want. On average, global cement has a clinker factor of about 78 percent. Industry leaders intend and expect that to drop to 60 percent by 2050.[5]

At present there are two main types of SCMs in use, both of which are byproducts of other industries. Coal fly ash, usually just called fly ash or even just ash, is the particulate matter collected from the stack of a coal-fired power plant. You get about a ton of ash for every 10 tons of coal burned, and it is a very, very effective pozzolan. (We clearly need to phase out coal-fired power as fast as possible, but even the most optimistic scenarios see it still with us for a few decades. And, to answer the question we sometimes hear: No, making effective and economical use of coal fly ash in concrete is not a big enough driver that it will ever prompt the construction of another coal-fired power plant.) Unfortunately, a lot of ash doesn't get used because of formidable obstacles such as the cost of the equipment for collecting it from the power plant's stack or the cost and lack of infrastructure for storing and transporting it. Much ash gets stored semipermanently in constructed ponds, where it is rightly considered a hazardous material, mostly because of some heavy metal content. Those metals get chemically bound to portland cement when the ash is used in concrete, so using it for concrete is the most economical and environmentally preferable means of disposal for as long as we're still producing it.[6]

The other main pozzolan in the marketplace today is ground, granulated blast furnace slag, usually called either GGBFS or just slag. As the name implies, blast furnace slag is a byproduct of raw steel production and is in some ways an even better pozzolan than fly ash for its better workability and light color. Slag from other steel and metal production, as in electric arc furnaces, is also useful but more problematic.

There are a number of less prominent materials in the field of SCMs, either in use or possible. Yet all of them, with one exception (box 5.3), put together with ash, slag, and current cement making capacity, don't yet supply much of the expected needs of the next few decades, even aside from climate and emission considerations. We need to reinvent concrete. We'll get to that, but for now let's look at what is currently (2021) available.

New and Alternative Cements

With both climate and so much money at stake—after all, concrete is a trillion-dollar industry—there is a lot of investment and intellectual capital working to develop less carbon-intensive binders than portland clinker. Many new cements have been developed and are moving, at one stage or another, along the so-called Valley of Death—the grueling path from "good idea" to "readily available in the marketplace." That valley is especially long and grueling for construction materials (compared with, say, new smartphone apps), even more so for materials that will have anything to do with health and safety. Any effort to introduce new concrete technology takes very big, very patient capital, typically by developing ideas first spawned in academia.

Here is a cursory review of current efforts to develop alternative cements around the world.[7]

GEOPOLYMERS AND ALKALI-ACTIVATED CEMENTS

There has been quite a lot of work on this technology of "activating" certain precursor minerals with (usually) sodium silicate to produce quality cements and concrete without portland clinker. At first glance, alkali-activated cements (AACs)[8] promise

Box 5.3   Supplements to Portland Cement Concrete

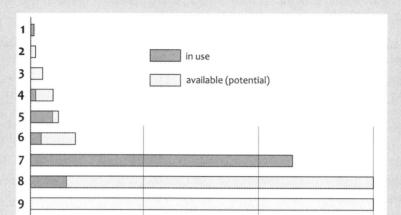

Global cement supplements / million tonnes per year

1. **Silica fume** is the byproduct of silicon production, as for computer chips. It is a very high-grade pozzolan, a fine black powder that is typically a part of very high-strength concrete. It is also difficult to work with and expensive.

2. **Waste glass** is coming into use both as aggregate and as a pozzolan when very finely ground. Its practicality as a climate-friendly ingredient in concrete will vary greatly with local conditions and will always require the energy of collecting, cleaning (with heat or water), and grinding it. In some cases glass shards must be treated so as to avoid an adverse chemical effect, the well-known alkali–silica reaction between the silica glass and alkaline cement paste.

3. **Plant ash.** When certain silica-rich crop residues such as rice husks and sugar cane bagasse are burned at controlled low temperature and then the ash is ground, you get a very high-quality pozzolan much like silica fume. Many millions of tons of such residues are available each year, but making effective use of them, as has been tried in many contexts, is problematic. Field burning is too hot and erratic, and optimal temperatures for burning in cogeneration power plants is too hot; in both cases, the resulting ash is crystalline, not amorphous as needed.

4. **Natural pozzolans.** In certain parts of the world such as Greece and the west coast of the United States, remnant bands of loose, ashy rock from ancient volcanism can be harvested and used in concrete (that is what the ancient Romans did in the area now called Pozzuoli, near Mt. Vesuvius). Natural pozzolans exist only in certain locations and vary in quality, but they can be and now are being used.

5. **Slag,** as discussed earlier in the chapter.

6. **Fly ash,** as discussed earlier in the chapter.

7. **Portland cement clinker,** as discussed earlier in the chapter. Note that the quantity in use dwarfs SCMs 1–6. Unfortunately, even if we make full use of all available portland cement, ash, slag, and the rest, we won't have the capacity to make the concrete the world will need in the coming decades. We will need 8 and 9 also.

8. **Filler.** Fillers are fine particulate minerals that can partially replace clinker and do not need calcining; their production needs only energy for grinding. Because many minerals can be used as fillers, they are abundant everywhere, but by far the most commonly used mineral is limestone. Fillers might have some mild pozzolanic properties, but when used with water-reducing admixtures, they mainly fill the smaller voids in concrete. Fillers are in common use worldwide, typically in the range of 5–35 percent clinker replacement.

9. **Calcined clay (metakaolin).** Clays, especially kaolinite clays as used by ceramics industries, act as very effective pozzolans when heated to about 800°C (1,500°F) and then ground. The world has a lot of clay deposits and, especially, many deposits of unusable (to the ceramics industry) clay that work just fine as pozzolans after heating and grinding; the raw material and necessary infrastructure are all in place together already. Calcined clay from companies such as LC3 is emerging to be a large-scale decarbonization method for the near term.

10. **Pure carbon** *(very recent developments not shown on chart).*

    Biochar is a charcoal-like substance made by burning organic material in an oxygen-free process called pyrolysis. Already well known as a soil enhancer because of its enormous internal surface area, biochar is beginning to show promise as an additive to concrete, both as fine aggregate and as a pozzolan (thus reducing cement content and carbon footprint). Biochar improves the toughness of concrete, but maybe even more appealing is the possibility it provides of transforming both agricultural and municipal wastes into climate-friendly concrete improvements.

    Similarly, graphene is a one-molecule-thick carbon sheet or lattice (in many possible configurations) that is showing huge promise in all sorts of industries, including as a concrete additive. Like biochar, the addition of modest amounts (much less than 1 percent) to concrete improves both compressive and tensile strength and decreases permeability.

    Research and pilot projects with both biochar and graphene continue apace, and we expect to see carbon's role in the concrete industry grow quite a bit further: to durably store carbon, to deal with waste products, and to diminish cement demand.

a much-reduced footprint, but there are substantial emissions associated with manufacturing the sodium silicate. More importantly, the usual and primary activated minerals are slag and fly ash—the same things that are currently our most abundant SCMs. To remove them from their role in supplanting clinker in portland cement concrete for use as AACs is not broadly promising for reducing emissions, although there may be local exceptions.

Magnesium Oxides

There has been much excitement about magnesium oxide (MgO) cement, based on research with magnesium carbonate rock. The CO_2 footprint of such cements is far higher than that of limestone (CaO) based cement, but the promise is that we will work out how to make MgO based clinkers with globally abundant ultramafic rock (magnesium silicates such as periclase and serpentine) instead of $CaCO_3$ limestone as the main raw material. That would be a big breakthrough in that it would eliminate the chemical CO_2 emissions (±60 percent of clinker's footprint) associated with portland cement. (The other 40 percent is from burning enough fuel to bake rocks.) To date there has been promising research, and we hope to see more, but there's no product at scale in the market.

CO_2-ACTIVATED BINDERS

Conventional portland cement–based concrete develops its strength through hydration, where water reacts chemically with the mineral oxides in the cement to produce hydrates. Another approach being touted by companies such as Solidia in the United States is carbonation curing of processed calcium silicate clinkers. This uses much less energy but has distinct limitations: The concrete has to be cured in controlled factory conditions with CO_2 gas, and it is insufficiently alkaline to protect steel reinforcements. Even so, the technology already has a place in the sizable market for unreinforced, precast products. It also has the limitation, for now anyway, that currently available industrial CO_2 gas is itself manufactured and thus has an emission footprint. Like the technologies next to be discussed, this one will look even better as an industrial ecosystem for CO_2 gas captured from emissions develops. Some have speculated that there is further promise, potentially substantial, in applying carbonation curing to the abundant magnesium silicate rocks discussed previously.

How Do I Make Low-Carbon Concrete?

How you can make low-carbon concrete today depends on who and where you are. We'll discuss this question separately for structural engineers, concrete suppliers, policymakers, and builders.

Dear Structural Engineers

It took me until I was this old to figure out what not to play.

—Dizzy Gillespie

We engineers have an important role in reversing the emission engine, for most of the carbon in construction, especially new buildings, is in structure and enclosure. We who design with heavy, bulky, high-carbon materials need to become a great deal more careful in their use, for just by paying a little attention we can reduce (or raise) a project's emissions substantially. Like jazz trumpeter Dizzy Gillespie, we're old enough now that we've figured out what not to play. It's time to step up and respond to the call of the times.

We have to change our habits. How many times have you called for a 5-inch slab when 4 might do, or a 24-inch beam when 18 might work fine, simply because time was short and the client was waiting. Most engineers in most situations are pressed for time, will probably never be penalized for overdesign, and have little or no reward for reducing steel and concrete volumes. This seems to be generally true everywhere: We have plenty of reason to be conservative and heavy-handed and almost no reason to lighten up. If our designs add appreciable extra cost to a client's budget, it's unlikely that anyone will ever know. As always, there are exceptions; some developers are aware of how efficient engineers are with their money, as measured in pounds of steel or framing lumber per square foot of usable space. So we can't be too cavalier in design or we get a bad reputation. But most projects have plenty of latitude to be lazy—that is, to increase cost by overdesign, be it deliberate or just from not paying attention— without much if any penalty.

Ramped up computing power won't change that, but it does make it easier and quicker to reduce volumes, fine tune strength requirements, and design with an eye on climate. Soon enough, you'll be able to track your project's footprint as you design, with the projected emission counter running in a window on your screen.

Meanwhile, here are a few basic suggestions regarding concrete. For more resources developed by and for structural engineers on every material and aspect of our trade in terms of climate, go to the SE2050 website (se2050.org).

Do You Want Strength or Durability?

We engineers define the concrete we want mainly by its compressive strength, partly for the obvious reason that we usually want it to carry compressive load in one way or another, but also because compressive strength is a rough indicator of other properties such as durability and elastic modulus. But that durability connection is sketchy; high strength does not guarantee long life, and it's possible to have too much cement in a mix. Engineers for the new San Francisco–Oakland Bay Bridge, for example, used high-pozzolan concrete because it dramatically reduces permeability to salt air and water. If you're just designing an everyday sidewalk, you don't need strength so much as durability against abrasion and, in many places, icy conditions. You can get that by calling for a modest strength level but putting a ceiling on cement content. As a general rule, of course, we shouldn't call for strength we don't really need, although there are cases where use of high-strength concrete can enable use of smaller cross-sections (reduced volume).

Hands off the Steering Wheel

Most young engineers are trained to specify a minimum cement content, typically more than needed, in every concrete. That made sense once; it doesn't now. To issue exacting concrete specifications, in which an engineer essentially designs or constrains a concrete mix's ingredients and proportions, is an outdated practice. Don't give them a recipe; just tell them what kind of cake you want. Write specs that stipulate strength, time to strength, any exposure, shrinkage, permeability, embodied carbon, or other requirements as may be important, and let the supplier work it out. One of the easiest and biggest ways for engineers to lower concrete's emissions is to let the concrete suppliers do what they do best: design the concrete. Don't tell them how much cement or water or anything else they should or should not use; just tell them what parameters matter and what are the maxima and minima for those properties. In short, don't be prescriptive but instead write performance-based specifications. Recognizing the need to reimagine concrete and improve its quality, the American Concrete Institute dropped its requirement for minimum cement contents in concrete, as written into their standard ACI 318, which serves as the basis for most modern North American building codes. As stated in their commentary,

> There is no requirement for minimum cement or cementitious materials content in ACI 318. . . . Historically, when concrete was proportioned with only portland cement, a minimum cement content was commonly specified to ensure that the strength and durability requirements were met. As concrete technology and industry expertise have evolved, there is a better understanding of factors affecting performance of concrete, thereby rendering minimum cement content requirements obsolete. . . . There is no technical basis for specifying cement content if the performance requirements are defined.[9]

If there is ambiguity or uncertainty, as there so often is, then pick up the phone and talk to the project concrete producer. A radical notion, yes, and one that can be difficult in public procurement situations, but nonetheless one of the most important ways for you to bring emissions down. Relax your grip and start communicating.

Don't Be Moonstruck!

Another big way to reduce concrete's footprint, possibly the simplest, biggest, and most cost-effective, is to give it time. That is, give the concrete as much time as you can to come to strength, because the more time you can give it, the less cement it will need to meet strength requirements. Much of the concrete we specify doesn't need strength for many months after placing, especially foundations. The 28-day strength benchmark, deeply habituated throughout the industry and enshrined in building codes, is often irrelevant—often, one size *doesn't* fit all.

The 28-day benchmark was historically justified because it allows quality control within a reasonable time frame; after all, no one wants to find out after several months that their concrete doesn't pass muster. But that justification has been rendered obsolete by new technologies for embedding monitors in the wet concrete that will broadcast key data as it sets; we can now tell without coring or breaking cylinders, and very soon after placing, how well a concrete is curing and how it will perform. Even without high-tech sensors, modern concrete suppliers have a much more refined sense than earlier generations of what their materials will do. Just by relaxing time-to-strength criteria to 56 or 90 days, you can save both emissions and cost, because cement is usually the most expensive ingredient in the concrete. Of course, very often a concrete mix *does* need to gain strength fast by being on a project's critical path—that is, when everyone will be waiting impatiently for it to reach some proportion of its strength. Here there are two types: high early strength with high ultimate strength and high early strength but modest ultimate strength.

There are plenty of examples of high early strength with high ultimate strength: tilt-up panels, precast work, retaining walls that must be backfilled right away, post-tensioned slabs above grade, or anything above grade where the removal of formwork as soon as possible is desired. The usual ways to get high early strength are by use of more cement or type III high–early strength cement—that is, high-carbon solutions. There are set accelerators such as calcium chloride, but there are costs, limitations, and problems with their use.

Typical examples of high–early strength concrete needing only modest ultimate strength are sidewalks, curbs, and pavements. They may never need to be particularly strong, but they almost always need to be put in service as soon as possible, and they do need to be durable.

In both cases, there are unfortunately no easy and inexpensive paths to low-carbon concrete (other than to not specify more strength than needed), so this is an area calling for research and innovation. Some might suggest that we should just relax and slow down, take it easy, don't be in such a hurry, but such an admonition invariably falls on deaf ears in a world where time is money. Still, it's worth noting that these are but a few of many examples of "hurry" causing extra emissions: Saving time = saving money = causing more climate disruption. A tough nut to crack, but we need to try.

A fairly simple way to track concrete's footprint is by monitoring its *binder intensity*: the amount of binder (clinker plus reactive SCMs) per unit volume and per strength category. Binder intensity for a great number of in-use concrete mixes has been well studied and found to vary substantially. That is, for a given strength class, some concretes are far more climate-friendly than others, signaling that just by paying attention, we engineers and concrete suppliers can deliver the same quality product today, with extant, available technologies, without such substantial emissions.

Dear Concrete Suppliers
The old joke says there are two kinds of concrete: one, cracked, and two, about to crack. In a similar way, there are two kinds of concrete suppliers: those who are tracking and reducing their carbon emissions and those who soon will. In just the past year (2020), the number of reported concrete mix Environmental Product Declarations (EPDs) has exploded from just a few hundred to tens of thousands.

Most of the burden of decarbonizing concrete falls on you, fairly or not. The growing awareness of climate emergency is rapidly translating into market dynamics and policy initiatives that will very much affect producers everywhere and favor climate-friendly practices. Your customers will be asking, if they're not already.[10] Government procurement mandates will require that you know your footprint, and it will be considered in awarding contracts. The price of cement will be driven upward by pricing emissions, and some of the SCMs described previously will be more and more readily available, as well as cost-competitive with cement.

There will of course be big differences in the scale and nature of change, depending on where you supply concrete and to whom. Supplying infrastructure projects in Toronto is not the same as rebuilding your home in the hills above São Paulo, which is not the same as re-creating the Silk Road across Asia. Changes in the concrete market typically first affect the big urban producers, then work their way out to rural and smaller ones.

It will be no trivial thing to add silos to a plant so as to add an SCM option for mixes; it costs a lot, and more importantly it takes up a lot of space that is already allocated. Nonetheless, it will be easier for bigger producers to adapt because they have more and more automated control over mixing and, in the case of precasters, curing. The other extreme of a rural builder mixing concrete from bags in a temporary mixing pond to make concrete to dry in the sun is about the worst, most wasteful, and most carbon-intensive way to make concrete. For that and other reasons China, by far the biggest concrete producer in the world, is making a big effort to consolidate and automate production as opposed to the now-widespread use of bagged cement and ready mix. It might complicate life for the small builders, but at a national scale it means getting better use out of the cement plants they have and sometimes avoiding needing new ones (which are typically coal fired).

The simplest change for most producers is to seek out the lowest-carbon cement available, whether it be from more efficient producers, or as blended cements (pozzolan or limestone bulk-mixed with clinker). Blended cements are rapidly gaining market share, led by Europe, but they currently lag in North America. In part this is because they are new, and we haven't fully tested them for use with local aggregates, but it's also because the regulatory and standard-writing environment hasn't fully caught up and adopted them. Where that is the case—where we have twentieth-century standards governing twenty-first-century technology—engineers and producers must both push for reform.

There will be an increased push to reuse old concrete as aggregate. There are problems with that, of course: collecting, sorting and crushing the materials, assessing the strength, and allowing for the added water (or admixtures) needed to maintain workability. But the push will and should be there nonetheless, if only to save having to haul and dump it in landfills.

Finally, note that much of what has been discussed in this chapter is available now. Liquid carbon injection such as CarbonCure is available now, and artificial limestone aggregates such as Blue Planet soon will be. Water-reducing admixtures are readily available that make use of filler much more practicable. The daunting task of developing accredited EPDs is made easier and less expensive by private enterprises such as Climate Earth and national concrete associations. Tracking and publishing your carbon footprint may seem like yet another annoying burden that impedes your ability to just make the damn concrete, but consider it a basic cost (or it soon will be) of working in an open society. Just as we expect to know the mileage of a car or truck, the fat content of prepared food, or the presence of cancerous substances in anything we might use before purchase, we as a society, as a world in climate disruption, must know the climate impacts of what we use. Concrete, probably more than anything else, will be among the first to be subject to that expectation.

Dear Builders
You can help decarbonize concrete and construction by doing what you already spend most of your time doing: communicating. Ask your concrete suppliers what they are doing to reduce emissions or changes they might suggest for any particular

project or concrete pour. Ask your engineer the same things. Get them both on the phone to find ways that maybe no one had thought of but might just pop out of a conversation. Ask. Talk. Question. Most builders I know started as carpenters or electricians and then graduated up to contracting—to managing all the many people and suppliers who team up to build. Quite a different skill set than pounding nails, but if you've lasted a few years then you've gotten the hang of it. You know how to talk, so talk (and listen): Talk to everyone in your building ecosystem, announce your intent for climate-friendly building, ask for help, and let everyone below you in the food chain (the ones to whom you write checks) know that you'll be looking to see what they do to reduce emissions.

To repeat, here's the *worst possible way to make concrete*, both for climate and quality of the finished product: Acquire and store paper-bagged cement, use what hasn't been ruined by moisture to hand-mix with gravel and hose water in an open pit (plenty of water, of course, so it will be easy to pour), and then get as much as possible into the formwork before it sets. Then add a bit of water to loosen up what has set and get it also into the forms. Strip the formwork as soon as possible so the concrete can dry in the sun and wind. That's how you make really bad concrete, but that is how a very large portion of the world's concrete gets mixed and placed.

Partly for this reason, China is aggressively moving to shrink the bagged cement market and industrialize a process that needs industrializing. For the climate, that's a good thing. Still, throughout this book we describe and support localized (vs. industrialized) building, even as we see concrete for the odd case that it is: already localized (you can't import or export ready mixed concrete very far) yet necessarily heavily mechanized in both manufacture and placement. You as a builder can make better concrete by doing the opposite of everything just described above. Design and mix your ingredients carefully, taking advantage of the best available knowledge (not merely "what we've always done"), using the best available equipment and ingredients (hopefully including SCMs), and curing your concrete as slowly as possible, meaning keeping it moist for as long as possible.

Some of the above might seem to construction veterans like dreamy stuff disconnected from the real world. Who has time to chat about it, right? Indeed, time is money, and there very often seems to be nowhere near enough of either. But across a very wide variety of structures, a lot of time and money gets wasted, and extra emissions generated, just because people didn't or couldn't or wouldn't communicate. Over and over again; that's what people have been not doing: *not* asking questions, *not* listening to intent, *not* noticing what everyone else on the project is doing. By contrast, many projects both large and small dramatically reduce emissions (and costs; they tend to go hand in hand) by simply getting the right people into the room together as early as possible in the project design. Just plain old-fashioned respectful communication, especially where and when it's not "normally" done, can be the most potent single driver of low-carbon design. It's also more fun and can lead to startling other benefits such as getting stakeholders excited (*They actually wanted to hear my ideas!*) or yielding cost savings far beyond just eliminating a few hundred pounds of cement, as in the house project described in endnote 10.

Dear Policymakers

General policy ideas are discussed in chapter 11, but there are a few matters—and precedents—specific to concrete. This is no surprise, for as governments at every level rise to the challenge of reducing the up-front emissions from construction and materials, concrete is the obvious starting point. It has by far the biggest footprint of any material we make and has far more room for improvement (both disruptive and nondisruptive) than steel or any other material.

As with embodied carbon in general, concrete-related policy initiatives are of two basic types: establishing procurement guidelines and setting limits.

ESTABLISH PROCUREMENT GUIDELINES

Establish embodied carbon guidelines for public construction procurement that favor low-carbon concrete by monetizing and rewarding reduced emissions (or penalizing high emissions, depending on how you look at it). Governments around the world at local, state, and national levels are already moving this way, as are some major corporations such as LinkedIn and Microsoft.

SET LIMITS

Develop building standards and code amendments that put a ceiling on emissions, always allowing for exceptions and special conditions. (At this writing, ASHRAE is working on language for its 189.1 standard, the basis of most green codes.)

In both cases, the trick is in defining limits that are feasible yet also effective in reducing emissions and also announcing a schedule of revisions by which the limits will be tightened in years to come. That "trick" must be a local or regional effort to survey common practice among local concrete producers—what are the global warming potentials and cement contents of concrete mixes of every strength category from producers in the area?—and then work with local stakeholders to set initial limits.

The first such effort we know of was in Marin County, California. There we

(Bruce instigated the effort) crafted and adopted a code amendment in late 2019 that is written in the format and language of the International Building Code (the basis for most North American building codes) and is freely available for adoption by others.[11] It comes with a very large caveat: The limits established for Marin County (or more generally the San Francisco Bay Area) were calculated based on a detailed study of local concrete suppliers. We had a lot of data about the global warming potentials and cement contents of concrete mixes of every strength category from many producers in the area, as well as more collected around northern California by the Structural Engineers Association of Northern California and regional average values published by the National Ready Mix Concrete Association. The stakeholder group reviewing the data and code language included the Marin building official, local structural engineers, the National Ready Mix Concrete Association, local concrete producers, the cement trade group, several academic engineers, the Sierra Club, general contractors, and more.[12]

We already have, of necessity, some adaptability built into our concrete regulations. Unlike other structural materials such as steel, wood (with all of its now well-cataloged grades and properties), or concrete masonry, ready mix concrete is not a commodity; the supplier in Chicago is generally not competing with a supplier from Denver or Boston, because he has to use the sand, rock, and cement available in Chicago, and especially because you just can't move wet concrete very far. There are plenty of exceptions to this rule, and modern (read: fossil fuel–based) transport infrastructure makes it feasible to move huge masses of heavy material across the planet if the project is big enough to warrant it. But for most concrete placed anywhere, the sand and gravel are local, even if the cement might be from afar, and the ingredients, including water, are mixed at the plant; concrete is a local business. Not as local as your neighborhood grocer, but not as bland and generic as a big box store or a steel wide flange beam.

Regardless, adoption of low-carbon concrete provisions must start with the most careful and thorough survey possible of local or regional standard practice. A map is no good until you know where you are to start. With that, start! At the very least, begin requiring EPDs and get your local industry monitoring and thinking about carbon footprint. Set achievable goals along with a schedule for ratcheting carbon limits down over a short but workable period of years.

Thinking Outside the Cement Box: Other Paths to Decarbonization
Portland cement, for being so carbon intensive, is the obvious first target of decarbonization efforts: Make concrete with less cement, and make lower-carbon

cement. However, a great many other pathways are opening up that lead not just to zero but to the possibility of durable, carbon-smart concrete that absorbs more emissions than it creates.

Bring It Home: Carbon Capture, Utilization, and Storage
There is plenty of innovation around capturing carbon gases, either directly from the air or in concentrated form at the stacks of energy and heavy industry, and then durably using or storing them. Indeed, that is a central notion in this book, along with making skillful use of the carbon captured and stored by plants via photosynthesis.

In many ways, concrete stands to be a durable and massive place to store carbon—to absorb the greenhouse gases that it has to date been copiously emitting. But, as mentioned earlier, any efforts to store and use carbon in concrete will be efficacious only as captured (not manufactured) carbon gas becomes more readily available. With that said, here are the ways we can durably store carbon in concrete.

- *Natural carbonation* of concrete is happening already, naturally, everywhere. You will hear of how concrete reabsorbs carbon dioxide via carbonation, and the concrete industry likes to remind us that all the concrete everywhere is sucking up the carbon dioxide made in its manufacture. That's true to an extent, but because concrete is dense, carbonation of concrete can occur only where air might reach: in the outer few centimeters, and only very, very slowly. In fact, that's what drives the minimum cover requirements for reinforcing bars in building codes: Carbonated concrete—the outer few centimeters—is chemically less alkaline and thus doesn't protect rebar from corrosion. Everything below the surface (which is most of the world's concrete) is quite free of carbonation. If we could somehow expose all concrete everywhere to moist air, we would start a slow but massive carbon drawdown. Hardened concrete is a thermodynamically out-of-equilibrium material; you might say that, over the past hundred or so years, using intense fossil fuel heat, we forced carbonate minerals to be something they didn't really want to be, and now they are trying to revert to their preferred mineral/chemical state. Like everything else, concrete is always changing, even if very slowly. Recent estimates posit that global carbonation of concrete is absorbing CO_2 at the rate of a quarter of a gigaton per year—not as trivial a number as many had previously thought.[13] (Alarmingly, the Intergovernmental Panel on Climate Change recently identified cement infrastructure as a carbon sink that reabsorbs a large fraction of the emissions resulting from cement manufacture. That assertion has come under intense criticism for grossly overstating the effects of carbonation by ignoring the long time horizons needed, ignoring that the great bulk of extant concrete is not exposed to air and may never be, and ignoring emissions from the fossil fuels burned to heat the limestone.)

- *Gaseous carbonation* of calcium and magnesium silicate clinkers (as discussed previously, e.g., Solidia).
- *Liquid carbon curing* of wet concrete (e.g., CarbonCure): Liquid carbon kept at low temperature and high pressure at the ready mix plant can be injected into newly mixed concrete in a way that mineralizes it and adds strength (thus diminishing cement requirements). This can reduce carbon footprint by as much as 5 percent, per CarbonCure.
- *Carbon curing* of various minerals and especially of industrial byproducts (e.g., Calera in the United States, Carbon 8 in the United Kingdom, Mineral Carbonation International in Australia). A lot of things we have been throwing away in great bulk, such as bottom ash from various municipal and industrial incinerators, can be processed with CO_2 to get useful minerals, pozzolans, or artificial aggregate for concrete.
- *Carbon aggregate.* The nonglue solution: Accrete carbon retrieved from plant emissions around sand or other particles to create artificial limestone aggregate (e.g., Blue Planet). This may be the most promising path forward because it is indifferent to the binder, can constitute the bulk of the concrete (and thus the bulk of potential carbon storage), and can be manufactured next to any cement or fossil fuel power plant to sequester its emissions. Simple, powerful circularity. Biochar may also come to have prominence here if we can learn to pyrolyze various waste products in bulk so as to replace natural aggregate.

There are especially high hopes for carbon curing and carbon aggregate because they can capture and durably store very large quantities of atmospheric carbon, and in the latter case they can also spare the destruction of the riverbeds that we currently scrape for sand and gravel. These technologies and companies (and many more) are at the end of 2021 at various stages on their way to market (e.g., Solidia is well established, CarbonCure is well established in North America and moving into Asia, and Blue Planet, building a first plant in Pittsburgh, California, is partnered with Mitsubishi to enter Asia). The landscape of companies and available decarbonizing technologies will surely be evolving and changing for the foreseeable future at a brisk pace. In fact, we are astonished at the furious pace and volume of innovation in this market space, and we expect that by the time you read this, other promising technologies will emerge.

I Never Thought of That! New Life to Designing Concrete

Computers are changing design not just with compelling 3D visualizations but also by empowering smart design choices by keeping useful knowledge at hand. Ever more powerful computers and engineering software are making it easier to design ever more daring structures or just do a better job with everyday structures. Real-world architecture is usually constrained by budget and doesn't soar or dare so much. That's fine, yet all but the simplest projects still need engineering and thus present opportunities to reduce carbon emissions by more careful design. Computers, software, and building information modeling (BIM) are like most technologies: agnostic. They can help us design ever more exciting or safe or climate-friendly architecture, but they are just as ready to help accelerate the trashing of the planet. It's up to us to decide which way to use them.

By its sheer volume concrete stands poised, perhaps more than anything else in this book, to transform from a major climate disrupter into a major climate healer. "Zero" is not the goal; we propose that an industry now responsible for one twelfth of humanity's emissions flip itself around in a generation to become a major absorber of the greenhouse gases now in the air. Tepid goals to try and do better by a long time from now are far worse than disappointing, because slowly doing less bad is basically losing to climate catastrophe.

Starting right now and for the immediate future, decarbonizing concrete—getting to zero—will be achieved mostly by minimizing clinker use and maximizing use of SCMs and filler along with finer aggregate gradation and plasticizing admixtures. As carbon utilization enterprises get traction, especially in China where most concrete gets placed, we will also be able to build carbon permanently into concrete in multiple ways and start to move beyond zero.

Still, it makes you wonder: What else haven't we thought of?

The chances are good that there are plenty of things we haven't yet thought of, plenty of ways to make artificial rock to serve various purposes. It helps to notice that we use concrete to do a very large number of very different things. Sometimes we want it to support buildings as foundations or be building frames that won't collapse during blizzards, dance parties, or earthquakes. Other times we just want it to be a wearing surface for floors and walls, streets and sidewalks, highways and runways. Sometimes we want it to contain or transport fluids, such as water and sewage, or animals, as in stockyards and zoos. Sometimes we want it to be a sound or fire barrier, like stucco or gypsum board, or to insulate like foamed mineral board. We use it to build bridges, some of which are soaringly beautiful, and we use it to build prisons, which never are. You can make a boat with concrete, or a tunnel, or a harbor safe from the storm. You can kill with concrete, and you can save lives with it. You can make it purely for art. All these things are artificial rock, and it may be that we've hardly begun to imagine all the expressions of that simple idea. Nor have we fully imagined the technological means to make it what we want without wrecking the stable climate we depend on.

Somehow in the past century we've turned these many forms, uses, and functions into one thing: concrete as portland cement, sand, and gravel, period. Our building codes make that very clear, and our engineering and construction educations train us into that very narrow tunnel of thinking. Climate emergency compels us, and our vastly greater knowledge enables us, to reimagine concrete—artificial rock—as using the resources at hand to serve the purposes needed without the huge damage to the environment that supports us.

Old Tech Is Climate Tech: The Renaissance of Earthen Architecture

One way to start reimagining concrete is to take a look in the rear-view mirror at the concrete of our ancestors: clay concrete, or earthen architecture. The world's oldest surviving buildings date back at least ten thousand years at sites in China, Europe, and the Middle East. They are typically stacked and fitted stonework, or one of the packed earth construction systems cob, adobe, or rammed earth, essentially the first concretes using the original binder, clay. The Great Wall of China, for example, was built by running horses back and forth over layers of soil within the containing stone facade walls. Still standing today is the famous city of Shibam in Yemen, the "Manhattan of Mud," multiple twelve-story structures built entirely of hand-packed earth, continuously occupied for a thousand years, and another testament to the surprising durability of clay-based concrete.

Earthen architecture has thrived everywhere during the past two hundred years, attracting the attention of J. Paul Getty, Antonio Gaudi, Frank Lloyd Wright, and these authors, among many others, and is now seeing a growing renewal—and multiple upgrades. Though not as strong or durable as cement or lime concretes, clay concrete in its many forms holds increasing promise for the modern world, as it is safer and far less expensive for both builders and the climate than the modern default of portland cement concrete. Even so, a stigma remains that conflates earthen buildings and poverty. A radio interviewer in Northern Ireland once asked Bruce, on the air, "It took us thousands of years to get out of these mud huts; why would we want back into them?" That was a fair question, to which the answer was, "Because they're affordable, easy, far more durable and comfortable than you think, and don't cook the climate." And because so many modern people have no experience of earthen architecture, we might also add, "Go see for yourself! Go listen to the quiet of a rammed earth or adobe home, see the subtle beauty of a clay plaster, feel the toe-wriggling pleasure of a well-done earthen floor! Now imagine all that in your modern school or office building." With that as introduction, we now turn to three modern pioneers to describe each one's unique experience with earthen building.

After completing her doctoral thesis on modern earthen building at Carnegie-Mellon, Prof. Lola Ben-Alon has taken up a teaching post at Columbia. Coming as she does from the land of Jericho, whose walls are among the oldest samples we have of *any* architecture, she is more than qualified to speak about the original concrete and its place in modern society (box 5.4).

Box 5.4   The Case for Modern Earthen Building
by Lola Ben-Alon

Imagine a building constructed of raw earth from the building site, mixed with fibrous byproducts from locally grown food. Think about it like "farm to building": The shorter the supply chain, the more environmentally, socially, and economically sustainable the product is. By using these "natural" materials, we minimize the transportation, chemical and thermal processing, and intermediate storage that make up the high carbon footprint of conventional building materials.

This shorter supply chain makes earthen building—modernized versions of ancient technologies—a promising component of climate-friendly design. Homes made with earthen and bio-based materials also provide a more affordable alternative for low-income housing. And just as "you are what you eat" rings true, so do the spaces we live and work in affect our lives and health; indeed, modern research shows that earthen materials provide optimal indoor environments for human health.

Despite these environmental and health advantages, earthen buildings are not widespread in mainstream construction. Furthermore, they are being excluded from many regions that had used primarily earthen construction until the last couple of decades. There are four main reasons for this exclusion: lack of technical or engineering information, durability challenges, negative cultural image, and omission from building codes and training programs for building professionals.

Several earthen building techniques appear within prescriptive U.S. regional building codes (e.g., Appendix U, *Cob Construction*, 2020, New Mexico Earthen Building Materials Code). Even so, they are often excluded from construction projects because of their low thermal insulation values (in addition to the reasons named above), which in most cases do not meet energy code requirements. To some extent this reflects on the crude state of energy codes in that they often look only at the thermal insulation, or R-value, of materials and assemblies. Earthen walls do not rate so well by that one metric, but they do have well-documented thermal mass and hygroscopic properties that are often unaccounted for in

continued

Box 5.4 *continued*

energy modeling programs. Thermal mass provides a sort of temperature-stabilizing flywheel, and the porous and permeable material structure provides hygroscopic and humidity buffering capacities.

Earthen construction systems display a range of thermal properties and so can be tuned by the technique used. Assemblies such as cob, light straw clay, and rammed earth can each be designed and built to take advantage of their different thermal abilities. Rammed earth and cob are dense and so have more thermal mass, often needing added insulation. By contrast, light straw clay can be lightly packed to capture air pockets and so is often used as insulative infill within a light frame construction.

Unlike conventional insulation materials, light straw clay's porosity and mass, along with the "quasi-phase change" effect of raw clay with humidity, make for a temperature and humidity "flywheel" mechanism that provides a much steadier indoor temperature, absorbing moisture from the ambient air and desorbing moisture into the air to maintain optimal relative humidity levels for human health. These thermal properties bolster passive conditioning, improving the comfort and survivability of buildings under changing urban climates and power outages. As figure 5.8 shows, the indoor temperature in a light straw clay house can provide an average 3°C warmer indoor temperature than a conventionally insulated wood frame in cold winter with no heating.

Earthen Materials in the Big City

Most earthen building codes today constrain earthen structures to one- or two-story buildings (notwithstanding the presence of centuries-old, multistory earthen structures around the world), but what about taller structures and other urban building types? Earthen materials are not limited to structural assemblies and can be easily used in finishes, regardless of building scale. Light straw clay can be used as an insulative infill within almost any structural system, clay-based plasters can be applied on top of any wall system, and earthen floors and partitions provide both warmth and sound control.

Earthen surfaces can be of any color, from earthy tones to bright colors or plain white, and earthen plasters can be made rough or highly polished as desired. Earthen (clay) surfaces will also make for healthier indoor environments by passively removing toxins such as volatile organic compounds, and reducing the ozone levels in a room. Well-built earthen finishes dissolve the pervasive negative perception of natural and bio-based materials as "funky," nonhygienic, or simply low-tech "poor man's materials."

Policy Gaps: Bringing Health and Embodied Carbon to Energy Codes

Energy codes in the United States (and elsewhere) mostly ignore both the health aspects and embodied energy and carbon associated with the making of buildings. To foster an earthen construction industry, and for other reasons, we need to consider both in mandatory energy and code requirements.

Energy codes should account for not just the operational energy and carbon but also how insulation materials (and all material components of the thermal enclosure) were produced, how much of a carbon footprint they have, how they are demolished at the end of service life, and how toxic or recyclable they may be. We need to develop building models that capture mass and hygrothermal benefits, and we need to account for chemically benign surfaces such as clay.

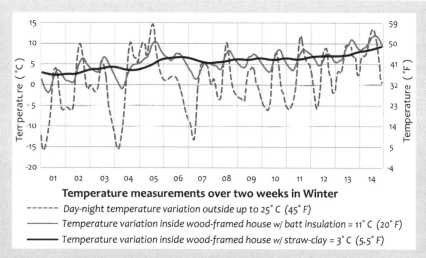

Temperature measurements over two weeks in Winter
----- *Day-night temperature variation outside up to 25° C (45° F)*
—— *Temperature variation inside wood-framed house w/ batt insulation = 11° C (20° F)*
—— *Temperature variation inside wood-framed house w/ straw-clay = 3° C (5.5° F)*

FIGURE 5.8. Light straw clay can provide a steadier indoor temperature than a fiberglass-insulated wood frame, shown here for a passive house in Denver, Colorado. (L. Ben-Alon, *Natural Buildings: Integrating Earthen Building Materials and Methods Into Mainstream Construction*, 2020. Carnegie Mellon University Thesis. https://doi.org/10.1184/R1/11908032.v1)

To address widespread misperceptions of natural building as primitive and only for the poor, we also need to develop better design and testing protocols. Appropriate protection of exterior earthen walls includes a good "pair of boots" (high footing or splash protection) and a good "umbrella" (deep roof overhang) to reduce rain-driven erosion (as illustrated in ASTM E2392-M10 2010). As with any buildings or materials, earthen structures need maintenance, as was historically an integral part of community and family life in many parts of the world. It can be again, or at least it doesn't require special skills or unpleasant chemicals.

We hope the use of earthen and other healthy, low-carbon building materials will increase over the next few years. As it does, it is our responsibility as building professionals to make sure this growth is made sustainably without incurring unwanted environmental or social outcomes. For earthen and bio-based materials, raw material extraction would need to follow responsible practices and protect arable land, akin to permaculture and sustainable farming for food.

Future Directions

There is plenty more we want to know, and we hope to see academic research and innovations around better understanding of clays, maintenance and durability issues, indoor environmental effects, environmental benefits, optimal mixtures, and fabrication technologies. It may be that the use of water-reducing admixtures, such as those discussed for portland cement concrete, can impart the workability, toughness, and durability that we want to improve in clay concrete. By investigating these issues, we can contribute critically needed environmental quantification leading to Environmental Product Declarations and better acceptance in the construction industry.

With degrees from Harvard and Stanford, Gaya Datar was poised to make an easy million in Silicon Valley or Wall Street. Instead, she followed her dream of riches—understanding as she does what real riches are—and the people of Rwanda and beyond are the beneficiaries. The ready smiles of EarthEnable's staff and customers belie the magnitude of their achievement and its potential for simultaneously fostering both affordable, healthy housing and climate-friendly technology all over the world.

Box 5.5 More than a Floor
By Gayatri Datar

It started with a dream to improve health outcomes through simple and affordable solutions. Founded in 2014, EarthEnable is an East Africa–based earthen construction company on a mission to make living conditions healthier and more dignified for the world's poor by providing healthy, sustainable, affordable housing products to rural families. EarthEnable's flagship product is an earthen alternative to dirt floors: locally sourced earthen floors that are 80 percent cheaper than concrete. EarthEnable is the first organization to offer affordable and green housing products to the rural poor—products that clean up the unsanitary conditions that jeopardize their health. EarthEnable's mission is based on the deep-seated belief that improved earthen construction (or earthen concrete) is the cross-sectoral solution to many economically developing countries' greatest challenges across the health, housing, employment, and environmental sectors.

The enterprise began as a class project through Stanford's School of Design in 2014. EarthEnable's founder, Gayatri Datar, and her team from Stanford visited Rwanda and saw vivid examples of serious physical and mental health complications caused by dirt floors, which are ubiquitous in rural areas of many developing countries (especially Rwanda, where 75 percent of the population lives on dirt floors). According to a 2009 World Bank study[a] conducted in Mexico, replacing a dirt floor with a clean one causes a reduction in diarrheal disease by 49 percent and parasitic infection by 78 percent. Further region-specific research conducted by the Stanford team showed that concrete was the only alternative flooring material available to rural communities, but impoverished families were unable to afford it. In addition to being a significant financial investment, concrete causes major environmental problems, being responsible for 8 percent of global carbon emissions. After transport and energy generation, concrete production alone is the third-ranking producer of anthropogenic CO_2 in the world.

The Stanford team discovered that the solution to these issues was combining earthen construction techniques used for thousands of years with modern innovations. In the United States, earthen floors have been refined to make them easy to clean, abrasion resistant, and modern in appearance. Unlike concrete, earthen floors are made without mechanization, using only a hand-packed mixture of gravel, sand, clay, and fiber (e.g., corn husks or dung) tamped into place. However, the team quickly discovered that although most of the materials used to build earthen floors could be found in Rwandan villages, the commercial linseed oil sealants and binders used in the United States were prohibitively expensive for rural families. Undeterred, Datar and her team recruited biochemist Rick Zuzow, who set out to

Photo courtesy of EarthEnable.

engineer an oil-based floor sealant that would be both environmentally friendly and more affordable. The result is EarthEnable's proprietary seed oil varnish, used by several hundred masons and floormen to finish earthen floors across Rwanda and Uganda.

With ongoing R&D, EarthEnable has developed durable, aesthetically pleasing floors and in 2019 also began offering an earthen plaster to ensure that a range of earthen products are available to address housing needs. EarthEnable has found that the main challenge for customers concerns product maintenance knowledge: The earthen floor's unique requirements must be acknowledged and made clear. This requires moderate behavioral change, without which customers can inadvertently misuse the product, which in turn can lead to deficiencies. A well-made and maintained earthen floor can last a generation, but without proper knowledge, customers may treat it as they would a dirt or concrete floor. Accordingly, EarthEnable has instituted extensive measures to address and correct these misconceptions.

Today, EarthEnable is able to provide earthen floors that are 80 percent cheaper and 90 percent less carbon intensive to produce than concrete, and they have provided flooring and other products to almost 40,000 people across Rwanda and Uganda. To deliver these products, EarthEnable has upskilled local masons across central Africa to become flooring entrepreneurs who independently sell and build earthen floors in their communities. By delivering EarthEnable products, these small business owners (called micro-franchisees) are able to double their previous income while serving their communities. In addition to providing training, EarthEnable supports these micro-franchisees with a robust quality assurance department to oversee quality and ensure that customers are satisfied. As a result of these efforts in 2020, 99 percent of EarthEnable's customers indicated on customer surveys that they would recommend EarthEnable's floor to a friend.

continued

Box 5.5 *continued*

By continuing to develop products and empower micro-franchisees to deliver those products in Rwanda and Uganda, EarthEnable seeks to be the guiding force in market-based best practices and policy development for the nascent earthen construction industry. After 6 years and more than 8,000 earthen floor installations, EarthEnable has developed insights about the growth and progression of the developed economy floor construction industry. Although earthen construction is used by nearly a third of the global population, especially in rural areas of low-income countries, most legal construction standards across the world apply only to construction using high-carbon materials such as cement and steel. Several developing countries either explicitly prohibit building with earth or lack appropriate frameworks for regulating earthen concrete. Efforts to create standards for earthen construction have been met with resistance from skeptics.

Fortunately, as the planet's resources become scarcer, and as a growing population needs affordable housing solutions, many countries are starting to allow for earthen concrete in their building codes. EarthEnable has invested significant resources to work alongside government to demonstrate the benefits of earthen construction technologies and encourage the development of engineering standards to ensure that earthen concrete is responsibly regulated. EarthEnable's efforts resulted in the creation of a think tank in Rwanda to develop legal standards for earthen construction in 2019. The Local Building Materials Think Tank is in the process of writing a standard for constructing houses from adobe blocks in Rwanda, which EarthEnable hopes can be used as a legal standard for earthen construction across the world. EarthEnable does not believe that one company can meet all of the demand for affordable

Photo courtesy of EarthEnable.

housing, so their mission is not only to build a company but to build an entire industry. Through earthen housing product innovation, empowering and certifying local masons to become earthen construction entrepreneurs, proving profitable business models, and developing policy standards to legalize earthen concrete, EarthEnable is catalyzing an industry for affordable housing improvement.

EarthEnable aims to profitably deliver its products to rural customers through a replicable business model, and mobilize replicators to franchise the business or license the technology to expand earthen concrete solutions to new countries. EarthEnable will shift from implementer to coach by providing replicators with all the tools and methods they've used to build affordable housing products in Rwanda and Uganda. Just like microfinance and solar home systems started with one company that was then replicated by others, EarthEnable aims to be the first company proving the business model to profitably serve this market need. Through these efforts EarthEnable seeks to ensure that affordable, sustainable construction options will meet the growing demand for housing in Africa and across the world.

Note

a. https://openknowledge.worldbank.org/bitstream/handle/10986/7295/wps421401update1.pdf;sequence=1

As a civil engineer, a builder, and a mother, Lisa Morey brought a lot of experience into founding Colorado Earth, LLC, near Denver. She knows as well as anyone the rewards and difficulties of trying to do anything even slightly different in today's construction market, and she brings us her report.

Box 5.6 Entering the North American Market as an Earth Block Producer
By Lisa Morey

Promoting earthen construction in North America has been one of the most challenging and inspiring experiences of my life. Some things are instant loves, like the first sight of your child, or the ocean, or gelato, and they become life anchors that you couldn't let go of even if you tried. The pursuit and practice of earthen construction has been like this for me, a love that comes with purpose and drive.

As an advocate for earthen building I am an educator, researcher, and businesswoman. I have often found myself in conversations where the question arises, "What is earthen construction, anyway?" I reply that I work with adobe, to which I receive the response, "What a great program! Are you on the software development side?" Long, long before Adobe Acrobat was even a thing, the walls of Jericho were being built with *adobe*: mud bricks with clay plaster. After covering that little bit of history, I go on to explain the actual type of adobe I make and its many benefits that got me excited long ago. The blocks use an abundant resource—dirt (or rather, clean subsoil with no organic material)—with a well-proven durability. Earth blocks are fireproof (dirt doesn't burn), bulletproof, and moldproof. In addition, the finished walls are aesthetically like a natural environment, have superior acoustical properties (nothing is as quiet), can passively regulate temperature and humidity, are low maintenance, and make

continued

Box 5.6 *continued*

a very low embodied carbon system. The construction process produces minimal waste while being cost-competitive with conventional "stick" framing. One of two responses typically occurs in these conversations. Perhaps I have gained a potential client or supporting advocate. Usually, this person responds with "Oh, my grandfather built his own adobe home!" or some other personal experience that validates the material. Or maybe the listener is confused and uninterested in asking further questions. For the latter, it's difficult to connect the images of crumbling structures in poor, far-away countries to the high-end buildings I build and had just described. If only I could take each person into a crafted earthen building and allow them to linger and experience the solidity and quiet beauty of the walls!

The thrilling part of owning and operating an earth block yard is opening new possibilities for people, revealing things they had not seen or considered before and showing why a shift away from conventional building materials should occur. In addition, there is pride in knowing that the block walls will be standing for hundreds of years, as can be seen in historical earthen structures around the world.

For this college student who went through the usual civil engineering curriculum, earthen construction was not even briefly mentioned in materials classes. Instead, I learned in my mid-20s, while obtaining my construction engineering and management degree, that "earth" in construction pertains only to subsurface soil composition, a place to put a concrete foundation. From there it was a huge and delightful leap to discover that earth can be screened, mixed with a designed amount of sand or other additives, moistened and—voilá!—adobe. Formed bricks are left to air-dry (or compressed for added strength and durability, as my company does), laid with mortar, and finished with a plaster, all from the same raw material.

I was introduced to adobe in New Zealand, the country that has produced the most comprehensive and detailed earthen construction code in the world, where I initially practiced designing and building homes out of "mud bricks." Now I am now designing, manufacturing, and constructing adobe bricks but primarily compressed earth blocks (CEBs) in Golden, Colorado. Situated alongside a local quarry, the overburden material from their excavation activities is delivered to the block-making site just a few hundred yards away and placed directly into our manufacturing equipment. Interested in incorporating other additives into the mix design, I have been exploring the inclusion of natural fibers such as hemp, as well as material that could be recycled rather than taken to a landfill. The benefit of these additives is that they improve the blocks' thermal performance, strength, or carbon footprint. This research is being conducted in collaboration with a local university, where I have also had the opportunity to teach students about natural building.

I am inspired by the many connections I've made with promoters, innovators, and achievers in the industry. Many of these relationships have been formed through networking and at conferences where I've shared my work and research, such as Earth USA in New Mexico. My partnership with Ital-Mexicana, a manufacturer that produces the equipment to make earth blocks, also provides the collaboration to improve the technology. But above all, I am inspired by the clients I support and continually encouraged by visionary people who seek high-performance building materials and practices that contribute to the well-being of our planet.

Though inspiring, the challenges are substantial for a lone wolf businesswoman working to sell this "new" building material in a North American market. Competing with established manufacturers and industry habits presents major challenges. My hope is for earthen construction to be recognized and used as a credible building material for the applications and projects it best fits: one- and two-story structures in most climates. With access to the knowledge and raw materials needed, the possibilities are many and the opportunity for growth and inspiration enormous. Compared with wood framing, earthen concrete is better for the climate and better for those in ever more fire-prone regions such as the arid U.S. West.

Although earthen construction has been around for thousands of years, it gives us a new means to be pioneers in supporting better management of our natural resources and restoration of the climate. The humble adobe block serves as both a tie to our past and a demonstration of a better future that uses innovation, building science, intuition, and common sense to guide a path beyond the outdated conventions of industrial building.

Grow It and They Will Come: Biological Concrete

We very deliberately end this long chapter on concrete with a piece about algal materials, because it points out their enormous potential and also segues to the larger world of plants and how they all can help us develop a climate-healing architecture. Efforts to grow building materials are already entering the marketplace, such as the North American companies Ecovative (insulating foams made from fungi feeding on waste wood or paper pulp) and BioMASON (bricks grown in factory conditions with bacteria). We asked our friend Wil Srubar at the University of Colorado to report on efforts in his lab and the industry at large. Prof. Srubar, we should add, has fast emerged as one of the leading thinkers and innovators around carbon in the built environment, in part because he consistently gets more done in a day than most of us can manage in a week. Here he talks about his work to grow concrete, but we also relied heavily on his work to establish a monetary value to carbon sequestration at the end of chapter 3.

Box 5.7   Can We Grow Carbon-Storing Buildings?
By Wil V. Srubar III

If you think about it, buildings are not unlike a human body. A strong, stiff skeleton provides structural support and protection from external forces. A multifunctional skin provides protection from the elements. Buildings are electrified. They breathe, consume energy, regulate temperature, and produce waste. Buildings are organisms, albeit inanimate ones.

What if buildings of the future—the walls, floors, roofs, windows, and foundations—were grown (and perhaps even maintained) by *living* organisms? What if those organisms used carbon dioxide (CO_2) exclusively as a raw material resource?

continued

Box 5.7 *continued*

Growing carbon-storing buildings may seem like science fiction, but naturally occurring organisms such as plants, algae, and bacteria have been producing strong, stiff, durable carbon-storing structural materials for millennia. Modern-day researchers are taking note and leveraging the carbon sequestration and storage mechanisms exhibited by these organisms to produce—no, grow—high-performance, carbon-storing materials for applications within and beyond the built environment.

Nature's Carbon-Storing Solutions

The natural world has evolved two of the most effective carbon sequestration and storage mechanisms on the planet—photosynthesis and carbonate biomineralization—two mechanisms that are being exploited and should be further leveraged to purposefully grow carbon-storing building materials. Photosynthetic plant fibers, including timber, straw, and industrial hemp, have been used for millennia to manufacture building materials. In addition, biological organisms such as algae and bacteria have evolved to produce the tough, hard carbonate minerals that make up shells, coral, and limestone. Because of marked advances in biotechnology in other fields (e.g., bioenergy, agriculture), a grand opportunity now exists to harness the ability of plants and other biological systems to grow new high-performance carbon-storing materials at scale.

Photosynthesis: Growing Materials with CO_2 and Sunlight

The chemical equation for photosynthesis is quite simple: $6CO_2 + 6H_2O \rightarrow C_6H_{12}O_6 + 6O_2$. In other words, plants breathe in six molecules of CO_2, which they absorb from the air, and take in six molecules of water, which they absorb through their roots. Using only energy from the sun, the plants convert the CO_2 and water into various sugar molecules, most notably cellulose, hemicellulose, and lignin—three of the most common biopolymers on the planet (as opposed to the petrochemical polymers we call plastic). Cellulose gives plants and trees their load-bearing structure, while hemicellulose and lignin glue the cellulose and hemicellulose fibers together, much as concrete and steel rebar work together to make reinforced concrete.

Photosynthetic algae and cyanobacteria are single-celled organisms that are very similar to plants. Most species of algae and cyanobacteria secrete carbonic anhydrase, an enzyme that helps pull in atmospheric CO_2. The algae absorb the CO_2 through their cell walls and use it, along with water and light energy from the sun, to exponentially replicate their own biomass through mitosis (i.e., cell division) and perform other biological functions (e.g., produce and secrete carbonic anhydrase).

Nearly all dry biomass—dry wood, stems, roots, even algae—is about half (45–50 percent) elemental carbon by mass. The only source of that carbon is atmospheric CO_2. In fact, 1 kg of biomass actually takes about 1.83 kg CO_2 out of the atmosphere. How is that possible? Fun with chemistry: 1 kg of biomass contains 0.5 kg of elemental carbon. To get the total mass of CO_2 that it took to produce 0.5 kg of carbon, we have to multiply by 44/12, or the molar ratio of CO_2 (44) and carbon (12). Multiplying through, we find that 1 kg of dry biomass actually takes 1.83 kg of CO_2 to make.

With photosynthesis, nature has certainly evolved an efficient carbon capture and storage mechanism, and we humans have been converting a lot of that biomass into building materials for centuries.

We use trees to make lumber, plywood, oriented strand board, and, now, glulam and mass timber. We use raw cellulose, hemp, and straw as insulation and fiber mats and forestry residue for cabinetry. We use other natural fibers in carpets and as reinforcement in fiber-reinforced plastics and fiber cement board. Cellulose-based admixtures are used in concrete.

Most of the photosynthetic biomass we use in buildings today relies on forests. Trees are cut to make lumber and other structural wood products, and the residues (such as sawdust) are used for fiber reinforcement and other secondary products. Some might argue that, because we rely on so much forest biomass, we should plant more forests and convert more forest products into usable building materials if we are to transition buildings into carbon storage batteries. Plant more trees! It's a simple plan, right?

But there's a catch: Trees are certainly exceptional organisms that from a genetically encoded single seed will grow strong and stiff while sequestering and storing carbon. But there are two major downsides to using trees: They need land, and they need time.

Land use is important. Deciding whether to plant more forests or to plant more food crops is a dilemma increasingly faced by most populations around the world; an acre might be more valuable as a corn crop than a forest. In fact, most would argue that food should always take priority over the other two basic human needs—clothing and shelter—if one ultimately has to choose. At any rate, land use is very important, and the fight to protect the forests we still have rather than plant additional acreage will continue.

The other downside to forests is time. It takes anywhere from 20 to 30 years for a tree to reach maturity. Indeed, each tree in the forest will store and sequester CO_2 every single year it grows, and one could argue that a tree is more valuable in a forest than in a building from a climate perspective. But trees are not as productive from a CO_2 storage perspective as one might think.

In other words, not all biomass is created equal, and figure 5.11 quantifies and compares the carbon storage productivity of different photosynthetic organisms. Each organism's carbon storage productivity is expressed in tons of CO_2 per hectare per year. From the graph, it is clear that the softwood forests common in the northern temperate belts cannot fix carbon as well as the alternatives. This limitation is caused by the slow growth rate of trees and the land needed for each mature tree to flourish.

The carbon storage productivity of straw is somewhat higher than that of trees. One planting of straw per year can sequester and store approximately 5 tCO_2/hectare/year, almost twice that of forests. Straw has two other advantages: We will always grow straw, because it is the byproduct of primary food (e.g., wheat, rice, barley) production, and multiple harvest cycles can occur in many climate regions, so the carbon storage productivity can be two times higher.

In contrast to trees and straw, industrial hemp plants are carbon sequestration machines. Industrial hemp, which is grown primarily for fiber, is very tall (up to 3 meters) and can be planted densely. Thus, the carbon sequestration and storage efficiency of hemp biomass is an order of magnitude higher than that of trees or straw.

However, photosynthetic algae are carbon sequestration champions. The carbon storage efficiency of algae (about 200 tCO_2/hectare/year) is due in large part to the exponential growth and carbon fixation efficiency of algal cells. For the most part, algae are cultivated in large-scale outdoor cultivation ponds. The basic idea of cultivating algae as a source of fuel and food dates back nearly half a century.

continued

Box 5.7 *continued*

Methane gas production from algae, proposed in the early 1950s, reached its peak during the global energy crisis of the 1970s. From about 1980 to 1996 the U.S. Department of Energy supported small efforts toward the goal of producing oil from microalgae. Most recently, advances in biotechnology, including the ability to genetically engineer algae to produce even more oils and convert light energy into biomass even more efficiently, have accelerated algae cultivation. This acceleration has been fueled mainly by peak oil concerns and the systematic decarbonization of U.S. energy industry. The primary end-use application of algae has been biofuels, so, as when we compost straw, stems, and other organics, much of the stored CO_2 is (to date) re-released back into the atmosphere.

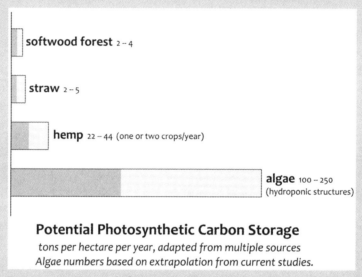

softwood forest 2 – 4

straw 2 – 5

hemp 22 – 44 (one or two crops/year)

algae 100 – 250
(hydroponic structures)

Potential Photosynthetic Carbon Storage
tons per hectare per year, adapted from multiple sources
Algae numbers based on extrapolation from current studies.

FIGURE 5.11. Potential photosynthetic carbon storage.

Figure 5.11 sheds light on a few grand opportunities with hemp and algae on which the building industry could (and should) capitalize to maximize carbon sequestration in usable biomass while minimizing land use. New industrial hemp and algae bioproducts are a prime example. The recent legalization of U.S. industrial hemp cultivation comes at a time of rising demand for durable, bio-based building materials. As one of the strongest, stiffest, and fastest-growing of all natural fibers, industrial hemp exhibits a remarkable potential for use as reinforcement in advanced composite materials for buildings. Hemp fibers, fabrics, and shiv can be purpose grown for building materials and used as feedstocks by structural wood composite and hemp-based insulation companies (e.g., Hemwood, JustBioFibre, Isohemp) to manufacture high-performance industrial hemp-based building materials. Instead of relying on land resources, advances in soil-free seed germination could be leveraged to purposefully grow fibers without burdening land for food production.

Large-scale cultivation of algae for advanced biofuel production is already common in many regions of the United States. Although much of the biomass is currently incinerated for energy production, biochar can be used to produce high-performance building materials (e.g., concrete, carbon nanofibers). Opportunities also abound for storing the captured carbon by engineering algal biomass systems for buildings. To date, translucent algae panels have been used for building facades in daylighting applications by world-class architecture and engineering firms (e.g., Arup). Algal systems have the potential to be engineered for near-site fuel and food production and indoor air purification (AlgenAir). Some species of algae also precipitate solid carbonate minerals, which are currently being explored for carbon-neutral cement and concrete production at scale by some early-stage companies (Minus Materials).

More research and development is needed for straw, hemp, and algae to be converted to high-performance construction bioproducts. Advances in U.S. industrial fiber processing must occur for these products to be cost competitive with other materials. Currently, most fiber processing is done overseas, which imposes an economic challenge for straw-, hemp-, and other fiber-based products to be competitive in a commodity market. Relatedly, supply chains must be established that link fiber processing with material manufacturers. The cost of building material testing and certification also makes rapid uptake of new, innovative materials difficult. Without these innovations, the opportunity to store and lock up the carbon absorbed through carbon farming would literally float away.

Carbonate Mineralization: Growing Carbon-Storing Minerals

Biomineralization is a process by which living organisms produce minerals. Of all the minerals that are produced through biomineralization, calcium carbonate (essentially, limestone) is the most prevalent in nature. Massive limestone deposits, shells, and coral are all composed predominantly of biogenic $CaCO_3$.

The basic chemical equation for calcium carbonate mineralization is straightforward: $Ca^{2+} + 2OH^- + CO_2 \rightarrow CaCO_3 + H_2O$. For every 1 kg of $CaCO_3$ that is formed, 0.44 kg of CO_2 is sequestered and permanently stored in the mineral. $CaCO_3$ is a relatively stable carbonate mineral, meaning that it is not easily dissolved in water. You need an acidic condition or heat to be able to dissolve or drive off the lime (CaO) and re-release the CO_2 in the atmosphere. Acid dissolution is the primary concern with acid rain, which wreaks havoc on limestone monuments and statues that are placed out in the elements for centuries. Heat release of CO_2 is the primary issue with portland cement manufacture, in which limestone is heated to extreme temperatures to drive off the CO_2 and leave behind the valuable CaO needed to make portland cement. The chemical process of calcination is responsible for about 50 percent of CO_2 emissions of cement manufacture.

For natural organisms to produce $CaCO_3$, the reaction is almost always aqueous, meaning it is performed in a liquid environment. In other words, organisms take and use CO_2 and elemental calcium, which are both dissolved in the water. For example, seawater is 410 ppm calcium (or 1.2 percent of all of the solids dissolved in seawater), which is small, so additional calcium is usually added when this natural process is replicated in the laboratory. $2OH^-$ are two hydroxide molecules. If you recall high school chemistry, hydroxides are responsible for higher pH, or alkalinity. This doesn't mean that *all* of the seawater has to be extremely basic (high pH)—that would kill almost all living things in the ocean. What this does mean, however, is that if there is a tiny spike in the pH at a *very* localized area near the

continued

Box 5.7 *continued*

organism, the calcium will react with the CO_2 and the hydroxide molecules to form $CaCO_3$ and H_2O. Through their normal metabolic activity, many species of bacteria can spike the pH near their cell wall by secreting chemical OH^-. In this way, many microbes and coral are thought of as tiny microcatalysts to induce biomineral formation. The systematic, microscopic pH spike and subsequent biomineralization reaction are responsible for most of all coral reefs in the world. It is a slow process because of the low concentrations of calcium in seawater.

This naturally occurring biomineralization process in bacteria, often called microbial-induced calcium carbonate precipitation (MICP), has been exploited in a number of applications in buildings and infrastructure. So-called self-healing concrete, which originated at Delft University of Technology in the Netherlands, leverages MICP technology. Since the first demonstration, the technology has been the focus of extensive research across the globe. Self-healing concrete, in principle, is concrete designed to seal its own cracks. Bacteria that are capable of MICP are mixed into fresh concrete, along with the nutrients needed for survival. As cracks form in the concrete, the bacteria produce $CaCO_3$ minerals, which fill the cracks. This self-sealing approach could be particularly effective for preventing chloride exposure and subsequent corrosion of rebar, which reduces the longevity of reinforced concrete structures. Actual regains of strength have been achieved only in laboratory conditions, which has minimized MICP use in real-world structural applications.

Although MICP may be an effective crack repair method for cement paste and concrete, the local environment within concrete is harsh. It doesn't take long for most bacteria to lose their ability to reproduce (and thus to produce minerals). In fact, less than 0.5 percent of the initial bacterial inoculum has been shown to last more than 30 days in cement paste, mortar, or concrete.

Growing Carbon-Storing Concrete and Limestone Fillers

My research team at the University of Colorado Boulder sought out to leverage MICP to help us grow a concrete alternative. In collaboration with professors Sherri Cook, Jeff Cameron, and Mija Hubler, my interdisciplinary research team at the Living Materials Laboratory grew portland cement–free concrete materials. In one of our studies, we used photosynthetic cyanobacteria as tiny biocatalysts within a cement-free mortar to precipitate biominerals that helped bind the sand particles together. We also engineered an internal environment more suitable for the photosynthetic bacteria to survive within the sand, thereby creating a carbon-storing living building material (LBM). In these LBMs, photosynthetic marine cyanobacteria capable of MICP were encapsulated in a biocompatible hydrogel–sand matrix. We demonstrated that the biogenic minerals produced by the bacteria significantly improved the mechanical properties of the materials compared with bricks without cyanobacteria.

The result? A grown photosynthetic, carbon-storing composite material with a compressive strength (f'_c) of more than 500 psi—on par with low-strength cementitious mortar and higher than that of adobe brick. Microbial viability within our bricks greatly exceeds that of traditional self-healing concrete. Nine percent of our initial inoculum survived for at least 30 days in our cyanobacterial mortar. These mortars represent a new material paradigm in which carbon-storing microorganisms can produce carbon-storing materials—and even persist within the resultant material—thereby potentially imparting biological functionalities to an otherwise inert structural material. The technology is now being commercialized by Prometheus Materials, an advanced materials biotechnology startup located in Boulder, Colorado.

In one of our more recent studies, we leveraged the capability of algae species to produce carbon-storing biogenic limestone. This invention has become the technological foundation of Minus Materials, another new biotechnology startup committed to growing carbon-storing limestone fillers for portland limestone cement using algae.

Toward Genetically Programmed Living Architecture

We are only beginning to scratch the surface of possibilities for using biological organisms to grow buildings. Different materials and building systems could be engineered by combining photosynthetic bacteria, plant, and algae species. Energy and daylighting systems, as well as on-site food, fuel, and material production, would spur a new paradigm for architecture. If nature can do it, we believe that living materials can be engineered to do it, too.

Considering the challenges humans will face in the 2020s and beyond—climate change, disaster resilience, infrastructure, and space exploration—we should look to the power of biological organisms and living materials at the building scale to help solve some of the most critical environmental crises of our time. By doing so, we could harness the ability of living organisms to create materials that would help us build more sustainable buildings and communities—both on Earth and beyond—that better blur the boundaries between, and bring harmony to, the built environment and natural world.

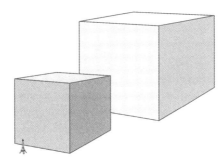

FIGURE 5.12. Eiffel Tower next to global concrete production next to global waste straw production.

If we took all the straw left over from growing our food (2 billion tons of waste straw annually, making a 1.6-mile cube) and turned it into durable building products (which we know how to do), we could negate almost all of the 4 billion tons of emissions from making our 10 billion tons of concrete (making a 1-mile cube) annually. Let's now look at how we can do that.

6. Biological Architecture: Wood and Mass Timber, Agricultural Byproducts, Purpose-Grown Crops, Waste Stream Fibers, and Lab-Grown Materials

Meet Your Friends, the Plants

Wood, grasses, and animal products combined with stones, clay, and baked limestone were the sum total of all building materials for thousands of years of human history (as discussed in chapter 5). Indeed, the historical architecture we flock to admire—the cathedrals, castles, mosques, and ancient historical districts—used nothing more than local versions of these natural materials. Collectively, we invented and refined countless ways of using and combining these basic materials.

The Industrial Revolution eclipsed the rich, varied, and central role of plant material in buildings, widely replacing it with artificial rock (concrete), steel, and eventually plastics. What was once fundamental to building cultures worldwide was largely reduced to a few product types: kiln-dried dimensional lumber and sheet goods (e.g., plywood, oriented strand board, and medium-density fiberboard). In recent years, mass timber elements (e.g., cross-laminated timber, glue-laminated beams, and mass plywood panels) have attracted the attention of architects and engineers because of the potential to reduce the carbon footprint of large buildings by substituting mass timber for concrete and steel. That is why mass timber occupies the central role in architecture's current vision of plant-based, carbon-storing materials. We don't expect it to be the game changer that its proponents claim, but nonetheless we hope that mass timber will prove to be a sort of "gateway drug" to the wider world of carbon-storing material possibilities.

The range of plant-based materials is an embarrassment of riches, including common materials that have been used in modern construction for decades, alternative materials with a long history of use that are experiencing resurgence in applicability and form, and entirely new materials emerging from labs and testing facilities around the world. In this chapter we group these materials into five categories—wood and timber, agricultural residues and byproducts, purpose-grown crops, waste stream fibers, and lab-grown plants—and introduce you to the vast world of plant-based building materials.

The sales pitch for a return to more plant-based building materials is simple and, in the face of the climate crisis, very compelling.

Plants Are Made from Atmospheric Carbon

As the world develops the processes and machines needed to extract pure CO_2 out of the atmosphere (as we increasingly need for industry; see chapter 11), we would be wise to remind ourselves that *this is what plants do.* They turn atmospheric carbon into more solid forms of carbon, using only sunlight, water, and soil minerals (and in the case of most human-grown crops, additional inputs such as fertilizer). Every year, the natural growth of biomass on the planet removes billions of tons of CO_2 from the atmosphere. And as a great byproduct, they produce the oxygen needed for survival of all self-propelled critters on the planet, including us humans.

Plants Transform CO2 into a Staggering Variety of Fibers Full of Promise as Building Materials

From massive oak trunks capable of holding up a cathedral roof for 500 years, to reeds and grasses that can be bundled in different ways to provide structure, enclosure, and insulation, to individual fiber strands that can be tied, pressed, twisted, and glued (and even chemically transformed) into myriad useful forms, it is possible to find a plant-based solution for nearly every part of a building assembly.

Plants Are an Abundant and Renewable Resource

We will certainly address the complex issues necessary to ensure regenerative plant use, but plants are quite simply the most renewable building material options available to us. The other building elements discussed in this book are available in varying degrees of abundance, but with the exception of the carbon that we may mechanically extract from the air, we deplete the resource with each use. Whether grown in natural settings such as forests, in human agriculture, or in labs and factories, only plants have the potential to keep coming back, providing a clever species like ours with a continuous supply of building materials. Opportunities for co-beneficial uses of plants—such as using agricultural residues like stalks, stems, and shells—can increase abundance without increasing our planetary footprint.

Plants Provide Opportunities for Simple, Affordable, Accessible Manufacturing

There is much talk about the "moonshot" approach to mitigating climate change, but usually a thousand "little shots" will be better than one big one. The beauty of adopting plant-based building materials as a central effort in climate mitigation is the sheer simplicity and low bar to entry. Making carbon-storing building materials from plants is a low-tech, low-investment opportunity; the limitations are largely issues of mindset, adoption, investment, and regulation rather than technology. The majority of the material options we discuss in this book are already being manufactured on some scale. To embrace plant-based architecture, we don't need to wait for the technology to develop and mature in order to get to work. Even at the high-tech, experimental end of the spectrum, the breakthroughs needed to bring new materials to market are about bringing scale to manufacturing, not inventing entirely new processes. To a great extent we already know what we need to know and have the manufacturing know-how to make it work.

As a stacked benefit, manufacturing of plant-based materials tends to be more about shaping, aligning, and binding fibers than transforming plant material into new compounds; it doesn't require that we "make molecules be something they don't want to be," as green chemist John Warner puts it. Conventional industrial material production relies largely on the "heat, beat, and treat" approach, transforming raw materials into the products we want via sizable inputs of fuel, mechanical, and chemical energy. Although it's certainly possible to produce plant-based materials in a high-intensity way, the current array of plant-based building materials typically features low-intensity production inputs because the source plant material already has most or all of the desired properties built into its fiber structure. Less intensive inputs and associated emissions only strengthen the carbon-storing benefits of plant-based materials.

Plants Are Well-Distributed Around the Planet

A symbiotic relationship exists between plants, climatic conditions, and the needs of humans living in the region. "Vernacular" architecture is an industrial-era term for buildings that demonstrate this remarkable symbiosis. The unique attributes of the plant-based materials used in vernacular buildings reflect the ability of locally sourced plant material to survive in local conditions and to grow at a rate that matches or exceeds the need to repair and replace the material in the building. Plant-based architecture offers rich solutions that are quite literally grounded in the soils and conditions of the region, providing local solutions to local building needs (box 6.1).

Box 6.1 How Much Biomass?

There's no mystery about how much biomass is available, from the local level to the global. The early 2000s featured a great deal of enthusiasm for and study of biomass as a potential replacement for fossil fuels. Although setting all that biomass on fire to replace fossil fuels seems like a shortsighted dead end, the research makes it easy to understand what kinds of biomass exist and in what quantities.

In the U.S. context, the Union of Concerned Scientists (UCS) produced a report in 2012 that attempted to take an inventory of the amount of biomass available while accounting for sustainable sources and scales (figure 6.1). They were reacting to a study by the U.S. Department of Energy's Oak Ridge National Laboratory (ORNL) that determined there was a billion tons of biomass available for bioenergy in the United States. UCS reassessed the ORNL numbers to reflect what they thought were ecological shortcomings in the assessment. This analysis gives us a good snapshot of biomass potential, which we would advocate prioritizing for building materials that will store carbon rather than bioenergy that will release it back to the atmosphere.

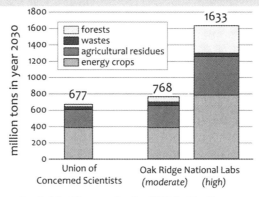

Available Biomass in the USA in the Year 2030

estimates from sources noted
based on "The Promise of Biomass," Union of Concerned Scientists, 2012

FIGURE 6.1. Varying estimates of the amount of biomass available in the United States, calculated to support biofuel energy but relevant for biomass building materials too. (Adapted from "The Promise of Biomass," Union of Concerned Scientists, September 2012)

The UCS analysis maps closely to our categories of plant-based building materials, showing more than 150 million tons of agricultural residues, 40 million tons of waste fibers, and 20 million tons of forest biomass residue. These numbers account for the volumes of each type of biomass needed for soil and ecosystem health and so represent a good indication of the potential supply of raw materials for carbon-storing building materials.

The largest potential source of biomass in this study is purpose-grown energy crops, such as switchgrass and willow. There is much debate about the sustainability of this type of biomass production. We would rather ensure that waste stream biomass is prioritized for building materials rather than expanding cropland for the sole purpose of generating biomass for construction. The potential for 400 million tons of purpose-grown biomass does indicate that, where appropriate (i.e., where ecosystem impacts are regenerative and where co-products improve value), it is possible to produce biomass with the central purpose of making building materials.

With 677 million tons of biomass—and a corresponding 2.5 billion tons of stored atmospheric CO_2—identified as being sustainably available in the United States annually, the raw materials for plant-based building materials are abundant and waiting only for innovators and designers to collaborate to get them.

Plant Materials Don't Generate Waste (If We Don't Want Them To)

Although we definitely throw away a lot of plant-based materials in a wasteful manner, most plant-based materials don't create persistent volumes of waste. Dumping wood and other plant-fibers into landfills is a bad idea; the decomposition of the material creates methane and returns much of the carbon stored in the material to the atmosphere as an intensive greenhouse gas (GHG) and leaves the remainder buried. But the fact that plant-based materials break down into natural elements is an opportunity for us to consider a more circular way of moving material through different life cycle use stages. Today, the notion of burning biomass to generate energy drives a lot of research into biomass growth and use. There is definitely potential to first use biomass as building materials and then as fuel (with carbon capture and storage technology preventing the carbon from reentering the atmosphere). But this seems short-sighted when plant-based materials could provide a wide array of secondary uses that can include new building materials or benefits to soil and agriculture.

Plant Materials Offer Biophilic Potential

The buildings humans enjoy most tend to have natural materials and natural forms. Today, we call this biophilic design—the incorporation of natural forms and materials to bring experiences of nature into our buildings—and people study its positive impacts on building occupants. Plant-based buildings are inherently biophilic, and as designers learn how to choose and use plant materials, the design opportunities will grow, both literally and figuratively.

Nature gives us endless versions of buildings with carbon-storing materials from which we can learn valuable lessons in material selection and construction techniques. From wasp hives to oyster shells, social weaver bird nests to spider webs, there is a whole world of remarkable, carbon-storing architecture to study and emulate, as the burgeoning field of biomimicry is doing.

But we're not wearing rose-colored glasses: Such a transition to plant-based materials is eminently achievable and brings not only climate benefits but a wide range of co-benefits. However, we need to be careful that a transition to plant-based architecture is not done in a short-sighted way; achieving good "carbon numbers" can still wreck people and the planet in the process. First and foremost, we don't want to encourage efforts to simply cram tons of industrially grown plant material into questionable composite materials, creating off-gassing, wasteful, single-use materials that ruin ecosystems when growing and spewing toxins during manufacture, inside buildings, or in landfills. Each subset of plant-based materials requires unique considerations to create wins for the climate, growers, manufacturers, builders, and building occupants.

What follows is a snapshot of our five categories of plant-based material options. Despite using the widest possible lens through which to view this burgeoning material sector, we know there are lots of worthy materials, approaches, and products we are not able to call out specifically. We hope this chapter inspires you to explore more widely, knowing that we are showing you but a fraction of what's already out there.

Timber: The Good, the Bad, and the Potentially Ugly

Builders have a long and productive relationship with timber. We've used wood to build structures, and make floors, walls, roofs, cladding, doors, windows, trim, shelves, and cupboards. It's hard to think of a building in which wood has not been put to some use, from earliest known history to today.

The fiber structure of wood is remarkable in many ways. It comes in large sizes, both in length and diameter, and is often usefully straight in its natural form. It is strong enough to handle remarkable loads yet soft and flexible enough to be cut, shaped, drilled, nailed, screwed, or doweled in many ways. It is very stiff but also elastic, able to bend without breaking. It is dense enough to repel most of the water that lands on it but porous enough to absorb paints, stains, and finishes. And regardless of species, the structure of its grains and the colors of its fibers are beautiful to behold. In so many ways it is the perfect building material. Even its abilities to withstand fire—at least in the form of mass timber—are impressive. What's not to love? It even stores atmospheric carbon.

We are poised before a potential explosion in timber usage in the building industry. Growing interest in and acceptance of mass timber for constructing large buildings could increase demand for timber manyfold, and the low emissions resulting from producing timber products combined with the volume of stored carbon are a key driver of this emerging swell in wood use.

You might think that a surge of mass timber buildings would be celebrated in a book promoting plant-based, carbon-storing architecture, but assessing the degree of carbon storage offered by timber products is not at all straightforward. Far from being the poster child for carbon-storing building, the use of timber in buildings requires a very nuanced understanding of supply chain issues and forest-level carbon stocks in order to be certain we're not doing harm in the process of trying to do good. Although there is no doubt that we can pack a lot of carbon atoms into timber buildings, it is far from certain that we are doing well by the climate in doing so (figure 6.2).

In the simplest form of carbon accounting, we can assess the mass of timber in a building and estimate that about half of that mass is carbon (tree species vary in carbon content, but most softwood species used in construction are about 50 percent carbon by dry weight). Given the large volume of timber in a mass timber building, this kind of accounting generates impressive carbon storage numbers. However, there are many reasons for rejecting this overly simple analysis.

A Lot of the Wood in a Tree Doesn't Make It into a Building

Modern timber building requires turning round logs into squared, planed, and evenly sized dimensional lumber. Of the total mass of a tree harvested in the forest, only 30–50 percent actually ends up in a building (not including root matter, which reduces that percentage even more). The pathways for the remaining mass will vary: Roots are left in the ground, where they will eventually break down; branches and other "slash" are typically left on the forest floor, where they also break down; bark and sawdust are often used as fuel to heat kilns for drying lumber. In all of these cases, the carbon stored in those parts of the tree is going to end up back in the atmosphere, not in a building. If only half the carbon in a tree goes into a building and the other half goes back into the atmosphere, we haven't meaningfully stored a net amount of carbon despite the presence of many carbon atoms in our building, and we will probably have incurred an immediate carbon debt from the 50 percent of the tree that is not in the building.

Cutting Down a Tree Eliminates an Ongoing Carbon Sink

Trees draw carbon out of the atmosphere over their whole natural lifespan. Under standard forestry practices, a tree is harvested when it reaches a productive peak, when it stops "putting on weight" rapidly but far from the end of its natural growth cycle. Cutting the tree down at this point removes the potential for many more

What about wood?

If we build a lot of timber structures . . .

. . . but end up with fewer mature forests

then we haven't helped the climate

Always use sustainably harvested lumber

FIGURE 6.2. **Can't count the carbon for the trees.**
Moving carbon atoms from forests into buildings isn't
necessarily good for the climate. We need to ensure
that forest carbon stocks grow at the same time that the
amount of timber in buildings grows.

decades of carbon drawdown, because a mature tree with a slow growth rate can
absorb more carbon dioxide than a young tree with a fast growth rate. Therefore,
our accounting for the carbon stored in the tree at the time of harvest should also account for the lost carbon storage potential. This effect can be minimized by length-
ening the harvesting cycle to allow trees to get closer to their full maturity before
culling them, but this would disrupt long-established forestry planning cycles and
could lead to timber shortages if adjustments in harvesting cycles were made too
quickly.

Cutting Down Groups of Trees Can Release a lot of Soil Carbon
Woody biomass is not the only place in a forest where atmospheric carbon gets
stored. Root systems fix carbon in soils, as does natural decomposition of forest
floor litter and the workings of all the complex life forms in the soil. Depending

on the climate, forest type, forest maturity, and many other factors, there can be as much carbon stored in forest soils as in the woody biomass above ground. For the vast northern boreal forests, as much as 75 percent of forest carbon is in the soil. When trees are harvested in a way that exposes an expanse of forest soil to sun, wind, and rain, a lot of this soil carbon is lost to the atmosphere. Currently, even the very best forestry certification standards do not require accurate accounting of soil carbon before and after harvest, so there is no way to be certain how much carbon is being released due to logging and therefore no way to add soil carbon emissions to the total emissions associated with harvesting.

Some form of soil carbon monitoring and reporting is likely to make its way into forestry certification standards in the future, and this will help make our accounting for timber products more accurate. Until this is common practice, all we know is that we are not accounting for all the carbon emissions associated with timber products.

Trees Take a Long Time to Grow

Trees can regenerate; if we cut one down, another can grow to replace it. And we can help the process by intentionally planting replacement trees. But because trees take a long time to grow, there is a carbon lag time during which the newly planted trees are absorbing a lot less carbon than the mature stand they are replacing. In a climate emergency, this matters a lot because we can end up skewing the carbon balance from forests to the atmosphere at exactly the wrong time.

Mature, Diverse Forests Store the Most Carbon

Regardless of the climate zone and forest type, a mature forest with maximum biodiversity stores the most carbon for that ecosystem type. Managed forests—especially monoculture tree stands—may be productive sources of timber but store a lot less carbon. Cutting into remaining stands of old-growth forests and mature ecosystems removes crucial planetary carbon sinks that are far more valuable in climate mitigation than the carbon atoms we could take from them and put into buildings.

Forestry Practices May Exacerbate Forest Fires

When a forest burns, the carbon release to the atmosphere can be massive. The 2018 wildfire season in California alone released approximately 68 million tons of carbon, equivalent to the state's electricity production emissions for a year. Many studies attribute the growing number of wildfires worldwide to a combination of drier, hotter conditions driven by climate change and industrial forestry practices that leave forests more vulnerable to fire spread. Although it may be impossible to accurately attribute forest fire emissions to a life cycle assessment (LCA) of timber products, we cannot remain blind to the fact that the current practices of the forestry industry play a key role in the new fire norms and the vast emissions they release.

Ecosystem-Scale Accounting Is More Important than Tree-by-Tree or Stand-by-Stand Accounting

Even if we are able to determine exactly how much carbon is in a tree (easy), how much carbon got emitted in the production of a timber product (LCA does a good job within its boundaries), how much carbon got left behind from the tree (a bit harder, currently not counted in LCA), how much carbon the tree was not able to continue absorbing (a bit harder, currently not counted in LCA), how long it will take a replacement tree to begin absorbing the same amount of carbon (a bit harder, currently not counted LCA), and how much soil carbon was released when the tree was harvested (a bit harder, currently not counted in LCA)—even if we could tally all these factors and determine that the carbon stored in our timber product outweighed all these emissions, it wouldn't really be a climate victory if overall forest stocks on the planet are declining. The value of forests for planetary-scale carbon sequestration is based not on whether a particular stand of trees owned by a timber company or government is being managed so that its carbon stock is increasing (with all factors accounted for) but on whether the total carbon stocks in all forests collectively are increasing or decreasing.

Even if LCA allows a building to count carbon stored in a timber product because it meets high standards of forest management practice, if the national and global forest carbon stocks are decreasing we may have been better off leaving those trees alone. Accounting for forest carbon stocks at the national level is complex, and there are many ways that figures can be manipulated. International efforts are under way to improve data collection, modeling methods, and reporting, but right now it is difficult to see the forests for the trees.

An exploration of the issues around carbon storage in timber products reveals the complexity without always revealing a clear answer. The good news is that a great deal of effort is being made to clarify these issues; in the meantime, take this list as a reason to approach carbon storage in timber with caution.

Doing Wood Right

Okay, so measuring effective carbon storage in timber building materials is difficult. That doesn't mean we should give up and stop using wood in our buildings, but it does put a high value on doing wood right. We can't just turn to mass timber as the plant-based solution to our embodied carbon issues in buildings and gobble up the Earth's remaining thriving forests to do so.

As we've just reviewed, there are issues aplenty that need to be understood and addressed for accurate timber carbon accounting. But there is also a simple solution: We need to grow more forests than we harvest, creating more biomass in forests than is removed by humans and natural causes. Modeling indicates that it is possible to both increase forest carbon stocks to support more timber-based construction and increase timber harvests on a global scale.[1] This will need to be an explicit goal of the building industry if we are going to embrace mass timber construction: We need to take responsibility for ensuring that we are growing forests at a rate that far exceeds our removals from them.

Notice that we are talking about growing forests and not just planting trees. There is a crucial difference between encouraging and expanding the growth of forest ecosystems and merely creating monoculture plantations. Not only do monoculture plantations store much less carbon, they also do not support all the other critical natural services provided by diverse, natural forest ecosystems. The building industry does not just get to sponsor some tree planting schemes that create tree farms and claim to be solving climate change with mass timber buildings. We need to forge real alliances with forest owners and managers and invest in the research and work of building long-lasting and productive forest ecosystems. This is an achievable goal, but as consumers of timber products we will need to bring all our resources to the table in a cooperative effort to grow forests and make timber buildings.

Harvesting of timber is not the only pressure driving deforestation. More forest area is lost to development and agricultural expansion than to harvesting for timber products. It can seem counterintuitive, but a forest that is being carefully harvested and can provide sustained economic value is much less likely to be sold for conversion to development or agriculture. A building industry that is responsibly—and locally—supporting the activities of forest owners, foresters, and mills can help ensure that the value of these forests is maintained. As with growing forests, we will need to be intentional and committed to supporting productive forests and averting land use change when it results in deforestation. This includes more than being good customers for forests; it means actively defending them by making our voices heard by politicians and developers when forests are threatened and actively working to provide alternative solutions to the pressures of deforestation.

Climate change mitigation efforts in other industries are also likely to increase deforestation, as pressure mounts for makers of packaging and short-lived consumer items to turn to bio-based options (rather than plastic) to reduce their carbon footprints. The building industry can put timber to use as long-term storage, but if forests are being cut down to provide single-use products with a nominally lower carbon footprint, we may lose the ability to responsibly access enough timber to do so. We will need to put our understanding of LCA to use in demonstrating the value of concentrating valuable timber resources in long-lived, high-value buildings.

The large percentage of wood biomass that is not used for high-value purposes in a building offers us another way to improve our use of forest resources for long-term carbon storage. The timber industry is already investing in methods of productively using parts of trees that are not used for building products. For example, oriented strand board (OSB); laminated strand lumber; and low-, medium- and high-density fiberboard, which make use of forest fibers other than high-value dimensional lumber, are now ubiquitous. Such innovation has much room to expand. The bark of many tree species has been turned into insulation material (in loose, batt, and board form), and intentionally harvested bark has been turned into exterior cladding. Forestry residue is also being explored as a source of bio-based adhesives (see chapter 7).

With some concerted effort, a much greater percentage of harvested forest biomass could be captured in buildings, increasing productivity without expanding harvesting areas and putting more forest carbon into long-term storage in buildings.

Coppicing

Industrial forestry practices focus on the removal of an entire tree from a forest, but coppicing is an ancient practice that is benefiting from a new wave of interest from researchers and practitioners. Coppicing involves the cutting of tree species, mainly hardwoods, that will grow new shoots from the same root system after the main trunk has been cut. Rather than killing the tree and abandoning the roots to decay, a coppiced forest can continue to provide wood for a wide range of uses while maintaining the integrity of the forest ecosystem. Traditional coppicing practices produced everything from renewable fuel and charcoal to fence posts to timbers for ship building. Depending on the tree species, harvest cycles can range from 3 to more than 50 years, and the same coppiced trees can continue to produce for hundreds of years. As the building industry searches for ways to reliably store carbon without depleting forest carbon stocks, coppicing offers plenty of opportunities to rethink how we grow and gather timber.

Improvements in timber math are coming.

Getting Specific About Forest Data

Chapter 3 examines broad issues in LCA and carbon storage accounting. As this chapter shows, accurate modeling and assessment of carbon flows around timber and forests is daunting. Still, the real potential for meaningful carbon storage in timber products is spurring activity to address the shortcomings of existing methods.

These efforts require getting specific about forest data. Forests are valuable contributors to earth's climate control because they are such rich, complex ecosystems, but this can make forest carbon flows difficult to characterize broadly. Climate, terrain, proximity to water sources, and even insect and animal activity can change the carbon profile of a forest dramatically within very small distances. Adequate understanding of current and predicted carbon flows into and out of forest ecosystems needs to happen at both the micro and macro scale if we are going to understand the carbon impact—and other important ecosystem services—of removing trees from specific locations at specific times.

Dynamic accounting for forest carbon must include carbon stored in below-ground biomass, above-ground biomass, dead organic matter, and soil organic carbon. Improvements in mapping and sensing technology are helping researchers learn more about the carbon ecology of forests, and this, in turn, informs the creation of better carbon inventories and improved forestry practices. Remote sensing from satellites and robotic measurements on the ground are beginning to supply critical information to support on-the-ground researchers. There are many stakeholders needing this information and the methods for carbon accounting and forestry practices it can illuminate, among them national and state governments and forestry companies. The building industry has a unique perspective to bring to this table and a compelling reason to participate and ensure that the standards of this work are as high as possible.

Timber is such a tantalizing prize for carbon-storing architecture, offering the clearest and quickest path to wide-scale use of biogenic materials because wood is such a versatile, accepted material with strong historical pedigree supported by an established industry with the ability to offer a reliable supply chain, code compliance, design support, and, if we can make sure we keep growing forests and truly storing carbon, the ability to move large buildings toward net carbon storage.

Agricultural Residues and Byproducts

If we are attempting to imagine a transition to plant-based architecture, wouldn't we be lucky to find ourselves surrounded by billions and billions of tons of affordable, available, and suitable raw material just waiting to be turned into a vast array of building materials? And having just considered all the complexities of accounting for carbon storage in timber, wouldn't it be nice if all that raw biogenic material offered a straightforward pathway to meaningful carbon storage?

Welcome to the wonderful world of agricultural residues for building materials. We only need to open our eyes and our minds to the vast potential that is literally piled all around us as byproducts of growing the food we eat to see a remarkable opportunity for large-scale climate mitigation.

Human beings grow a lot of food, and nearly all food harvests include a high percentage of plant matter that we don't eat: agricultural residues. We expend as much time and as many resources into growing and harvesting the residues as we do the food, but we make very little use of this leftover plant matter. In some cases, there are established or developing uses for some percentage of this biomass, but more often it's a nuisance at least and sometimes a major ecological problem when residues are burned or stockpiled. We may look back in a few decades and wonder, "What took us so long to make hay with all this stuff?"

There is a bewildering array of agricultural residues, and nearly all of them already have historic, modern, or experimental uses as building materials. We could literally fill a book with example after example, but instead we offer an overview of the subject to outline both the exciting potential and the potential pitfalls.

At a time when we desperately need to draw CO_2 out of the atmosphere, we need to recognize the scale at which atmospheric carbon is drawn down into agricultural crops. Consider a single crop type: cereal grains such as wheat, oats, barley, rice, and rye. The food product from these plants is a bundle of seeds at the top of a long stem, but the stem itself, called straw, has no food value. Annually, the global straw harvest from these cereal grains is around 2.2 billion tonnes, and 45–50 percent of the mass of that straw is carbon that was taken from the atmosphere over the course of a single growing season.[2] This means grain straw is responsible for drawing down approximately 1 billion tonnes of carbon (3.67 billion tonnes of CO_2) each year, which is roughly the equivalent of all emissions from the global iron and steel industry or the country of India. If we start to count all the agricultural residues produced annually—100 million tonnes of rice hulls, 60 million tonnes of coconut shells, 1 billion tonnes of corn stover, half a billion tonnes of sugarcane bagasse, to add up but a few—we quickly see the equivalent of all the world's transportation emissions pulled out of the atmosphere every year, and perhaps even more.

This remarkable drawdown happens via human activity that is already taking place; we don't need to invent new machines, expend more energy, or use more land to achieve this scale of climate mitigation. Although agriculture is certainly a large contributor of GHGs, representing up to 20 percent of global emissions, these emissions are happening whether or not we take advantage of all the drawdown action inherent in the residues. Making use of agricultural residue as a climate intervention is a no-lose strategy, providing an excellent return on the GHGs currently associated with agriculture without driving up emissions any further. And as the agriculture sector undertakes its own efforts to reduce GHGs, the value of carbon storage from residues improves further.

Agricultural Residues for Biomass
The case for using agricultural residues as a potential feedstock for biomass energy to mitigate climate change has already been explored and developed. Biomass burning, *with* carbon capture and storage (CCS), according to the International Energy Agency, could be responsible for up to 10 gigatonnes of negative emissions by 2050 and is often posited as one of the few viable options for the scale of drawdown needed to meet the world's Paris Agreement targets. Such studies have been very helpful in identifying and quantifying the world's stocks of agricultural residues and their massive drawdown potential, and a well-developed carbon accounting method has been accepted within national and international climate mitigation efforts. A basic carbon accounting advantage of residue biomass is this: The emissions associated with planting and harvesting the biomass are shared or split with the primary food products; it's a two-for-the-price-of-one deal. The manner in which production-related emissions are attributed can vary (by mass, volume, or dollar value), but the result is the same: We're getting carbon storage value for the same amount of production emissions.

Despite the enthusiasm for and effort behind biomass energy with CSS, this approach raises some serious issues. Biomass energy with CCS schemes involve one of two approaches: burning all this agricultural residue to generate energy or heat and using carbon capture technology to prevent the carbon emissions from going directly back into the atmosphere, or using biomass to create biofuels such as ethanol and methane to be burned in place of fossil fuels. In both cases, the technology to accomplish this is in early development phases and far from being ready to deploy at scale. And both cases are also examples of using old-school thinking to address climate change: If we used to burn fossil fuels, let's just burn biomass instead.

The use of biomass, whether for building materials or energy, is not an inherently positive undertaking. It will take a principled and well-considered approach to ensure that we do not repeat the same cycles of exploitation and waste based on narrowly defined goals that have driven us into our current climate crisis. It is all too easy to forecast a new regime that values biomass in a way that drives destructive behavior, including deforestation, conversion from food-intensive to biomass-intensive crops, robbing soils of much-needed carbon and the transportation of cheap biomass from less developed parts of the world to industrialized and centralized factories, to name but a few of the potential pitfalls of pursuing a building industry founded on the use of agricultural residue. (See chapter 12.)

Well-funded efforts to perfect biomass energy with CCS will continue to develop and will probably have an important role to play in climate mitigation. We are not suggesting that this avenue should be closed down, but we think there is a highly compelling case for putting a lot of this biomass into long-lived building materials instead of torching it. This approach does not require the deployment of as-yet-undeveloped technology and is likely to be more economically impactful. We can maintain our hold on carbon that plants have already stored for free, and we can hold onto all that carbon while creating new manufacturing opportunities with more innovation and employment benefits than might be offered by setting all that biomass on fire and pulling the carbon out of the smoke.

There is no need to see these approaches as mutually exclusive. There will be some types of biomass in some regions that are better suited for energy purposes and others that are more productively turned into building materials. In the same way that the timber industry supports industries such as paper, packaging, and furniture as well as building materials, our collective and intentional use of agricultural residues will include many suitable purposes. We see building materials being centrally important in the drive to make better use of agricultural residue. And the case for accounting for all the carbon contained in biomass is well understood, regardless of the final destination for that carbon.

Better Biomass by Intent

At its best, the transition to biomass building focused on agricultural residues offers a chance to build a new supply and value chain based on the best principles we can bring to bear. The use of ag-residue for building materials is at its industrial infancy, young enough to be able to start from a place of higher ideals and yet technologically within reach of rapid deployment across the globe and the economy. In many ways, the transition to biomass building with ag-residues is an ideal test bed for our ability to manage the wider transitions needed to address the climate crisis in an equitable way. We hope the brief tour of possible feedstocks and materials that follows is inspiring at the practical, material-based level and as an example of what we may be capable of achieving more widely.

Types of Agricultural Residues

Ag-residues are as varied as the hundreds of food crops from which they derive, but some categorization can help us understand the many ways in which they can become building materials. The definitions given here all have blurry edges, and some plants offer more than one of these types of residue, but we can broadly characterize ag-residues as stalks and straw; shells, hulls, and pits; fibers; and pith.

STALKS AND STRAW

It is rare that the stalks of food crops are edible by humans (although some have high value as animal feed), making stalks an abundant and ubiquitous form of agricultural residue. For many crops, the edible seed or fruit grows at the end of its stalk, making it easy to separate food from stalk and therefore collect the stalks without significant loss of either food or useful biomass. In the case of cereal grains—by far the highest-volume crops globally—the stalks are called straw. Stalks and straw are often harvested from fields along with the seed or fruit and bound or baled for easy handling and removal from the field, making these ideal candidates for biomass building products. Stalks and straw have numerous established and potential uses:

- **Bales.** Compressed, tied bundles of straw have been used since the early 1900s as rigid insulation blocks. Today, there are thousands of custom site-built straw bale buildings and numerous manufacturers supplying prefabricated panels based on straw bales.
- **Compressed straw panels.** Sheet-style panels made from compressed straw (wheat straw, in particular, is coated in lignin that acts as a weak glue when heated) have been manufactured since the 1930s and are used as partition walls and insulated sheathing (figure 6.3). Compressed between two skins of rigid sheet material (such as OSB or other structural panels), compressed straw has also been used as structural insulated panels since the 1980s.
- **Loose insulation.** Chopped straw has historic and modern use as a loose-blown and dense-packed dry insulation.
- **Mineral-bound straw.** Long-strand or chopped straw is coated with mineral binders such as clay, gypsum, or lime to make sheets, blocks, or site-formed insulation. Many forms and combinations of straw and binder have historic and modern applications.
- **Glue-bound straw.** Long-strand or chopped straw is coated with glue (see chapter 7 and figure 7.3) to make structural panels (manufactured globally in many forms), blocks, bricks, and structural "timbers."

FIGURE 6.3. **Straw-based panels.** Numerous companies worldwide, including Ecococon (pictured here), are turning low-value straw into efficient, carbon-storing, and affordable wall and roof panels. This type of production can be created wherever straw stocks exist. (Photo courtesy of Ecococon, https:// ecococon.eu/)

SHELLS, HULLS, AND PITS

The seed or fruit of many crops is protected by a tough outer shell or hull, which come in a wide variety of forms, from thin sheathing such as rice hulls to thick shells such as coconut and palm kernel and everything in between. Similarly, pits or seeds can also be byproducts with valuable properties, including cherry, peach, date, and olive pits. These materials are gathered as an integral part of food harvesting and are therefore collected and centralized, making them straightforward to incorporate into building material supply chains.

Shells and hulls are essentially small buildings made to protect a seed, so they are naturally tough, resistant to weathering and decay and unattractive as food sources to animals and insects, all desirable properties for human building materials. Established and potential uses include the following:

- **Aggregate.** Tough shell and pit material can be used in conjunction with mineral aggregate (sand and gravel) or can replace it. These materials can be combined with mineral binders such as cement, lime, and clay to make concrete, mortar, and plaster materials, or they can be loose-fill aggregate in structural or semistructural roles.

- **Insulation.** Low-density hulls and seeds have uses as insulation, in both loose and bound forms. Rice hulls, abundant worldwide, are a particularly excellent example because of their light weight, high silica content (for natural fire and rot resistance), and a shape that traps lots of air but resists settling.
- **Compressed boards.** Numerous shell and hull materials have been turned into sheets, panels, and boards with natural binders in the shell material or a variety of glues (see chapter 7).
- **Biochar.** When biomass is pyrolyzed (burned in the absence of oxygen), the resulting biochar material (a form of charcoal) retains the majority of the carbon in the original biomass. Biochar can last for hundreds of years and has broad applications as a soil amendment. Many types of woody shells and pits are ideal candidates for creating biochar, containing ample fuel value in the dense biomass and creating biochar with desirable structural properties. In addition to its use in soils, some types of biochar have been used as carbon-storing aggregates and amendments in concrete, mortar, and plaster and as a stable, lightweight, and fire-resistant loose insulation. Biochar is an example of biomass being useful as both an energy source and a building material. Biochar also offers an excellent solution for dealing with biomass from buildings at the end of their useful lifespan. Any biomass material that cannot be reused or recycled can be converted into biochar to continue the carbon storage beyond a building's lifespan.
- **Ash.** When biomass with naturally high levels of silica is burned, the resulting ash may be used as a reactive supplementary cementitious material (SCM; see chapter 5) to replace or offset the quantity of portland cement needed to make concrete. Dozens of abundant shell and hull stocks—including rice, palm kernel, coconut, olive, and cotton—have been studied and their SCM properties determined to be suitable. Ash use for SCM is an example of biomass being useful as both an energy source and a building material.

Fibers

Numerous crops are grown specifically for the quality or abundance of fiber they produce, including cotton, jute, flax, and hemp. A small percentage of existing fiber crops already have established building-related uses (such as jute backing for carpet and linoleum flooring and an increasing use of hemp fiber insulation). Attempting to divert these sources of fiber for additional building materials may create competition for the resource, raising prices and possibly resulting in deforestation in favor of cropland. Of more interest are the fibers that are currently unused or underused.

Fibers can be anything from tiny strands pulverized from stalks to thick, fibrous stalks, and uses vary depending on the size and characteristics of each kind of fiber. Established and potential uses include the following:

- **Glue-bound fibers.** Fibers of varying lengths can be glued or compressed together to make a variety of board and sheet products (figure 6.4). These can range from natural wallpaper finishes to laminated structural materials such as flooring, cladding, and composite "timbers."
- **Insulation.** Fibers can be used to make loose-fill, batt, and board-style insulation products.
- **Reinforcement.** Fibers have a long history of being added to concrete, mortar, and plaster to provide these brittle materials with additional tensile strength and to prevent shrinkage cracks. Fiber reinforcement can include anything from microfibers in finishing plasters to long stalks of hemp or kenaf partially replacing steel rebar in structural concrete.

PITH

The core of many crop plant stalks is composed of pith or medulla, a lightweight, spongy substance that, when dried, produces chips of "natural foam" that can be used as highly effective insulation (because "insulation" is a matter of trapping and holding small pockets of air or other gases; air is the real insulator). Pith does not have the density to be useful as fuel or fiber content to be made into other value-added products, but pith can be a significant portion of the volume of a crop stalk. This combination makes pith an ideal source of building insulation material. Pith materials can be used as loose fill insulation or combined with mineral binders or glue to make board-style insulation.

There are many abundant crops that produce very high quantities of pithy stalks, including sunflowers, brassicas (such as collards, broccoli, and cabbage), hemp, and kenaf. The technology needed for converting thousands of tons of pith into insulation is no more complex than the age-old hammer mill and screen. Despite excellent properties for insulation, this category of agricultural residue is underused. Many lab-scale experiments have shown the potential for a range of pith-based insulation products, but only hempcrete, which binds hemp pith (called hurd or shiv) with lime, has seen much use in construction to date.

FIGURE 6.4. **Gluing fibers together.** Eschewing the toxic and wasteful petrochemical glues often used to bind fibers together, a new generation of materials are using natural, nontoxic glue. IXIM Bioproducts uses their glue to bond a wide variety of fibers, including hemp, corn, and sawdust into blocks, bricks, and sheets. (Photo courtesy of IXIM Bioproducts, https://www.iximbio.com/)

It would be difficult to overstate the potential for agricultural residue to become a widespread feedstock for building materials, given the vast array of raw materials and the many proven pathways to turn them into building products. We have barely begun to scratch the surface when it comes to inventively converting these residues into building materials. This whirlwind tour of the main categories and uses of annual food crop byproducts sketches out the broad possibilities; within each category there are existing products ripe for more widespread adoption and almost countless prototypes, startups and lab-bench developments. There is diversity not only of raw materials, approaches, and uses but also of scale. In areas with massive feedstocks supplied by industrial agriculture, it is possible to build large, automated factories mass-producing materials; in areas of small-scale artisanal growing there can be handmade, high-value products, and at every scale between there are opportunities for growers, manufacturers and builders to work together toward regionally appropriate manufacturing and building solutions.

Picking potential winners and losers from among all this activity is impossible, but regardless of which products end up becoming carbon-storing staples of the new carbon architecture, it is the climate and all of us who live and work in buildings who stand to benefit from a vast scaling up of agricultural residues in the material ecosystem.

Purpose-Grown Crops
Humans have long cultivated crops specifically for building construction purposes. Sometimes these crops have co-produced food or fiber, whereas others are grown only for their unique building properties. As with other facets of plant-based architecture, we are not treading on new territory as we explore the potentially positive role of purpose-grown building material crops in addressing the climate crisis. However, as we outlined in the case of timber, there are important considerations to ensure that any expansion of purpose-grown crops can have a meaningful and sustained impact on the global carbon balance and the connected human and ecological systems.

There are inherent dangers in promoting purpose-grown crops as raw materials for building products. The displacement of arable land from food production to material production is a constant threat, especially when food for less affluent people and societies is forced to compete with material production for wealthier countries. We want to avoid economic incentives that would cause land to stop feeding people and instead "feed" buildings. We also want to avoid expanding arable land at the expense of natural forests, removing all the potential good forests do for the planet and the climate in favor of growing building materials.

However, with that caveat made clear and always remaining central to the subject, there is a long and sustainable history of purpose-grown building materials that bring carbon-storing benefits to the building sector and a potential future for these materials to expand and be joined by others that are nascent or just beginning to enjoy a comeback.

The category of purpose-grown crops for building material use has its own unique factors for carbon accounting. In general, these crops follow the same kind of straightforward methods that would be applied to any product in LCA because the arc of a purpose-grown crop maps closely to any other kind of product: Measure the inputs and outputs and consider the dynamic benefits of the stored carbon. The key variables in the approach to accounting are the length of the crop cycle and the existence of any co-products from the crop. Both factors will be addressed as we tour through the main crop categories.

Bamboo
Bamboo for building construction has a long history, with many variations of bamboo housing and public buildings part of the vernacular throughout Asia. Strong bamboo poles serve as structural frames, and smaller poles with woven split bamboo

are used as enclosures and partitions, with regional variations in lashing, joinery, and fabrication. This versatility is central to the modern bamboo industry, which is well developed in several market sectors.

As a forest-based resource, bamboo is often compared with timber. Like timber, the fiber structure of bamboo has a high strength-to-weight ratio, and its significant structural properties are enhanced by an elasticity that allows it to bend repeatedly under loads without failure. However, bamboo is not a tree; it is a grass. This means bamboo regenerates via its rhizome (root) network, so that harvested bamboo stalks do not need to be replanted like trees but grow back from the same rhizome network. Bamboo also grows at a rate that far outpaces timber, with building-grade bamboo reaching maturity in 5–7 years compared with 30–80 years for timber. This has an important bearing on carbon accounting for bamboo versus timber, because the short growth cycle means the carbon stored in a bamboo stalk was removed from the atmosphere recently; the stalk is largely finished absorbing CO_2 when it is harvested, and a replacement stalk will regrow and continue absorbing atmospheric carbon at a rapid pace. This crucial difference in the carbon cycle of bamboo versus timber has been shown to offer significant advantages over timber for climate mitigation.[3]

Currently, the majority of construction-grade bamboo is grown in the Asia-Pacific region, with about 65 percent of total bamboo forest area compared with about 28 percent in the Americas and about 7% in Africa.[4] However, the climate and soil conditions for bamboo forestry exist beyond its current extent, and efforts are under way in the United States and sub-Saharan Africa to begin cultivation of construction-grade bamboo. These efforts are laudable but need to adhere to careful environmental analysis to ensure they do not cause more harm than good.

The hollow structure of a bamboo stalk gives "raw" poles unique structural properties, but bamboo is rarely used in its natural form in modern construction. Unlike timber, bamboo can't be sawn into consistent dimensional units required for standardized design and construction practices. All bamboo building products are laminates, requiring the stalk to be stripped into fibers that are then glued together to produce materials with stable, consistent dimensions. The fiber can range from continuous sawn strips to fine strands depending on the source bamboo species, product type, and structural requirements.

The need to create laminates with a high percentage of adhesive content means that bamboo products tend to have higher GHG emissions than comparable timber products, because of the additional processing emissions and the high emissions from current adhesive options. Higher product stage emissions can reduce the net carbon storing benefits of bamboo, a factor that must be considered in accounting for the dynamic carbon storage impacts of bamboo products.

As with timber, there is a lot of promise for achieving a lot of carbon storage by using bamboo in a "mass bamboo" approach, creating the structure of large buildings with a variety of laminated bamboo products. Mass bamboo can join more established uses for bamboo to expand on the carbon storage potential of bamboo forestry.

- **Mass bamboo.** Posts, beams and structural slabs of laminated bamboo are in early stages of development, with some products beginning to see use on full-scale projects.
- **Bamboo plywood.** Sheet versions of laminated bamboo are available for use as structural sheathing, and these products are beginning to be used as the skins of structural insulated panels for low-rise construction. A wide range of millwork and finishing products are well established in Asia and beginning to see wider use in North America and Europe.
- **Bamboo flooring.** The most common form of bamboo building product in North America, flooring products come in a wide range of plank styles and finishes and are available through mainstream building supply centers.

Hemp

Hemp is the "grandmother" of industrial agriculture crops, with hemp fiber at the heart of large-scale textile, rope, and paper manufacturing throughout history. Outlawed in the early twentieth century in many western countries because of its association with its cousin, marijuana, industrial hemp has been revived over the past 20 years in Europe and Canada and, as of 2018, in the United States. The lost century of hemp growing has resulted in a steep learning curve to reintroduce hemp cultivation with modern practices and the development of markets for hemp-based materials. Hemp enthusiasts have done much to promote the use of the plant for a variety of food, oil, medicine, fiber, and building purposes, and although it's true that hemp can be used for all of these purposes, there are typically specialized strains grown for each purpose, and one crop may not co-produce multiple products. But the potential for co-production of more than one end use is a strength of industrial hemp, especially from a carbon accounting viewpoint, where the input emissions can be divided over more than one end use.

Hemp is a high-yield crop, with annual biomass accumulations of more than 5,000 kilograms per hectare, and it has also been shown to store carbon in soils at a rate higher than other annual crops. Both of these properties make hemp an attractive crop from a carbon storage perspective.

Renewed hemp cultivation offers a lot of potential to restore agricultural production in regions with poorer soil quality, but it also poses the danger that other food-producing acreage or forest lands will be converted to hemp production. Maintaining a balanced approach to the growth of industrial hemp will be necessary to ensure we're not creating unintended consequences.

Building materials is not the leading driver of the hemp resurgence, but there are roles for this crop in the building sector:

- **Hemp sheet materials.** Chopped hemp stalks can be compressed with adhesives into structural and decorative sheet goods. With yields that exceed those of forests, hemp structural sheathing and millwork panels can provide a higher degree of carbon storage than similar timber products that currently dominate

FIGURE 6.5. **HempWood.** Among many ways hemp can be used for building materials, pressing and gluing hemp stalks into a wood replacement is very promising. Carbon-storing HempWood flooring and boards can be used throughout building interiors. (Photo courtesy of HempWood, https://hempwood.com/)

the market. Hemp stalks from seed or CBD production can be used for this purpose, making for a beneficial co-product arrangement.

- **Hemp lumber.** The hemp plant can be compressed with adhesives to produce a rigid, structural board material (figure 6.5). Currently, this type of product is being developed for uses in flooring and millwork, but early work to produce structural members is showing promising results and will probably result in new products entering the market.

- **Hemp fiber.** Although the primary use of hemp fiber is for textiles, many hemp crops produce abundant fiber of lesser quality, and this lower-grade fiber is ideal for insulation material. Batt-style insulation products are being manufactured on a small scale in several countries and are already competitive in price with established batt insulation materials.

- **Hempcrete.** Hemp grown for textile fiber generates a significant volume of hemp pith (known as hurd or shiv) as a byproduct, and this has resulted in the development of hempcrete (or hemp-lime, as it's called in Europe) products for building. This use of hemp fits more closely in the agricultural residue category. Hempcrete products developed over the past decade include a variety of insulation materials for in-situ installation, precast blocks, structural composites, and precast panels.

Cork

The bark of the cork oak has been harvested for centuries. Unique among forest products, the living tree is preserved through many cycles of harvest. Bark is harvested when a tree reaches about 25 years old and can continue on 9- to 10-year cycles until the tree is at least 150 years old. It is critically important for cork oak forests to retain their biodiversity to remain productive, and a healthy forest supports important Mediterranean ecosystems that would otherwise be prone to desertification. The need to maintain a healthy and diverse ecosystem as a prerequisite for a sustainable industry positions the cork industry as an outstanding example of how productivity and ecology can be complementary; as a model for production for a plant-based architecture, it is hard to imagine a better model.

Cork has typically been harvested to make bottle stoppers, but over the past 20 years the industry has diversified into building products as synthetic bottle stoppers have won market share from natural cork.

Cork is naturally water and fire resistant and can be produced as sheets and boards without glue because of natural adhesives in the cork bark that are released when the material is steamed. Cork building materials include the following:

- **Flooring.** Cork is formed into thin sheets that are either adhered directly to floor substrates or glued to a rigid backing (usually a wood fiber board) to make tiles or planks.
- **Insulation boards.** Rigid sheets of cork are produced in a variety of thicknesses and used as continuous insulation for walls, floors, and sometimes foundations.
- **Cladding.** Rigid cork boards are formulated to combine the properties of a rigid insulation board and finished cladding.

Oil Crops

Natural oils have long played an important role as paints and sealants for buildings. Largely replaced by petrochemicals in the twentieth century, many of these products have maintained niche markets for wood finishing and chemical-free paints. Growing interest in nontoxic materials for improved indoor environmental quality, as well as carbon storage, is rekindling interest in natural oil products (oils that polymerize when exposed to oxygen) for buildings. Natural oils can also be sources of polymers for new kinds of adhesives and binders (see chapter 7).

Where natural oils are a co-product along with food or fiber, expanded use of oil crops could be climate beneficial. However, large-scale expansion of oil crops to replace fossil fuels could lead to replacement of lands currently used for food production or deforestation.

Key oil crops include the following:

- **Linseed oil.** This oil has long been used as a base for paints and wood sealants, and several modern paint companies have developed linseed products that are affordable replacements for petrochemical paints. Linseed oil has a niche use as a binder in clay-based building materials, including flooring, plaster, and bricks.
- **Tung and walnut oil.** These nut oils continue to be used as wood sealants.
- **Vegetable oils.** This category includes castor, soy, peanut, and canola oils, all of which are sources of polyols used in manufacturing polyurethanes. These oils are typically highly processed and combined with petrochemical ingredients in current products. Research into expanded uses for these types of natural oils may lead to new uses for building adhesives, paints, and bioplastic products (see chapter 7).

Seaweed

Cultivation of seaweed has increased dramatically over the past decade, and developing practices and markets indicate that this trajectory is likely to continue.

Most cultivated seaweed is for food products (for humans and animals) but also as a source of food additives such as carrageenan and agar. As oceans soak up excess atmospheric CO_2, seaweed farming is increasingly being viewed as a viable climate mitigation strategy. A market for seaweed building materials can provide additional incentives to develop seaweed aquaculture, as building-grade seaweed products can come from material not suitable for food-grade requirements. Seaweed is also being explored as a source for binders and adhesives, which could also have uses in building products.

- **Insulation.** There are several variations of seaweed insulation products in small-scale production in different parts of the world, in both batt and board formats.
- **Thatch.** Coastal builders have long used scavenged seaweed as a durable, long-lasting thatching material for roofs and wall cladding. Small-scale production of panelized versions of seaweed thatch are currently available.
- **Algae-based materials.** Seaweed is a form of algae, and smaller algae have the potential to be grown and made into a wide range of products.

Reeds
Marshland reeds have long been used as a roofing material, often featuring useful lifespans longer than modern roofing products. Wetland reeds tend to have ideal characteristics for durable thatching because they naturally withstand damp conditions. As perennial plants, reeds can be sustainably and selectively harvested with minimal input while maintaining healthy wetland ecosystems. Reeds can be used in buildings for the following:

- **Thatch.** Traditional roof and wall thatching are a labor-intensive craft that survives today as a niche market for historical preservation and ecological building. However, efforts to manufacture thatch panels that can be easily mounted on walls and roofs are being explored and offer the potential to greatly reduce the time and cost of traditional thatch while maintaining the low input emissions and high degree of carbon storage.
- **Insulation.** Chopped reeds make an excellent thermal insulation and are a by-product of thatch harvesting and production, making use of trimmings and waste from the higher-value use of reeds.
- **Semistructural fibers.** Many forms of reeds are large, tough tubes that are ideal for compressing, gluing, or otherwise binding into sheet goods or lumber replacements.

Switchgrass

One of the main species of prairie grass native to North America, switchgrass has been experiencing a resurgence as a perennial crop that can be used to produce ethanol biomass fuel and contribute to climate mitigation. As with other biofuel crops, we suggest that a more beneficial use of switchgrass would be as a baled source of structural insulation or as a pulverized fiber. Perennial switchgrass has a deep root system capable of storing as much carbon in the soil as in its above-grade biomass, thereby doing double duty for climate mitigation. Switchgrass can be an important part of a regenerative agriculture system to rehabilitate depleted soils and provide fodder for rotational grazing of livestock, and producing biomass for building would be an additional added value.

To date, switchgrass bales have seen limited use in straw bale building, but they could be put to any of the multiple uses for straw detailed above.

Waste Stream Fiber

Our economy is overflowing with stocks of "waste" fibers. A lot of carbon-storing material used for short-term products ends up in landfills or incinerators but could serve a better purpose for climate mitigation by living a long second life as building products. This category includes several materials that are well established in the building industry and many more that could have greatly expanded market shares. Displacing materials with high emissions with carbon-storing waste fibers is a strategy that does more than offer climate mitigation; it can relieve pressure on landfills, provide additional revenue streams for municipal recycling programs, and create plentiful opportunities for regional waste-to-product manufacturing.

Carbon Accounting for Waste Stream Fibers

The use of recycled material in new products has well-established protocols in LCA practice for assessing emissions but also the same issues in assessing the value of stored carbon, as we've explored previously. There will be variations in the value of the stored carbon depending on whether the product is sourced from postindustrial or postconsumer waste and how emissions and storage have been assessed at the upstream stages. As long as we are preventing an otherwise inevitable, short-term release of carbon back to the atmosphere, products made from waste stream fibers should be considered an important and valid source of meaningful carbon storage.

Types of Waste Stream Fiber

WOOD

As discussed earlier, as much as 50 percent of the fiber in a harvested tree is not made into solid timber. The timber industry has already developed products that make use of some of the remaining material, including OSB and various densities of wood fiber board. Most of this waste fiber comes from sawing logs, but opportunities also exist to make these products from the "slash" that is commonly left on the forest floor during harvesting. A substantial amount of fiber could be reclaimed from wood that is not straight or large enough for use as dimensional lumber.

In addition to waste wood at the harvesting stage, a vast amount of wood fiber is sent to landfill or incineration in the form of construction waste. Although it would be difficult to recycle this wood as dimensional lumber, a concerted effort to reclaim this waste wood and turn it into products such as OSB and fiberboard, batt, and loose insulation would prevent a considerable source of emissions currently coming from the waste stream.

PAPER AND CARDBOARD

Cellulose insulation has been used in buildings for more than 80 years. Recycled newsprint is treated with borate fire retardants and used as a loose fill, dense-packed, batt, or wet spray applied insulation. As stocks of recycled newsprint shrink with the newspaper industry, growing stocks of fiber are being created by cardboard packaging from online shopping orders, and new cellulose insulation companies are tapping into this resource.

Recycled paper and cardboard fibers are also combined with resin to make cladding boards and panels, countertops, and other finishing materials. Several manufacturers are using or developing bio-based resins to improve the health and the carbon profile of their products.

TEXTILES

In the United States alone, more than 16 million tonnes of textile waste is generated each year, and nearly 11 million tonnes went directly to landfills. Global estimates of textile waste are around 100 million tonnes. This represents an excellent opportunity for recycling into higher-value building products.

Pressure is mounting on textile manufacturers and clothing labels to reduce their waste footprint, and much of their effort is expended on technologies to create viable recycled textile fibers for use in new clothing. Although this would bring valuable circularity to the industry, a market for building products from recycled textiles has fewer technological hurdles and could be more easily implemented. In the long term, building products could be made from fibers that are difficult or impossible to recycle into new textiles. Not all textiles are made from natural fibers, so the carbon accounting for recycled textile materials would require evaluation of the fiber content.

Currently, insulation products made from postindustrial textile waste are commercially available, but there are few products on the market made from post-consumer waste. However, numerous startups are demonstrating panels, bricks, insulation batts, and wall coverings made from recycled textiles that illustrate the vast potential for this to be another large-scale opportunity for carbon storing building materials.

DRINKING CARTONS

Approximately 4 pounds of milk cartons and aseptic liquid packages per person are sent to landfill in the United States per year. These products are made from 70 to 80 percent paper fibers, but they have polyethylene and sometimes aluminum foil layers to provide a liquid-proof barrier, and this makes them very difficult to recycle. Several companies have developed technology to shred this material and press it back together into sheet goods that can be used as sheathing and as a substitute for gypsum drywall panels (figure 6.6).

URBAN BIOMASS

Every year, thousands of acres of roadsides, airport fields, and parklands in urban areas are mowed to maintain sightlines and appearances, leaving millions of tons of biomass to decompose (or be burned) and sending carbon back to the atmosphere. Capturing any substantial portion of this biomass and converting it into building materials would result in carbon storage. Depending on the plant types (grasses, reeds, pithy stalks, woody saplings, and bushes), there are ways to incorporate this biomass into building materials. All of the pathways noted for agricultural residue above could be equally applicable to waste urban biomass.

As we consider plant-based architecture, stocks of waste fibers in the future may be found in the first-generation materials being suggested in this chapter. As these materials are removed from buildings at the end of their useful life, they will hopefully be part of a circular approach (see chapter 10) in which they are dismounted and reused in a new context so that the stored carbon is given longer residency out of the atmosphere. Eventually, even a product designed for circular use will no longer be recyclable in its intended form. At this point, we will be able to downcycle the

Figure 6.6. **Recycled drinking carton sheets.** Drinking cartons are an ever-growing waste stream that is difficult to recycle. However, the material can be shredded and pressed together into a nontoxic replacement for plywood, OSB, and drywall. (Photo courtesy of Endeavour Centre)

carbon-storing fibers into new waste fiber products such as those described below, as plant-based buildings become a source of waste fibers, which eventually become a source of biochar or other end uses that prolong the climate mitigation benefits.

Lab-Grown Fibers

We have so far been making the point that there is a lot of plant matter in the world that could be used to make building materials. Regardless of the source, the paradigm for acquiring this material is and has always been the same: Go out into the natural world and get stuff that has grown in the Earth. Whether grown in forests, on farms, or in ditches and whether grown naturally or intentionally, we've always obtained our plant fibers in this way.

This paradigm is being flipped in intriguing ways by a whole new category of building materials: lab-grown fibers. This may immediately call to mind vast indoor hydroponic forests, but not only is the method of growing different from that of typical plant crops, so are the organisms themselves. Researchers are working with the "little ones," organisms such as bacteria, mycelia, and algae, whose requirements for growth are minimal and whose reproduction rates are prodigious. This category of building materials didn't exist a decade ago, and yet today it is poised to disrupt the building industry in an unprecedented way.

It can be a long way from successful trials in the lab to full-scale production of building materials, but a number of very promising materials have graduated out of the lab and are beginning to make their way into production. Many others continue to be developed and start down the research and development path. The promise of this type of plant material is tremendous: We can grow carbon-storing materials to meet specific needs with minimal energy inputs, no waste, no land use change requirements, and often no pollution. We can grow these materials at a range of scales, in facilities that are located to minimize transportation needs and in ways that are both globally replicable and regionally specific.

Sound too good to be true? There is much work to be done to fulfill this promise, but the rewards will be transformative for the built environment and its impact on the climate.

Carbon Accounting for Lab-Grown Fibers

Lab-grown materials offer a very straightforward LCA analysis because inputs and outputs happen in a controlled setting and can be precisely measured with little of the vagary that can complicate carbon accounting for conventional biomass materials. To date, none of the companies producing lab-grown building materials have produced an Environmental Product Declaration, but the results are likely to show net carbon storage when they do. The central industrial process in the creation of these materials is the growth of the organisms, the biology makes the carbon storage easy to trace, and the inputs of light, water, and food for the organisms is much less energy- and GHG-intensive than those of conventional materials. In best-case scenarios the inputs for lab-grown materials can come from co-location of facilities with other industries that can provide waste heat, water, and nutrients and further reduce production impacts.

Types of Lab-Grown Fiber

MYCELIA

Mycelia are the "roots" of mushrooms. They are unique among plant-based materials because they do not use photosynthesis to grow. As carbon-storing building materials, they do not draw down atmospheric carbon but rather break down existing carbon-rich materials such as cellulosic plant fibers. In this way, mycelium materials may more properly belong in the "residue" and "waste" categories of plant-based materials, because the food that enables them to grow comes from growing media such as straw, hemp, wood, and other plant-based wastes. The carbon storage in mycelia therefore is not additional but is a transfer of some carbon from the growing medium to the mycelia.

Despite not offering an increase in the pool of stored carbon, the role of these materials can still be important as the mycelia transform the properties of the growing medium by binding loose fibers into solid form. Alterations in the type of mycelia and the growing medium and conditions can create anything from lightweight insulation to dense structural composites. A sweet spot may exist somewhere between these two extremes where a mycelium material can offer an ideal combination of structural integrity and thermal performance.

Mycelium materials are grown for a short period of time (often 2–7 days) during which growth is rapid. Once grown to the right extent and density, the material is dried or heated to kill the organism and prevent additional growth and the creation of fruit (mushrooms) that would generate more spores to fuel another round of growth.

Among the advantages of mycelium materials is a natural resistance to combustion that is unique among plant-based materials and a desirable property for building materials.

Small-scale production of mycelium insulation sheets exists today, exhibiting properties that mimic the high thermal performance of petrochemical foam materials without the need for toxic flame retardants and the avoidance of the pollution associated with the production and disposal of plastic materials.

Products such as structural blocks and tubes that can potentially replace masonry and timber materials are showing a great deal of promise, and some are in limited production and use (figure 6.7). We may never reach the just-add-water dream of mycelium buildings that grow in place, but it's not difficult to envision a wide range of myco-materials that revolutionize the industry.

Algae

The term *algae* includes such an incredibly diverse and large category of photosynthetic organisms that it's no wonder that the range of algae-based materials currently under development is so broad as to defy easy categorization. Algae can be harvested from natural blooms, stands, and shorelines or can be purpose-grown in a wide range of conditions. From specks of carbonate minerals to 150-foot-long strands of giant kelp, the ways in which algae can become building materials touches every aspect of the built environment. Algae materials belong in every chapter in this book; in addition to plant- and mineral-based materials, algae can provide raw ingredients

FIGURE 6.7. **Mycofoam.** Mycelium-based insulation from a "grow-your-own" kit from Ecovative is grown in situ on a panelized wall to replace foam and mineral wool insulation products. Naturally fire retardant and with excellent thermal properties, this type of insulation could have a wide variety of applications. (Photo courtesy of Endeavour Centre)

for glue and bioplastics and have also been used as a fuel source to power and heat buildings.

In the form of plant-based building materials, various types of algae have uses that are similar to other plant-based materials. There are small-scale producers of algae insulation batts and semirigid boards, and algae thatch has a long history of use as roofing and cladding in some maritime regions. Algae have been pressed into structural bricks and blocks with natural binders such as clay or algae-based glue. It is possible to envision a building in which the structure, floors, walls, and insulation are all algae materials.

Carbon fibers derived from algae are currently receiving a lot of research attention. Carbon fibers have been explored for many uses in building materials, including concrete reinforcement, composite structural frames, panels, and insulation materials. Typically, these carbon fibers are derived from fossil fuels. Algae can be used to produce photosynthetic carbon fibers that could bring carbon-storing benefits to the many uses for carbon fibers, in building materials and beyond.

Box 6.2   Landscape Architecture: Connecting to the Carbon Conversation
by Pamela Conrad

When *landscape* and *climate change* are used in the same sentence, the most common reaction is, "It's green, so what's the problem?"

To many landscape architects, the word *landscape* means everything outside the building: the streets, plazas, sidewalks, drainage channels, and yes, the parks and gardens too. Some parts are very green and others not so much, but each plays a unique role in the carbon story. Whether reducing carbon emissions in material selection or maximizing carbon sequestration by planting more trees and woody shrubs, landscape is a critical piece in the built environment puzzle of climate change.

We can do better in designing these elements, surfaces, and areas. And we *must* do better if we are to stave off further warming of our planet.

Both built and natural landscapes are complex, living ecosystems that are constantly changing and evolving over time. Their carbon impact is neither a static object, such as a building material, nor a constant increase of active carbon sequestration over time. Landscapes are both alive and inanimate. Fixed and dynamic. And, until recently, overlooked.

This gap became apparent and increasingly frustrating for me in 2015 when I wanted to review the carbon impact of some past landscape architecture projects of ours at CMG Landscape Architecture. I assumed I could go online and download a tool that would tell me what I needed to know, but surprisingly that didn't exist. I thought this strange because calculators existed for measuring the embodied carbon of building materials and operations, and some resources existed for understanding types of carbon sequestration. But nothing could provide a comprehensive carbon story of the places that we created. So, with the stubbornness of a farm girl from Missouri and with some masterful spreadsheet skills from my husband, I started putting the puzzle pieces together.

With even the first basic and crude landscape carbon calculator we created, the results were shocking, enlightening, and honestly even a bit embarrassing. As designers who hold sustainability as a priority, we thought we were doing all the right things, but carbon was never part of the conversation.

Though not the worst carbon emitter on the scene, surprisingly "business as usual" landscape design practices show the average site emitting more carbon than it can sequester over its lifespan. If we pay attention to the selection of materials and ongoing maintenance operations, emissions can easily be cut by half and the sequestration doubled. When we apply those basic strategies to site design around the world, the exterior built environment can go beyond carbon neutral and become climate positive (also called carbon smart by my fellow authors here), collectively sequestering more than a gigaton of CO_2 beyond project emissions globally in aggregate by 2050. This solution would thereby enter the ranks of the top eighty *Drawdown*[a] solutions, which when combined will reduce atmospheric greenhouse gas concentrations. Although these standards could and should become best practices, just imagine what we could accomplish if designers of the exterior environment along with our city, architect, civil engineer, and developer collaborators pushed beyond making "easy" improvements.

To put this climate solution into motion, in the fall of 2019 I launched the Pathfinder, a web-based app, and the Climate Positive Design (CPD) Challenge, which sets target time frames for offsetting carbon footprints and guides designers of the exterior built environment to improve the carbon performance of sites. Development of the app, the challenge, and the corresponding action strategies outlined here was jumpstarted by a research fellowship through the Landscape Architecture Foundation and collaboration with the environmental consulting firm Atelier Ten.

Most critically with this guidance now for the exterior built environment, the carbon conversation for the entire built environment is whole and can be advanced collectively, increasing overall impact. For improving the carbon impact of the exterior built environment, the three main components are outlined below: embodied and operational carbon emissions, and active carbon sequestration.

Embodied Carbon in Landscapes

For landscape project sites, the terminology for emissions is the same as for buildings. Embodied carbon includes emissions from the manufacturing, transportation, and installation of materials.

Based on the 560 site design projects that logged full details in the CPD Challenge within the first two years, 75 percent of all project emissions are coming from the embodied carbon of materials. Although there are general design strategies by which to decrease these emissions, innovation in materials will also improve impacts.

Design Strategies to Reduce Embodied Carbon

As a rule, *plant more, pave less*. This strategy may sound obvious and easy to some but insurmountable to others. We've paved paradise and put up more parking lots, road lanes, and concrete water conveyance channels than is probably good for us. Being responsible for everything beyond the building, we must question every bit of paving shown on plans.

Below the surface, thousands of miles of pipe crisscross under our feet, transporting stormwater runoff away from paved areas. As an alternative, the use of vegetated swales, biofiltration basins, and other green infrastructure is gaining momentum as city regulations are making them easier to implement. These low-carbon solutions come with the additional benefits of water treatment, water infiltration, habitat creation, and greater biodiversity.

Reusing materials from the site also provides significant carbon savings. The asphalt of abandoned parking lots can be crushed and reused as subbase material for new roads. Found objects such as boulders and wood from removed trees can be repurposed and crafted into site elements such as stairs and seating. On Yerba Buena Island in San Francisco, the Habitat Management Plan prescribed invasive eucalyptus tree removal so as to allow indigenous plants and animals to recolonize. Instead of mulching the fallen trees according to standard practice, we brought on a local artisan to mill and convert 30,000 board feet of eucalyptus wood into more than 100 benches and tables for the site (figures 6.8 and 6.9). In addition, during the mass grading operation we discovered more than 200 boulders ranging from 1 foot to 6 feet in diameter that are integrated into the site design, saving money and carbon and becoming unique features of the open space system.

continued

Box 6.2 *continued*

Photos courtesy of CMG Landscape Architecture.

Material Considerations to Reduce Embodied Carbon

As with architecture, the main material offenders are concrete, steel, imported stone, and highly processed materials such as plastics. Because of the sheer volume of concrete typically applied to sites, it is often the largest source of emissions for site design projects. Fortunately, concrete's huge footprint can decrease (see chapter 5), and its presence in landscape architecture need not be such a climate burden.

Alternatively, there are lower-carbon paving options such as stabilized crushed stone paving, aggregate paving, or wood decking or boardwalks. These can have far less embodied carbon than concrete paving with cement substitutions.[b] One area of opportunity for manufacturers is developing more stabilized crushed stone products that meet accessibility requirements, because the options are currently limited. If the concrete is a vertical application, it may be substituted with rammed earth walls because they can be built with a much lower carbon footprint.

Hidden sources of embodied carbon often lie below ground, such as steel rebar, piping, and structural foam. In the case of steel rebar, it is worth asking whether it can be substituted with welded wire mesh or fiber reinforcement. Maximizing the recycled content of all metal products on a project will help reduce some of the largest per-unit embodied carbon of all building materials; however, cost is a factor.

Other unnoticed sources of embodied carbon are in the structural "sandwich" required for certain assemblies, such as green roofs and rubber playground surfaces. Structural foam blocks are used in vast quantities for intensive roof systems. Without lower-carbon alternatives, the additional embodied carbon that goes into the green roof structural foam may never be offset by the sequestering green it supports. Some alternative products and systems do exist, but more are needed because green roofs are increasing in number and size. Alternatives to typical rubber playground surfacing include engineered wood fiber, which has substantially less embodied carbon per square foot than a typical rubber surface playground and allows natural water infiltration.

Although these strategies can be included in the upfront design documents, it is critical that the details be recorded in the specifications. Using the latest specifications with a focus on sustainability, especially for concrete and steel, will help ensure that the intended carbon goals are met while avoiding conflicts and changes in the field during construction.

Operational Carbon

Operational carbon emissions include activities with one-time or ongoing impacts. Because a landscape site contains living carbon, from the microorganisms in the soil to the vegetation above, any disruption to it can be considered a carbon emission. Although there are many fewer operational emissions on a landscape site compared with the energy needed to operate a building, additional operations over time occur through maintenance or functions such as lighting. These totaled roughly 25 percent of overall emissions reported by the two years of CPD Challenge projects.

Site Disturbance

When soil is disturbed, air reaches organic matter, which causes decay and releases carbon. Although only about 20 percent of the carbon that is sequestered by a tree is converted into long-term below-ground carbon storage, destroying greenfield sites releases large amounts of carbon from the soil and the above-ground vegetation.[c] Carbon stored in the soil increases its quality through improved structure, chemical composition, and biological productivity. Those properties increase oxygen and water content and therefore increase the plant biomass and carbon sequestration.[d] Minimizing soil disruption whenever possible will keep the carbon we currently have stored in the earth where it belongs.

Although the example of wood reuse from the Yerba Buena Island project above did remove trees to support regional biodiversity goals, a general approach of protecting as many trees as possible should be considered a best practice. When trees must be removed, the wood can be milled into building materials. If those options are not possible, consider partnering with a local biochar facility to convert the wood into a long-term carbon storage soil amendment or a cogeneration facility that uses heat from burning the wood to convert to energy.

Avoid mulching the trees and spreading or hauling off site because the wood will quickly decay, and about 80 percent of the total carbon sequestered in its life will release back into the atmosphere. One approach to prevent bare soil carbon release and increase soil quality is to plant cover crops such as legumes, grasses, brassicas, and buckwheat. Whenever possible, try to use the native site soil by adding amendments in place if necessary rather than importing from off-site, which produces significant emissions from hauling.

continued

Box 6.2 *continued*

Maintenance and Operations

In most cities our ears have become numb to the constant buzz of a lawn mowers or leaf blower in the background while passing through a plaza, on our way to work, or walking through a residential neighborhood. It is the much too common sound of a commonly overlooked problem. The gasoline it takes to operate those millions of mowers and blowers for our highly manicured favorite green places powers the same gas guzzlers we drive around. According to the U.S. Environmental Protection Agency, the emissions from landscape maintenance equipment annually in the United States in 2011 was 20.4 million tons,[e] equivalent to 4.4 million passenger cars driving in a year.[f] With a projected 12.3 percent increase by 2018 and California's Air Resources Board expecting those emissions to exceed those of cars in 2020,[g] this is an aspect not to be overlooked.

Beyond the obvious solution of specifying electric maintenance equipment, there are a few other alternatives to consider. One is to avoid overmaintaining. Every time a tree limb is cut, it is commonly chipped into the bin, and most of its carbon releases once it is spread. Landscapes often are maintained more for form than for function, but those unnecessary emissions can be avoided by installing native and regionally adapted plants. If we install those types of landscapes, the maintenance effort and costs will inherently be lower, as will the carbon footprint.

Native and regionally adapted plants also need less fertilizer, which commonly contains nitrous oxide, a greenhouse gas 298 times[h] more potent than carbon dioxide. Alternatives to typical fertilizers include organic mulches and compost, which can often be cultivated onsite and thereby reduce emissions associated with transport, storage, and packaging. Using native and regionally adapted plants reduces the carbon emissions associated with water distribution (because they typically need less), and they need fewer pesticides, which leads to healthier ecosystems and communities. Incorporating edible plants or community gardens may increase water consumption but is another option to consider for minimizing carbon intensity of available produce.

Active Carbon Sequestration

Although there is no doubt that landscape architects, planners, engineers, developers, land owners, and municipalities can reduce embodied and operational carbon emissions, active carbon sequestration is perhaps the greatest and most overlooked opportunity to positively affect the climate. As shown by the projects logged in the first two years of the CPD Challenge, sites have the potential to sequester at least three times as much as they emit through a handful of best practices.

Designed Landscapes

The U.S. Department of Energy reports that the 40 million acres of lawns[i] in America exceed the area of any irrigated crop.[j] It's a shocking amount, but it presents exciting potential. If we were to convert those lawns into groundcover plantings or no-mow meadow grasses, those same spaces could be active contributors to climate healing by taking 4.8 billion tonnes of CO_2 out of the atmosphere in the next 50 years rather than emitting 1.5 billion tonnes. That's the equivalent of taking 1 billion average cars off of the road.[k] The opportunity is significant, and although it is costly to make those changes, it is largely a cultural shift for us to overcome as a society. We need to ask ourselves, "Is that fluorescent-green, water-hungry, unused carpet necessary for decoration around housing, highways, and byways?" and switch the paradigm to "We are climate healers, the places we've designed and developed are places that build a better future."

As to trees, plant as many as possible! In traditional landscape design tree spacing is often determined from a cultural or aesthetic point of view rather than the spacing at which trees would grow in their natural environment. Through the work of Afforestt and Shubhendu Sharma, research shows the incredible carbon sequestration opportunities when we approach tree planting with a "tiny forest" strategy. "Tiny forest" does not mean cute little baby trees. Rather, it means creating the whole forest ecosystem through a multistrata approach in a very small footprint. It's called the Miyawaki technique, and in some cases it includes planting 300 trees in the area of eight parking spaces. This method can increase carbon sequestration by 30 percent.[l]

Not every site may be fit for a tiny forest, but these little ecosystems can be a larger part of the urban forest network. As part of urban forestry initiatives, not only can cities plant empty tree wells, but they can begin using overlooked and abandoned places near freeways, parking lots, industrial sites, or vacant hillsides. Trees should be integrated into our streetscapes and green infrastructure to improve air quality and water quality and increase biodiversity. Our societies can also experience additional health and spiritual benefits of urban forests through biophilia, the human natural affinity, love, and connection to nature.

The best way to maximize tree sequestration potential is to identify the species in your area that will get the biggest (because the carbon sequestered relates directly to biomass), will live the longest, and will need the least amount of supplemental resources (thus increasing its chances of survival). More often than not, this is a native species to the region, but as the climate changes, so will the answer to this question.

Protected or Restored Natural Ecosystems

Protecting natural ecosystems should be a top priority, and we should no longer be developing greenfield sites. Carbon-rich environments such as forests and grasslands have absorbed roughly 29 percent of global CO_2 emissions each year since the 1980s, and blue carbon ecosystems have removed 20–30 percent of the world's emissions.[m] Where we can protect, we must. Where we can restore, we should.

Forests are perhaps the first image that comes to mind when we think about a carbon sink. The world's forests contain 45 percent of the world's carbon[n] but are being removed at a rate of 41 million trees per day.[o] Tropical rainforests are especially vulnerable to demands for converting land to palm plantations, which provide the palm oil used in many of our daily products. But interestingly, according to the United Nations, because of the presence of water and high organic content, the world's peatlands, also referred to as bogs, fens, and mires, store twice as much as the world's forests.[p] It has been an overlooked type of ecosystem that exists in most countries, but 35 percent has been destroyed since the 1970s. Land management practices must change to prevent further impact and carbon release of these types of wetlands.

Grasslands are becoming increasingly important, especially in fire-prone areas. Although these ecosystems hold much less carbon than forests, because of their large underground networks of roots and a thick thatch layer, after a fire the majority of their sequestered carbon remains in the soil. Much of a forest's carbon destroyed in a fire is released back to the atmosphere.

Blue carbon ecosystems refers to carbon that is stored in ocean environments, primarily salt marshes

continued

Box 6.2 *continued*

with seagrasses and mangroves. Because the soil beneath these plant types is anaerobic, the carbon is stored for long periods of time and holds five times as much as the world's tropical rainforests.[q] Gaining attention because of increased storms and rising oceans, the flood protection capacity of mangroves can increase the resilience of coastal communities while sequestering a significant amount of carbon. Kelp farming is also on the rise for its ability to sequester carbon and its use as a sustainable food source.

Alameda County's Depave Park, designed by CMG Landscape Architecture, could be one of the first projects in the San Francisco Bay area that will serve as a model for a living, resilient shoreline that is designed to capture and store as much carbon as possible in its restored salt marsh and constructed wetlands (figures 6.10 and 6.11). As a tarmac for a former navy base, the project proposes to reuse all of the materials for a reconfigured nature park while creating habitat for dozens of bird species, fish, and harbor seals. When constructed the new project would sequester more carbon than emitted during its construction within 4 years. Through its increased sequestration capabilities, it will also mitigate the carbon footprint of its original tarmac construction in 25 years opposed to the 220 years it would currently take.

Photos courtesy of CMG Landscape Architecture.

Going beyond Neutral with Climate Positive Design

The path forward to climate positive design is not exactly a straight one, but we are on the right track. Conversations between designers and developers, cities, and municipalities on reducing emissions and increasing carbon sequestration is becoming more common. LEED and SITES rating systems are embracing new pilot credits for the exterior built environment to have better carbon performance. It will require more talking and collaboration, and time is of the essence. This is an opportunity to redefine our position as stewards of the environment to becoming climate positive actors contributing solutions to a global crisis. Our projects can be greener, healthier, and better for people and ecosystems *and* be beautiful.

When we start to think about the built environment as a whole, we can together develop holistic solutions to the climate crisis. The opportunity for sites to globally sequester a gigaton of carbon beyond emissions is worth pushing for and striving beyond. Now, with a way to measure and improve site impacts, we connect and accelerate the interdisciplinary global conversation on how to solve climate change through better design of the built environment.

Notes

a. Paul Hawken, *Drawdown: The Most Comprehensive Plan Ever Proposed to Reverse Global Warming* (New York: Penguin, 2017).

b. *ATHENA→ Impact Estimator for Buildings V5.2 Software and Database Overview* (Ontario, Canada: Athena Sustainable Materials Institute, 2017).

c. Eli Corning, Amir Sadeghpour, Quirine Ketterings, and Karl Czymmek, "The Carbon Cycle and Soil Organic Carbon," Cornell University, 2016. http://nmsp.cals.cornell.edu/publications/factsheets/factsheet91.pdf

d. Corning et al., "The Carbon Cycle and Soil Organic Carbon."

e. Jamie Banks, "National Emissions from Lawn and Garden Equipment," U.S. Environmental Protection Agency. https://www.epa.gov/sites/production/files/2015-09/documents/banks.pdf

f. U.S. Environmental Protection Agency, "Greenhouse Gas Equivalencies Calculator," https://www.epa.gov/energy/greenhouse-gas-equivalencies-calculator

g. KQED, https://www.kqed.org/news/11310630/more-pollution-than-cars-gas-powered-gardening-equipment-poses-the-next-air-quality-threat

h. C. Gu, J. Crane, G. Hornberger, and A. Carrico, "The Effects of Household Management Practices on the Global Warming Potential of Urban Lawns," *Journal of Environmental Management* 151 (2015): 233–42.

i. "Clean Cities Guide to Alternative Fuel Commercial Lawn Equipment," U.S. Department of Energy, 2011. https://afdc.energy.gov/files/pdfs/48369.pdf

j. C. Milesia, C. D. Elvidge, J. B. Dietz, B. T. Tuttle, R. R. Nemani, and S. W. Running, "A Strategy for Mapping and Modeling the Ecological Effects of US Lawns," 2012. https://www.epa.gov/sites/production/files/2015-09/documents/banks.pdf

k. U.S. Environmental Protection Agency, "Greenhouse Gas Equivalencies Calculator." https://www.epa.gov/energy/greenhouse-gas-equivalencies-calculator

l. Afforestt, https://www.afforestt.com/methodology#

m. Hawken, *Drawdown.*

n. Michael Carlowicz, "Seeing Forests for the Trees and the Carbon: Mapping the World's Forests in Three Dimensions." Earth Observatory, 2012. https://earthobservatory.nasa.gov/features/ForestCarbon

o. Hawken, *Drawdown.*

p. UN Environment Programme, "Peatlands Store Twice as Much Carbon as All the World's Forests," 2019. https://www.unenvironment.org/news-and-stories/story/peatlands-store-twice-much-carbon-all-worlds-forests

q. Project Drawdown, "Forest Protection." https://www.drawdown.org/solutions/forest-protection

Future Developments

We are entering a period of burgeoning research into biomaterials, and it is impossible to predict which of today's lab experiments will turn into tomorrow's building materials.

Promising work is being done to produce in vitro antler materials. The antlers of ruminant mammals are the fastest-growing mammalian tissues and are both stronger and lighter than wood; the ability to grow antlers into structural components would be revolutionary.

Growth of synthetic silk and spider web has long been a goal of material science, and researchers are getting ever closer to mimicking the incredible strength and flexibility of silk and web strands. Encouraging work is happening to create these threads from fully biological materials, and commercialized versions of these fibers could feature in a wide range of building materials.

Toward Biological Architecture

In a world desperate for immediate and impactful climate action, the move to biological architecture stands out as one of the easiest, quickest, and most positive pathways we could begin to follow. The feedstocks are abundant and well distributed, the technologies already exist to turn billions of tonnes of plant matter into building materials, the investments needed are comparatively low, and we could get going right now. Plant-based materials can both eliminate current emissions from the materials they replace and provide vast amounts of durable carbon storage.

In its simplest form, plant-based architecture could be based on direct material substitution, one carbon-storing material replacing one emitting material. If we currently use a mineral or petrochemical form of board insulation, we can just substitute a plant-based version of that same product. Or if we currently use thick slabs of concrete for floors, walls, or roofs, we can substitute thick slabs of wood or bamboo, and so on. It can make sense to swap out materials without introducing any other type of change because a one-to-one replacement of one material for another allows everybody in the sector to clearly understand the intent and function of the new, plant-based product and be able to specify, cost, and install the replacement with the least amount of disruption. If we add up the potential carbon-storing benefits of all available (and soon-to-be-available and could-be-available) plant-based materials that can be directly substituted into buildings worldwide, the results would be phenomenal. It is quite possible that we could achieve net carbon storage in the built environment by following this path alone.

But architecture is so much more than a bunch of materials stuck together. Architects, engineers, and builders are more than mechanical assemblers; we bring vision and intent and craft and coherence to our projects. Plant-based architecture is a wide-open invitation to think outside our current patterns, and that is why this book expands beyond these material-based chapters.

We are excited about the abundant opportunities to make our buildings more biophilic, letting the grain, strand, and fiber of plant-based materials bring both a new warmth and new levels of visual intrigue to our buildings. Perhaps we can let go of perfectly flat and smooth synthetic surfaces and begin to enjoy the calming way natural fiber surfaces reflect light and sound. Perhaps we can embrace the potential when pressing plant fibers together to emboss and embed patterns, whether muted and barely perceptible or bold and captivating. Perhaps we don't need to paint every surface with petrochemicals anymore but let the materials present themselves and work to enhance the inherent beauty of products without surface coatings.

We are excited about the opportunities that become available when we think about design for disassembly, not just because it can reduce waste and lengthen the lifespan of carbon storage but because exposed, accessible fasteners offer new ways to see buildings, an aesthetic of assembly that becomes part of each building. Instead of hiding joints and fasteners (and mechanical services), we can design them to be beautiful and functional.

We are excited about ways to let plant-based materials be themselves, whether that be round trees or bamboo stalks, woven strands of fibers thick and thin, or factory-grown materials to take on shapes and forms that speak to their unique genesis.

Building beyond zero is more than just packaging carbon into the same old buildings. As inspiring as the vast array of plant-based materials may be in their ability to transform our relationship with the climate, we also hope they transform our relationship with our notions of buildings themselves.

7. Witches' Brew: Plastics, Chemistry, and Carbon

The European talks of progress because by the aid of a few scientific discoveries he has established a society which has mistaken comfort for civilization.

—Benjamin Disraeli

We all enjoy better living through chemistry. We have fresh, clean food, warm, safe buildings, cheaper and better clothing, and we have Wi-Fi and devices to access it. We have the world at our fingertips. We have cheap cars and cheap gas and the open road stretching ahead. In a great many ways, even some of the poorest among us have it better than any of the wealthiest people on Earth up to a century ago. And it's largely thanks to the fossil fuels oil, gas, and coal. The industry that provides them also provides the jaw-dropping array of chemicals, especially petrochemical polymers, commonly called plastics, that underpin our lifestyles. That industry has given us, or rather sold us, a level of comfort and pleasure that was literally unimaginable to our ancestors—a level of comfort that Prime Minister Disraeli already found alarming more than a century ago as he witnessed the early days of the Industrial Revolution captivating nineteenth-century England.

But, as the saying goes, "there ain't no such thing as a free lunch," and the bar tab is being presented to us today. So far, that tab is being paid almost entirely by the poorest among us, the rest of nonhuman life, and soon enough by our descendants. Plastics bring a lot of short-term value but intractable longer-term problems to society as a whole and to buildings, and thus they deserve our attention.

The rest of this book is focused on climate disruption, but here we look at other disruptions caused by the petroleum industry: petrochemicals, primarily plastics and adhesives, and their proliferation in the built environment. Nearly a billion tons of global warming emissions result from their production, along with the noxious chemical emissions resulting from their manufacture and disposal, but a great deal more danger and destruction is caused by our love of plastics and glues. We have covered the Earth and filled her oceans and killed her creatures with our petrochemical detritus, and we're far from done. Here we address some ways to cease the harm and reverse the damage.

Plastics

The COVID-19 pandemic and accelerating green growth around the world have eviscerated many of the oil industry's dogmas: that renewables would suffer from high costs, that governments would slow-walk environmental commitments, that investors would continue to reward long-term bets on oil with generous market values.

But one nugget of wisdom has survived everything the market has thrown at it, and now oil companies like ExxonMobil and Shell are wagering billions on it: that the world's demand for plastics is still growing, with no end in sight. . . . Even as demand for gasoline or jet fuel is seen stagnating or falling, plastics demand will only continue growing, underpinned by growing consumption in populous and fast-growing nations like India and China. . . . Consultants at McKinsey declared petrochemicals the industry's one clear "bright spot."

—Scott Carpenter in *Forbes*[1]

Bright spot, indeed! In yet another hockey stick curve defining the past half century, the production of plastics has skyrocketed, with only a slight hiccup during the recession of 2008–2009 (figure 7.1).

Judith Enck, president of Beyond Plastics explains,

The effects of plastic pollution are more far-reaching than most people realize. In addition to the fifteen million metric tons of plastic entering our oceans each year, scientists have found plastic particles in the most remote places on earth, from the peak of Mt. Everest to thirty-six thousand feet underwater, in the Mariana Trench. . . . Microplastics can be found in everything from drinking water to soil to beer to table salt to a cup of tea. In fact, we're all ingesting roughly a credit card's worth of plastic each week. Stunningly, scientists recently found plastics in human placentas.[2]

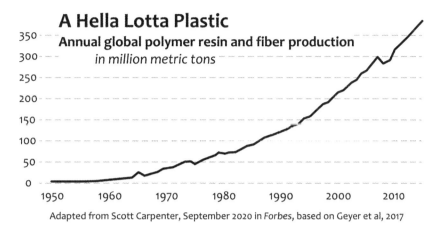

A Hella Lotta Plastic
Annual global polymer resin and fiber production
in million metric tons

Adapted from Scott Carpenter, September 2020 in *Forbes*, based on Geyer et al, 2017

FIGURE 7.1. Global plastic production since World War II. The industry's current plans will make this climb very much higher in the decades to come.

As Stan Laurel might have said, "It's a fine mess we've gotten ourselves into!" The question before us, as chemists, engineers, businesspeople, and society, is: Can we keep the thousandfold utility of plastics, or even just some of it, without wreaking such devastation on ourselves, our descendants, and on the other species? Plenty of people have been working on this, not least the New Plastics Economy (www. newplasticseconomy.org), who boil the problem down to three components.

- We must **eliminate** the plastic we don't need: the throwaway straws, cutlery and cups; unnecessary packaging and items that can be replaced with better alternatives.
- We must **innovate** so all the plastic we do need is designed to be safely reused, recycled, or composted.
- And we must **circulate** everything we use, making sure the plastic we produce stays in the economy and never becomes waste or pollution.

Let's look at these in turn.

Eliminate the Plastic We Don't Need
Simple to say, daunting to make happen. There are certainly plenty of people in every country who are voluntarily reducing their consumption of plastics, but these virtuous few haven't had much noticeable impact. Still, awareness is always the beginning of change, and there is growing public pressure on industry, all over the world, to reduce redundant plastic packaging and usage. But as figure 7.1 makes

brutally clear, that has not yet had much effect. The same pressures to minimize use of plastics and adhesives are brought to bear in the construction industry, but generally they influence only the rare project trying to achieve some green building certification such as LEED or the Living Building Challenge. "Need" may be the key word here, for once we've had a taste of some sort of great benefit, such as plastic cups, water bottles, and grocery bags, we tend to soon regard them as necessities. This is especially true of wealthy nations, as Beth Gardiner explains.

> *Convenience—like consumers' taste for eating and drinking on the go—is a big driver of plastic use in wealthy nations. And the developing world has become an important new market, too. In parts of Asia, international companies sell single portions of products such as shampoo, soap, and lotion to low-income consumers in individual packets. But while industry points to a lack of waste management infrastructure in poor countries as a cause of the ocean plastic problem, Americans use dozens of times more plastic per capita than Indians, five times more than Indonesians, and nearly three times as much as Chinese.*[3]

We will curb our societal usage only if made to do so—if we impel our bodies politic to pass legislation curbing at least the most egregious excesses of plastic usage (see chapter 11).

Innovate So All the Plastic We Do Need Is Designed to Be Safely Reused, Recycled, or Composted

The first synthetic plastic, Bakelite, was invented more than a century ago, following a series of cellulose-, milk-, or plant oil–based compounds that had already been around. It's hard to build a product, though, much less an industry, based on something in limited supply that others also want (such as for food). Soon enough, however, World War II kick-started a petrochemical industry and infrastructure. The postwar baby boom and newly contrived "consumer culture" then hastened the spectacular growth of a petrochemical plastics industry. As figure 7.1 shows, production is growing faster than ever—along with its many attendant problems. The question, then, is whether we can actually "innovate so all the plastic we do need is designed to be safely reused, recycled, or composted." Can we have the utility and service provided by plastics without their many ill effects?

This problem has two sides: demand and supply. Start with demand: Can we create a market for products that make use of the plastic already made and discarded? If we ever manage to retrieve the mangled messes in our landfills, rivers, and oceans, what will we do with it? There are plenty of well-funded ventures trying a great many ways to reuse recovered plastic, often in partnership with the businesses that use a lot of packaging. All are promising, but making small items such as skateboards and shoe soles can only use up so much volume; the predicament calls for an industry that uses material in massive quantities.

That would be us: construction, which uses an order of magnitude more physical material than any other on Earth. If anyone is going to make clever, safe, and scalable use of waste plastic, it will be construction, and we already have sheathing, blocks, insulation, roofing, and other recycled plastic products on the market. Not that they have been able to compete with great success in the brutal marketplace, but there is no lack of good ideas. There *is* a dearth of the steady, patient capital needed to penetrate the construction market, so more policy initiatives to foster greater recycling are much needed.

As to supply, it looks as if the future of plastic (even if yet a way off) is bio-based. *Bio-based* originally meant using some plant or animal matter that might also be food—always a problem in a hungry world (see chapter 6). New versions of the original idea appeared recently, perhaps most famously corn-based polylactic acid (PLA), touted for being biodegradable. PLA *is* biodegradable, but only under controlled conditions (not your backyard compost pile), and is made from corn, or anyway acreage, that might be put to better and less fertilized use. Soy oil is used in minor amounts in construction products, most notably sprayed foam insulation, whose manufacturers then somewhat disingenuously tout their "bio-based" product that is at most 10 percent soy.

Far more promising, though only just beginning, is a plastics industry based on algae and seaweed. Early generations of algae plastics can not only sequester carbon (see also box 5.7 in chapter 5) but derive their feedstock from the ocean, or even smokestacks, not land. The tantalizing possibility is emerging of a bioplastics industry that is a byproduct of pollution cleanup at power plants, rivers, and oceans.

Ryan Hunt, co-founder and chief technology officer at clean tech company Algix, said, "Algae [are] the fastest-growing organisms powered by sunlight. [We are] transforming air and water pollution (ammonia, phosphates and carbon dioxide) into plant biomass rich in proteins. When algae is used to clean the environment, the result is a biomass that we can convert into a bioplastic material."[4]

Concomitant with the advent of these algal materials is the notion of capturing CO_2 feedstock at the emission source to turn directly into plastic and the introduction of blockchain technology by which consumers can track and see the carbon footprint of whatever products they find.

> *Newlight CEO Mark Herrema said that "his company created the Carbon Date concept to appeal to consumers seeking to dig deeper into the environmental claims being made by consumer products brands." . . . Debbie Kestin-Schildkraut, market-ing and alliances lead for IBM AI applications and the tech firm's global blockchain ecosystem, says the importance of proving environmental claims is growing. "We are seeing in every study we do that more and more consumers are willing to change their shopping habits. . . . Blockchain can help build involvement."[5]*

There are many early-stage ventures developing algal and microbial materials. We wish them all well, knowing as they do of two basic challenges.

The first is that once you transform *any* substance into a polymer (plastic), you end up with something foreign (sort of by definition) to nature. If it can keep the moisture in the lettuce or shed the water from the windowsill, it is probably an unknown to the natural world as evolved to date. Unless we can design it other-wise—as, happily, people are working on—a bioplastic six-pack ring can choke a sea turtle just as much as one made of polypropylene.

But that's the easy challenge. The second one is the big one, at least for the next few decades: competing with Big Oil. According to Beth Gardiner,

> *"Because the American fracking boom is unearthing, along with natural gas, large amounts of the plastic feedstock ethane, the United States is a big growth area for plastic production. With natural gas prices low, many fracking operations are losing money, so producers have been eager to find a use for the ethane they get as a by-product of drilling. **Since 2010, companies have invested more than $200 billion in 333 plastic and other chemical projects in the U.S.** [our emphasis]. They're looking for a way to monetize it," Steven Feit [staff attorney at the Center for Inter-national Environmental Law] said. "You can think of plastic as a kind of subsidy for fracking." . . . "Recycled material is unlikely to contribute more than 10 to 12 percent of future plastic production," said Robin Waters, IHS Markit's director of plastics analysis and one of the authors of their report "Plastics Sustainability: Risks and Strategy Implications."[6] And the kinds of items covered by bans like Europe's only account for about 5 percent of plastic demand, he said. . . . The industry's critics fear the expansion of supply is likely to guarantee additional plastic usage regardless*

of whether consumers want it. Once new ethane cracking plants are built, producers will want to keep them running to maximize revenue, Feit said. "So then the next concern is that there will be an innovation in ways to get plastic on the market," he said. "This is what we've seen [in the past]—more and more things come packaged in more and more plastic. There is a whack-a-mole issue." Unless production slows, he added, "they'll just find something else to wrap in plastic."[7]

Circulate Everything We Use

Even before China stopped accepting plastic wastes from other countries in 2018, the recycling rate was only about 9 percent. Most plastic ends up in landfills, incineration plants, or simply on the landscape or in the water.

This dictum can be seen as a sort of mission statement for the second. We need to innovate in ways that not only provide the utility of current plastic compounds without the damage but also find ways to recover the solid and chemical wastes we've now dispersed and are still vigorously dispersing all over the Earth, including the oceans. The now famous Great Pacific Garbage Patch is a massive natural eddy in ocean currents that gathers anything floating to its core (figure 7.2).

Very few have seen this massive wad of trash. Most of the plastic is microscopic, and so it's invisible to the Hawai'i-bound tourists flying overhead or even to boats sailing across; it is literally out of sight and out of mind. Still, horrifically, it is killing creatures large, small, and very small who eat the bits of plastic that look like food, which then lodges in their guts and eventually chokes the life from them. As we said at the start, the price of bringing plastic into this world is being disproportionately borne by those who gain the least (the poor, living near the production facilities) or gain nothing at all (such as marine animals).

Dour news, for sure. Those 200 billion dollars' worth of new plastic production plants will draw fossil oil and gas from the ground, turn it into our bags and tubes, our shrink wrapping and styrofoam peanuts, and our toys and knick-knacks, for ever-so-brief usage, and then send it on its lethal way to the land and oceans. We can do better.

Adhesives

The petrochemical industry provides us with heat and light for our homes, gas for our cars, and the innumerable types of plastic that make our lives easier, safer, healthier, and nicer by just about any measure. Besides the fuel and plastic that underlie modern life, there is a third and relevant domain of petrochemical production: the

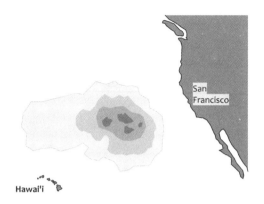

The Great Pacific Garbage Patch
80,000 tons of plastic in trillions of pieces over an area twice the size of Texas -- the weight of 500 jumbo jets mostly in microscopic-size pieces   Based on **The Ocean Cleanup**

FIGURE 7.2. The Great Pacific Garbage Patch.

innumerable solids, liquids, and gases we use directly or indirectly every day. These are the cleansers, solvents, paints, polishes, stains, backing, glues, and so much more that surround us in pretty much any kitchen, bathroom, or garage, not to mention schools and office buildings. They are cheap and so very handy, and they are almost always, to one degree or another, toxic. Each one has a label full of fine print about keeping from children and pets and about emergency medical procedures in the event of the wrong kind of exposure. Every firefighter knows that the smoke they often have to breathe during a building fire is full of unnatural toxins deriving from these burning compounds that, in aggregate, are likely to shorten their lives. In California, after the recent wildfires filled the skies with yellow smoke, it was discovered that the ash residue is toxic, sometimes requiring whole neighborhoods to be scraped clean (with the residue put where?) before anyone could rebuild.

We bring up this vast, complex, and unpleasant topic by necessity, as prelude to talking about a small subset, adhesives, that will play a crucial and pivotal role in a carbon-storing architecture. Petrochemicals and their (typically) plastic containers have their own carbon footprints, to be sure, but they are not our main concern here. Nor could we hope to address the stunningly complex and contentious world of toxicity in materials or buildings. Nor can we leave you hanging, however, and so before moving on to focus on adhesives we refer you to some of our friends in this business who have been working, thinking, writing, and advocating for many years for a healthier environment (box 7.1).

The Warner Babcock Institute for Green Chemistry has published its fundamental twelve principles of green chemistry, which are worth noting here (box 7.2). They are not all comprehensible to us nonchemists, but most of them will ring true as common-sense advice for a world that works for everyone and germane to any discussion of manufacturing carbon-storing products and materials.

We turn now to glues and adhesives because they stand poised to enable a thriving, carbon-storing architecture by binding the torrent of underused agricultural waste products (see chapter 6) into sheathing, insulation, lumber, and probably much more.

We've been making glue for a long time, having first figured out that by rendering animal hooves we could get a collagen-like substance that binds very well, and it is still in use for specialty items such as musical instruments. Those animal glues have their limitations and drawbacks, however, and so like many other things they have been replaced in construction products by petrochemical binders such as urea-formaldehyde and phenol-formaldehyde, polyurethane, epoxies, and diphenylmethane diisocyanate. The bulk of manufactured adhesives are used in construction, and of particular interest here is our fast-growing knowledge about how to bind cellulosic materials—mainly, to date, wood.

Our use of wood has evolved from logs to milled lumber to milled and glued lumber—first plywood, then oriented strand board and glued laminated (glulam) beams, and of late entire mass timber structures. In other words, we've become pretty good at taking smaller trees, reducing them to bits and pieces of fiber, then reassembling them with glue into the shapes we want. As we argue in chapter 6, mass timber structures are appealing in many ways, but we look with increasing skepticism on the unbridled claims of the timber industry about how terrific they are for the environment and how they are so much better for the climate than those

Box 7.2   Twelve Fundamental Principles of Green Chemistry

1. **Pollution Prevention**

   It is better to prevent waste than to treat and clean up waste after it is formed.

2. **Atom Economy**

   Synthetic methods should be designed to maximize the incorporation of all materials used in the process into the final product.

3. **Less Hazardous Synthesis**

   Whenever practicable, synthetic methodologies should be designed to use and generate substances that possess little or no toxicity to human health and the environment.

4. **Design Safer Chemicals**

   Chemical products should be designed to preserve efficacy of the function while reducing toxicity.

5. **Safer Solvents and Auxiliaries**

   The use of auxiliary substances (solvents, separations agents, etc.) should be made unnecessary whenever possible and, when used, innocuous.

6. **Design for Energy Efficiency**

   Energy requirements should be recognized for their environmental and economic impacts and should be minimized. Synthetic methods should be conducted to ambient temperature and pressure.

7. **Use of Renewable Feedstocks**

   A raw material or feedstock should be renewable rather than depleting whenever technically and economically practical.

8. **Reduce Derivatives**

   Unnecessary derivatization (blocking group, protection/deprotection, temporary modification of physical/chemical processes) should be avoided whenever possible.

9. **Catalysis**

   Catalytic reagents (as selective as possible) are superior to stoichiometric reagents.

10. **Design for Degradation**

    Chemical products should be designed so that at the end of their function they do not persist in the environment and instead breakdown into innocuous degradation products.

11. **Real-Time Analysis for Pollution Prevention**

    Analytical methodologies need to be further developed to allow for real-time in-process monitoring and control prior to the formation of hazardous substances.

12. **Inherently Safer Chemistry for Accident Prevention**

    Substance and the form of a substance used in a chemical process should be chosen so as to minimize the potential for chemical accidents, including releases, explosions and fires.

Source: Warner Babcock Institute for Green Chemistry, www.warnerbabcock.com/green-chemistry/the-12-principles/

All it needs is a bit of glue

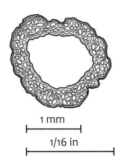

The tubular shape is the strongest there is, pound for pound -- and it traps air to insulate.

Glue a few thousand of these together and you have artificial wood that can hold up a roof and keep the family warm

1 mm

1/16 in

Straw in Cross-Section

FIGURE 7.3. The promise of straw.

icky, carbon-spewing concrete and steel buildings. Not at all necessarily so, and maybe only rarely so. (We look with equal skepticism at the countermarketing you will see from the concrete "Build with Strength" and steel representatives.)

While those three industry behemoths fight their turf battles in the public eye and in the various organizations that produce laws and building standards, we want to point out and promote the notion of introducing agricultural materials into the competition. The stage is set for making effective use of many other plant fibers (see chapter 6) besides wood, providing we develop an adhesive (or probably a family of adhesives) with all the functional properties we need but without the chemical hazards of the current petrochemical options. Let the trees grow (and absorb carbon), and use the plant material we're harvesting anyway, in combination with the right glues, to develop a truly carbon-sequestering material palette. Two billion tons per year just of grain straw, for example, are available with the added bonus that they have a tubular cross-section—meaning they contain air in small pockets, which is what every other kind of building insulation does because air is the actual insulator (figure 7.3).

And, as described in chapter 6, we see huge promise in bespoke crops such as hemp and bamboo that can provide stronger, faster-growing fibers to become structural sheathing and beams.

All this and more is possible with the right kinds of glue. Many bioadhesives, compliant with the principles of green chemistry, have been invented, but so far they exist only in private and university laboratories. Nature provides plenty of examples and clues for making nontoxic bioadhesives in species such as mussels and spiders. However, the introduction and scaling of these potentially game-changing materials is so far hampered in the same way as bioplastics: by an extremely risk-averse construction industry and by a petrochemical industry keen to keep and expand market share, especially as transportation turns increasingly to electric rather than gasoline propulsion.

Like concrete, steel, and timber, the petrochemical industry faces—and is vigorously avoiding—changes that may leave them with billions of dollars' worth of stranded assets. Economists talk about what they call "the tyranny of sunk costs," which are often followed by an escalation of commitment, a doubling down on a bad bet. We worry about the immense, destructive momentum these industries have, driven by the short-term demands of an unforgiving marketplace. We worry about their decisions to make ever more plastics of countless variety, decisions that are short-sighted and oblivious to the growing dismay of a populace and its legislative bodies and to the many pictures of tangled whales, choked birds, smothered rivers, and trash-covered beaches. We urge these industries to recognize the climate emergency for what it is and make bold changes accordingly.

Straw and other plant products (as described in chapter 6) are already here, using as placeholders the petro-adhesives that we already have and understand. Research with glue and cellulose is well on its way; now we just need to find or invent binders without the toxic and carbon footprints. How hard could that be?

8. Construction: On Site and Under Zero

So far we have put a lot of emphasis on greenhouse gas emissions (and potential storage) arising from the harvesting and production of building materials but not on the transportation of building materials to construction sites or the emissions that occur during on-site construction. These emissions tend to be the most visible to observers, with transport and concrete trucks loaded with materials crowding highways and city streets and earth-moving equipment and generators running nonstop on construction sites.

The plumes of diesel smoke associated with these phases of construction obscure an important fact: Only a small percentage of overall life cycle emissions arises from this part of the process. Even so, those plumes stink, are no fun for anybody, and deserve some attention.

The Impact of Transportation and Construction Emissions

Exploring studies of whole building life cycle assessments indicates that emissions from transportation and construction phases of building represent a small fraction of the building's whole carbon footprint:

- Transportation (Stage A4): 3–8 percent of life cycle emissions
- Construction (Stage A5): 1–5 percent of life cycle emissions[1]

Geographic location tends to be the dominant factor, as some cities and regions import a greater percentage of building materials from afar, and the carbon intensity of diesel fuel and regional electrical grids can vary widely.

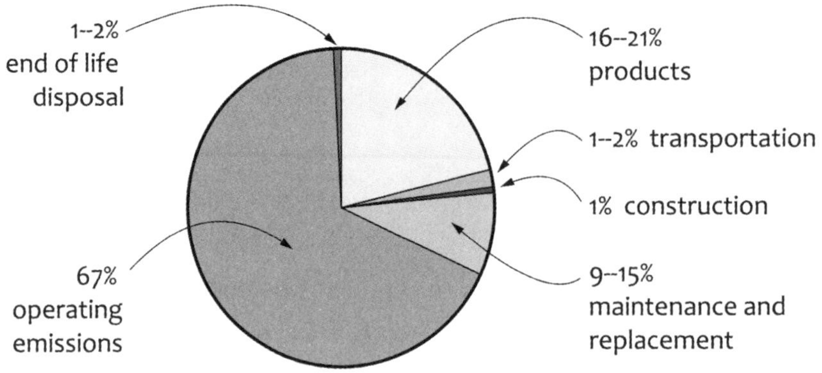

FIGURE 8.1. **A small slice with big impacts.** Construction site emissions are about 1 percent of the life cycle emissions of a typical building in the United Kingdom, and transportation of materials adds another 1–2 percent. But as with material/product emissions, these emissions happen up front and so carry significant climate impacts. And these emissions make for significant air and noise degradation in urban areas. (Adapted from the LETI Embodied Carbon Primer, https://www.leti.london/ecp)

The London Energy Transformation showed the proportional impacts of all the life cycle emissions for several common building types in the United Kingdom, in which transportation emissions ranged from 1 to 2 percent of up-front emissions and construction emissions were 1 percent (figure 8.1).[2]

Looking at these percentages it would be easy to simply dismiss these emissions as insignificant, but this is only because building operations and material emissions are so enormous. The total transportation and construction emissions themselves are definitely significant. Although few jurisdictions monitor and record construction site emissions specifically, the Greater London Authority reports that construction machinery alone accounts for 150,000 tonnes of CO_2e per year, and Oslo's Climate Agency estimates that between 120 and 240 million tonnes of emissions comes from construction sites in the C40 group of cities.[3] For municipal governments, these levels of emissions can represent a large proportion of emissions arising within their borders and are important for them to address.

Electrification

The pathway to getting transportation and construction emissions to zero (and to quiet and unstinky) is straightforward, if not easy to deliver quickly: replacing current diesel-based transportation and construction machinery and equipment with electrically powered options.

The beginnings of this sea change are starting to happen. European cities are beginning to include emission reductions or zero emission in tenders for city construction or in regulations that govern all construction activities. In 2019, Oslo initiated the world's first zero emission construction site, set by the terms of the tender for the project. The project was designed to set a high standard while minimizing risk and maximizing support for bidders. The project team included city staff, contractors, rental agencies, and equipment manufacturers, and cooperation between these parties enabled the project to meet its goals. The city created a list of ten tips for making construction emission-free[4]:

1. Set a clear goal that all the municipality's own construction sites should be emission free as quickly as possible, and no later than 2025.
2. Invite stakeholders as early as possible to a dialogue, to discuss possible barriers and solutions.
3. Create a market for emission-free construction machinery.
4. Ensure that the municipality's plans, guidelines and framework conditions build upon the overall goal of emission-free construction sites.
5. Clarify the project's approximate energy and power requirements early on so that the energy supply can be planned and put in place early in the construction process.
6. Set technology-neutral requirements that encourage competition and innovation.
7. Relieve risk where possible.
8. Favor the ones who take that little extra step.
9. Participate actively in forums where you can learn from other municipalities— and where they can learn from you.
10. Take the step—and follow up!

Other European cities, such as Amsterdam, Copenhagen, and Helsinki are heeding this advice and incorporating zero carbon construction targets into near- and mid-term climate plans.

On the equipment side, from electric pickup trucks and delivery vehicles to battery- and hydrogen-electric transporters to electrified site equipment, manufacturers are beginning to bring zero emission options to market. Nearly every major manufacturer of construction equipment has some electrified equipment on offer today, with many more models in development. Excavators, loaders, bulldozers, and cranes can be rented or purchased in all-electric versions. Generators are available with battery packs that greatly reduce running times for their diesel engines. Site lighting and hand-held equipment are also available in fully electrified forms.

As with the market for electric vehicles, there is currently a price penalty for all-electric equipment because of economies of scale. However, the operational and maintenance costs of this equipment are significantly lower than those of existing diesel versions. Sunkar, an equipment manufacturer, claims a 75 percent reduction in life cycle emissions for its 16-ton electric excavator over a comparable diesel model, using the current Swiss electrical grid intensity (figure 8.2).[5]

The company also predicts large operational savings over the lifespan of the equipment, based on a 50 percent longer life cycle as a result of fewer moving parts and greatly reduced fuel and maintenance costs.

Electrified construction equipment benefits from avoiding the "range anxiety" that plagues personal vehicles and road transportation. The use patterns of construction equipment are predictable, and the equipment stays in one area where dedicated charging infrastructure can ensure minimal problems with battery capacity.

The combination of technical progress, regulatory encouragement and pressure, and especially the anticipated financial returns could drive construction site electrification faster than we anticipate. Having leaders in the construction sector adopt and promote this strategy is crucial to the rapid success of construction electrification.

Stacked Benefits to Electrification
Climate change is only one compelling reason for the construction sector and governments to promote electrification of construction sites and transportation. Construction activity is heavily concentrated in dense, urban areas where fossil fuel use not only drives climate change but measurably increases air pollution and noise. Electrified job sites have the potential to dramatically reduce particulates, smog, and sound, although there are currently no independent studies to confirm the degree of reductions. The elimination of pollution and sound while equipment is idling—which is up to 50 percent of the average run time of construction equipment and generates a higher rate of some emissions—would alone make a large difference.

There is an additional and important benefit to electrification of construction sites: worker health. Hearing damage from working in and around loud equipment is well documented, with workers experiencing regular exposure to noise levels above 85 decibels from diesel equipment.[6] More dramatic is the health impacts of exposure to diesel fumes. More than 230 construction workers in the United

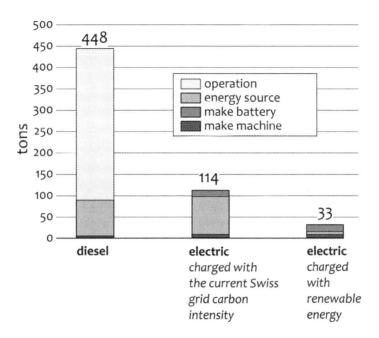

Comparison of Diesel vs. Electric 16t Excavators
lifetime emissions

FIGURE 8.2. **Disrupting emissions, quietly.** A comparison of the life cycle emissions for a 16-tonne diesel and electric excavator shows that if the batteries are charged on fully renewable energy, the electric model has just 7 percent of the emissions of a diesel version. Even on the Swiss electrical grid's current emission level, the emissions are still just 25 percent of what the diesel model would emit. (Adapted from Suncar, "Advantages of Electric Excavators," https://www.suncar-hk.com/en/electric-excavators /advantages)

Kingdom die each year from cancers caused by exposure to diesel fumes.[7] This impact is rarely studied, but it seems likely to be occurring worldwide where workers spend their days next to diesel equipment.

It is difficult to find studies that examine the emission impacts of construction workers traveling to and from work, but it is likely that this uncounted source of emissions could be quite high. Construction workers often top the lists of commuting time and distance surveys, with a U.S. national survey placing construction workers at the highest ranking of 33.4 minutes per direction of commuting time per day.[8] Add to this the high likelihood that construction workers and their employers use eight-cylinder pickup trucks and vans for personal transportation and to perform daily tasks, and a bit of rough math would probably indicate that worker transportation is another hidden emission factor within the construction industry.

Here, too, there is potential for electrification of vehicles to greatly reduce these emissions over the next decade. All major North American manufacturers of pickup trucks and vans are introducing all-electric versions of their popular models within the next few years, and upstarts are also entering the field intent on disruption.

Changes in How We Build

Construction is always going to require people and machinery on the job site, coordinating and performing the work that needs to be done in order to make a building where once there was none (or improve the one already there). Throughout the modern construction era, most building work has happened on site, where raw materials and products are assembled.

There are changes brewing in how we build that, at the least, will add options for how buildings are made and, if fully realized and adopted, may fundamentally alter the way buildings are put together.

Modular and Prefabricated Construction

The notion of creating large building components off site and assembling the parts in situ is hardly new. The Crystal Palace at the Great Exhibition of 1851 in London was a monumental example of an idea that accompanied the rise of the Industrial Revolution: Fabricate building components in a factory, under controlled conditions, and bring the parts to a site for speedy erection. The Crystal Palace was even an example of design for disassembly (see chapter 10), because it was moved to a new site after the exhibition. Through this lens, today's excitement about modular and prefab building seems quaint, because we've known how to do this for more than 150 years. What's all the fuss about?

A confluence of factors is fueling renewed enthusiasm for modular construction, including the increasing costs of site-based construction, financial benefits of shortening construction timelines, higher performance requirements, and skilled labor shortages.

Increasing costs of site-based construction. As the cost of living in large urban centers goes up, maintaining construction workforces in these hubs of development becomes more expensive, as do the logistics for material deliveries and waste removal.

Financial rewards of shortening construction timelines. Minimizing construction time on site, even if overall material and labor costs are the same, lowers the interest costs on construction loans and provides faster returns on development investments.

Higher performance requirements. The increase in requirements for energy efficiency is putting a premium on airtight enclosures and continuous insulation that is harder to achieve on site-built projects.

Skilled labor shortages in some markets. Higher performance standards require builders trained to achieve more airtight construction and other project requirements; existing labor forces are increasingly unable to meet those standards (see chapter 9).

It remains to be seen whether these factors will contribute to a rise in the adoption of modular construction. The Modular Building Institute's market report for 2019 shows that the market share of modular construction has risen from 2.43 percent in 2015 to 3.67 percent in 2018.[9] Although that means that there has been a 33 percent increase in modular projects in just 4 years, it is still a very small fraction of the overall construction market.

There are reasons to be excited about modular construction from a climate perspective. The development and application of newer, carbon-storing materials can be applied to modular construction designs without the need for widespread training of workers and development of retail supply chains. A modular construction company could work directly with manufacturers of carbon-storing materials to mesh product and component design and train a small number of installers in their facilities to use new materials. Once modular components are manufactured, site workers would not need to be familiar with new materials to successfully assemble the building.

We express our enthusiasm for design for disassembly in chapter 10 and the potential for building components to have extended lifespans as a result of easy dismantling and reuse. Well-designed modular buildings should be able to be taken apart and maintain their value as building components at the end of their useful life or when renovations are desired. Extending the lifespan of components will keep the carbon stored in climate positive materials out of the atmosphere for a longer period of time.

As dynamic life cycle accounting gets more accurate, construction site waste will become more identifiable as a source of emissions. Modular building facilities have an inherent advantage when it comes to minimizing waste and directing it to appropriate recycling or reuse purposes. This advantage may show up favorably in carbon accounting reports.

There is plenty of potential for modular construction to play a key role in building beyond zero, but there are systemic barriers that may slow or thwart this effort. Entrenched construction companies have a lot of incentive to continue hiring the site-based crews that have been their mainstay; disrupting the relationships and processes that drive site-based construction is a large risk for a reward that is measured not so much in total costs as in anticipated reduction in construction timelines. Modular construction companies have high startup costs, making investment in new facilities risky given the small market penetration that's been achieved to date. On the positive side, advances in computer-aided design and manufacturing allow a more seamless transition from plans to production and can improve the quality of the final products.

We can't predict whether modular construction will begin to fulfill its potential to transform the sector, and there are still plenty of stories about difficulties and outright failures of modular; we've been trying off and on for 150 years but are still just getting the hang of it. But we can see plenty of reasons for climate-conscious developers, designers, builders, and regulators to explore the idea, work out the systems, and coax out the many climate benefits.

3D Printing
Machine assembly of buildings dates to the 1960s with attempts to mechanize brick laying. This kind of construction automation was applied with limited success, particularly in Japan. The complexities of construction and limitations in automation software kept progress in check for several decades. Building-scale 3D printing became possible in the early 2000s but has yet to be put into widespread use.

Regardless of the technology used to make 3D printed buildings, from a climate perspective the limiting factor is the materials that have been used. Printed buildings require a medium that can be moved through the printer as a liquid or paste (or sometimes powder) form, which can then be set into a final product with the desired structural properties. Most printed buildings use either cement or plastic as the central ingredient in the paste, and these materials come with an inherently high carbon footprint. 3D-printed buildings using cement have typically used a very high percentage of cement to aggregate and therefore have a climate impact significantly higher than even the most carbon-intensive conventional buildings (see chapter 5). For printed buildings using plastic, only fully recycled plastics or bioplastics have any potential to have a lower carbon footprint than current buildings.

Inspiring work is being done in using natural clay materials as the medium for 3D-printed buildings. Clay can replace cement as a binder that meets the needs of 3D printers and has a fraction of the carbon footprint; combined with cellulose fibers for reinforcement, it may be possible to make a material with a neutral or even net carbon-storing footprint.

Current attempts at 3D-printed buildings are limited by the focus on building structure. Printed walls are either solid or made hollow with webs connecting the interior and exterior faces of the wall. These designs are inherently poorly insulated; until 3D printing can combine structure and insulation in accordance with the best building science principles for energy efficiency, they will need additional site work to properly insulate, seal, and finish. There are few climate zones where an uninsulated concrete, plastic, or clay building can be comfortably occupied without an excessive amount of operational energy.

There is a distinct possibility that someone—or many someones—will be able to combine the promise of inexpensive, fast 3D house printing with carbon-storing potential and a level of energy efficiency that will work in all kinds of climates. The field is new, and the climate effects of material selection have not been central to most efforts. The 3D printing revolution may yet disrupt construction.

A Lot of Partners at This Dance
Getting any building made is a complex dance that involves multiple partners, each with their own specialized knowledge and skills, all coming together to co-create. Even without the extra dimension of climate emergency, construction is a practice that is in constant flux, as building designs, efficiency, property costs, liability, technology, finance, trade skills, and regulations are ever evolving. Change cannot come from any single contributor in this process, and there is no way of centrally planning major shifts in construction practices. It may be that some or all of the ideas discussed in this chapter will make their way into the sector in various ways—maybe quickly and maybe very slowly. Pressure to adapt construction to at least the minimum requirements of local and national climate commitments will spur the changes that are most ready for widespread adoption and fuel interest in innovations that we haven't even considered.

The construction industry has never stopped evolving, mostly to increase scale and profitability and sometimes to minimize impacts on agreed environmental factors, such as energy efficiency. There is abundant talent in the sector—just look at the Burj Khalifa—and if they are put to use to help heal the climate, change could be rapid and profound.

9. Education: We All Need Schooling to Make This Possible

Any time proposals for broad social change are floated, there is an accompanying need for education to support and embed the change. But it can be a painfully slow process to move from a consensus that an idea is important to a broadly delivered curriculum that helps bring the idea into practice.

In the building sector, this movement can be even slower than the usual glacial pace of educational change. Architecture, engineering, and construction are complex undertakings, and there is a long career arc from schooling to internship or apprenticeship to junior staffer to experienced practitioner. This slow and steady building of knowledge suits these professions in which so much is at stake and errors are costly in both dollars and human safety. But this also means that when urgent change is needed—such as a rapid transition to carbon-smart architecture to reverse runaway climate change—the systems for educating about such change are not generally able to respond quickly.

Green building has slowly been integrated into curricula over the past few decades, often as an interesting option that is one among many niche areas a student may want to explore. It has taken more than 30 years for energy efficiency to approach a central role in building sector education, and even today many graduates complain that what they've learned about energy efficiency is inadequate or outdated.

We can't wait that long to teach people how to make carbon-storing buildings. If we follow the usual path, the climate will be long past repair by the time enough designers and builders have learned how to fix it. The urgency to educate is as important as the urgency to develop better materials, which has been central to this book. However, warehouses full of great, carbon-storing materials won't help solve the climate crisis if few professionals know how to design, specify, and install these materials.

We need to break the mold for designing and delivering curriculum if we're to build beyond zero. Typically, curricula are based on best practices, and these develop and change slowly. We've been capable of building net zero energy buildings for more than 20 years, but only a minority of design and construction professionals know how to do this, and most new graduates are woefully unprepared to do so. That's because we've collectively taken our time to watch developments in energy efficiency go through many cycles of iteration—trial, error, adjustment, improvement—allowing us to base new training on proven new approaches. But there is an inherent contradiction in "proven new approaches," because the approaches are no longer new by the time they're proven.

If we're going to collectively learn enough and fast enough to restore the climate, we can't leave education to schools and students. It will be incumbent on every person in the industry to learn how their work affects the climate and how to begin undoing that damage and transition to climate healing. Here are the homework assignments we'd like to give out to all our colleagues across the sector.

Architecture and Engineering Schools

Famous chemists John Warner and Paul Anastas launched the notion of green chemistry in 2000 with the publication of a book by that title. Each of them, in talks, will point out that a student could get graduate and postgraduate degrees in chemistry at any university in the world without ever being exposed to cautionary thinking about the possibly deleterious effects of chemicals on human health or the ecosystems around us. It was and is shocking, but it's not completely true today largely thanks to their work.

The same blind eye exists for young building designers: There is little or no discussion, much less training, to consider the effects of their future professional choices on the health of people and the planet. It's time for a version of the Hippocratic Oath for designers: "I will use the skills that will benefit the people and the place where I work according to my greatest ability and judgment, and I will do no harm or injustice to them." Design schools attract students with the offer of creativity, impact, and interdisciplinarity, and indeed these are central aspects of building design. Given the unparalleled impact of building design on the lives of people and the environment—acknowledging that buildings intimately affect every human being on the planet and are responsible for about 40 percent of global greenhouse gas emissions, not to mention massive impacts on ecosystems from the changes to landscapes and sheer amount of stuff that goes into buildings—it is well past time to ensure that the creativity and impact of building designers is put into service for people and planet.

Practically speaking, this means that all curricula in design schools need to embody and uphold this kind of oath. "Doing no harm or injustice" becomes a lens through which all the multidisciplinary facets of design are viewed, not out of ecological or political "correctness" but because we recognize that our profession is foundationally important to our societies and that our work is every bit as important to our collective well-being as that of doctors. We must go beyond commitments to "promote" sustainability, equity, and climate justice to a fundamental obligation to do so, and this notion can be built into curricula from the first 101 courses to the grading criteria for graduation.

In such curricula, climate literacy becomes as central a facet as form and structure, and understanding of the specifics of climate positive design—such as dynamic life cycle assessment and the use of carbon estimation tools—is as important as the specifics of building codes and design software.

Around the world, it is youth who are speaking out most strongly about climate change and who understand that, whatever their chosen profession or work in the world, climate mitigation will be a critical part of their futures. In fact, it will determine the very quality of those futures. Climate-centered curricula will be resisted by those embedded in the education system who don't want to share the primacy of their own chosen topics with climate design. The effort needed to update curricula and ensure that the most current understanding of the subject is significant, even if the idea itself is supported by the teachers and curriculum designers. Schools must support and demand these efforts, contributing financial resources and ensuring that the best practitioners and academics are part of the effort (box 9.1).

These efforts may seem onerous, but they might better be taken as opportunities to attract the best and brightest. Institutions that understand the motivations of a growing number of students will speak to their desire to enter professions that will allow them to thrive while doing meaningful work for the climate. As climate impact from buildings makes its way into policy and regulation (see chapter 11), graduates from schools that have taken a lead in climate-focused education will be in high demand in the industry. Honest and concerted efforts to combine climate and design as the twinned subjects they truly are can serve the interests of students, the planet, and the bottom line of design schools.

Box 9.1　Sweet 16 Student Competition Builds Carbon Footprint into Criteria

In late 2020, the founders of the BS (Building Science) & Beer Show, supported by Fine Homebuilding, GreenBuilding Advisor, and George Brown College, hosted the Sweet 16 Competition, an international wall assembly competition open to students in architecture, engineering, and construction programs. Participants are tasked with designing a wall assembly for their given climate zone with a focus on applied building science.

The competition organizers ensured that embodied carbon of the wall assemblies was among the six judging criteria, and the inclusion made the competition unique in placing the carbon footprint of assemblies at the same level of importance in the final judging analysis as thermal performance, cost, buildability, durability, and end-of-life characteristics.

It was encouraging to see that, even without the benefit of modeling software, three of the four finalists put forward designs that resulted in net carbon storage in their wall assemblies. The fact that experienced judges from across the residential building sector (including Chris) saw that these designs also met the highest standards in all of the criteria categories made a compelling case that residential construction is poised to move quickly toward net carbon storage without compromising on thermal performance, cost, buildability, durability, and end-of-life performance.

The embodied carbon analysis of each finalist showed that the carbon-storing entries could easily have used materials that would have greatly increased the overall carbon footprint and that the single entry with net emissions could easily have become a carbon-storing design.

The winning entry in the competition, from Dylan Ingui and Giancarlo Martinelli of Fiorello H. La-Guardia High School and Brooklyn Technical High School in Queen's, New York, proposed an exterior insulation wrap as a retrofit for an existing multifamily building in New York City (figure 9.1). Had the designers proposed a typical exterior insulation and finish system (EIFS) with foam insulation and synthetic stucco, their entry would have had a carbon footprint of about 65 $kgCO_2e$ per square meter of wall area. Because they selected a wood fiberboard insulation, their entry was essentially carbon neutral at −1 $kgCO_2e$ per square meter. On the large building for which their design is intended, this is a difference of many tons of emissions averted while meeting the competition goal of dramatically reducing operating emissions.

FIGURE 9.1. Sweet 16 student competition winners address embodied carbon.

Multi-Family Retrofit Proposal			Dylan Ingui and Giancarlo Martinelli
Component	**Emitted Carbon** - (kg. CO2e)	**Stored Carbon** = (kg. CO2e)	**Net Carbon** ("negative" = stored carbon)
Baseline Comparison Model			
Liquid applied air/vapor barrier	28	0	28
EIFS overcladding with XPS foam	459	0	459
Total carbon footprint for 80 ft²			28
Total carbon intensity per m²			459
Carbon Storing Model			
Liquid applied air/vapor barrier	28	0	28
Wood fiberboard insulation	163	361	-197
Aluminum clip system @ 48" OC	3	0	3
Z girt @ 48" OC, galvanized steel	14	0	14
Aluminum panel siding	145	0	145
Total carbon footprint for 80 ft²			-7
Total carbon intensity per m²			-0.9

Recognizing, incentivizing, and rewarding students to understand and implement building beyond zero, as the Sweet 16 organizers have done, is a way to accelerate learning and adoption of carbon-storing design and materials. Schools across the building sector can add to the success of the Sweet 16 approach by encouraging students to make carbon-smart decisions early in their careers and to build a set of criteria for success.

Construction Schools

North American trade schools have spent decades as repositories for troublesome male students who have struggled academically. In the postwar era of the 1940s to 1960s there may have been reasonable and expedient reasons to give these generations of young men a quick passage through their formal education and get them into work that was well paying. The assumption was that these workers only needed to follow instructions or repeat established processes, and this "worked" for quite some time—as long as disruptive change was not introduced.

Climate emergency is only one of many changes that have disrupted the notion that the building trades are a "simple" occupation; it is now much more difficult for new workers to enter their careers or to adapt to new changes that keep coming. Developments in building science, material technologies, and assembly techniques—as well as the digitization of design, procurement, and communication—have left the traditional curricula for the building trades sorely out of touch with current workforce needs.

In addition to these "hard skills," many trade schools have remained attached to recruitment and institutional cultures that are still focused largely on young, white men while the needs of the workforce and demographics have shifted significantly.

Trade school curricula need to respond to current challenges for reasons that include, but also go beyond, the climate crisis. The impending shortage of workers in the skilled trades has been noted for many years now, with attendant calls to actively promote entry into the skilled trades by women and BIPOC communities, yet the sector remains primarily white and male. As of 2015, less than 3 percent of workers in the construction and extraction trades were women; data on the percentage of lesbian, gay, bisexual, transgender, and queer (LGBTQ) workers in the trades is not available, which obscures but also underscores the issue.[1]

Trade schools need curricula that teach students more than a set of finite skills. Trade students need—and are beginning to demand—an education that enables them to grow and adapt to changes. Broadly speaking, this means training them to understand the "why" as well as the "how." A student trained to follow a prescribed set of steps to achieve a specific end will find it difficult to remain relevant as soon as those steps are no longer the norm. A student trained to understand the underlying reasons for today's standard practice can perform that practice to ensure best results but also adapt to new practices with knowledge of the underlying principles. Rather than rote learning, trade education can embrace conversation, inquisitiveness, and ongoing learning.

Trade schools are in an enviable position today: The jobs for which they provide training are in high demand and can provide their graduates with stable employment and good income. They have the additional attraction of offering meaningful work on behalf of the climate for the growing body of young people who desire an overlap between their own personal employment needs and the need to contribute meaningfully to climate change mitigation. Building retrofits and zero carbon construction, HVAC modernization, renewable energy, electrified transportation, and digital construction technologies are among the career options that combine hands-on work with knowledge and climate impact. Trade schools have the potential to greatly expand their pool of students by identifying these appealing and overlapping qualities of a new kind of trade education.

Unions and trade schools also have an important role to play in upgrading the skills of those already in the trades by providing accessible, affordable training that supports them where they are today. Both workers and employers will benefit from curricula that does not "force" workers to learn but rather gives them a purpose to learn that includes better wages as a result of training and a sense of contributing to an industry-wide effort to address climate justice.

Students and workers in the skilled trades can be shown that their work and their knowledge are essential to our collective success in addressing the climate crisis. They can be active participants in achieving our climate goals rather than passive recipients of change. As with design schools, the incorporation of a sense of responsibility must accompany an education that provides the tools to be an integral part of the climate solution.

Practicing Architects and Engineers

Design firms can help educate their next generation of employees by insisting that design schools provide them with the best in climate-centered education and collaborating with those schools to shape and deliver this essential curriculum. But waiting for a new influx of climate-responsive designers is not enough.

Licensed design professionals in most jurisdictions are required to take continuing education courses throughout their careers. This need for continuing education credits offers an ideal opportunity to bring climate-smart building practices forward on a short timeline. Regardless of the subject matter of continuing education courses, climate must find its way into the topic at hand so that it is not a standalone issue but embedded in all aspects of practice, from design to spec writing to costing.

Every member of a firm needs to learn about the principles of dynamic life cycle assessment and be familiar with the software tools being used to assess carbon performance. In-house training about design interventions that can dramatically reduce the carbon footprint of each building must become a regular feature of continuing education and incorporated into other training modules. As climate-related policies and regulations begin to take hold at both the government and corporate client level, firms that have grown their human capacity to respond and adapt to these new challenges will be best positioned to continue securing work.

Many professional associations are making climate commitments that can be adopted by firms–or outperformed by those who are more ambitious (box 9.2). Inclusive, firm-wide training is needed to ensure that climate impact is a central performance metric for all projects, not just the "green" buildings. Every team member in the firm can collaborate on setting ambitious emission reduction targets, and these targets need to be considered as important as budget and schedule. Incentives can be created to reward teams that outperform targets.

Most importantly, architects and engineers need to foster conversations among clients and consultants so that the climate change performance of projects is top of mind when projects begin to develop. Designers are often the "convenors" in building projects and as such can set the tone for the progress of goals and targets. If every member of a firm is well versed in climate-positive building practices and the subject is central to every aspect of project development, the subject may stop being relevant only to the self-identified "green" projects and become part of common practice.

Ambition regarding climate goals puts all the best and most important qualities of building design at the forefront: creativity, science, collaboration, innovation, and practicality. Design firms that have teams steeped in climate education will be the leaders in a field that, sooner or later, will have climate at its core.

All the Other Players

Policymakers and Regulators
Much of building policy and regulation has been reactive, responding to problems that have already occurred. The climate crisis requires an about-face, looking

Box 9.2   Professional Associations Get Committed

Professional associations across the design sector have begun to make commitments to take serious action on climate change. Although it remains to be seen whether these commitments turn into measurable actions on a meaningful timeline, it is encouraging to see climate action becoming a central facet of design practice. Publicly declaring an intention to take serious climate action seems like an important first step, and hundreds of individuals and firms have signed declarations and commitments.

In addition to strongly worded manifestos, many associations are providing important education, tools, and targets to their members as an integral part of these commitments. Some of these are highlighted here.

Architecture 2030. Established in 2003, Architecture 2030 was and remains a global leader in recognizing the link between architecture and the climate. The group's mission is "to rapidly transform the built environment from the major emitter of greenhouse gases to a central solution to the climate emergency." They hosted a global teach-in called CarbonPositive, with events hosted around the world focused on addressing climate issues in architecture. Their efforts have been met with encouraging uptake in the sector: 73 percent of the largest architecture and engineering firms, responsible for more than $100 billion in construction annually, have now adopted and are implementing the 2030 Challenge. According to a recent poll of design industry leaders by the Design Futures Council, approximately 40 percent of all U.S. architecture firms have adopted the challenge.

Architecture 2030 has been a leader in recognizing and addressing the importance of embodied carbon. They have issued a clear call to reduce embodied carbon emissions by 45 percent by 2025 and 65 percent by 2030 and to achieve zero embodied carbon emissions by 2040.

https://architecture2030.org/

American Institute of Architects (AIA). As an early signatory to the Architecture 2030 Challenge, the AIA placed climate action high on its priority list in 2009. To date, more than 700 firms have signed the 2030 Commitment and collectively tracked 3.3 billion square feet of design projects in 2019. The AIA has been focused largely on operational emissions, but awareness of embodied carbon is beginning to find its way in. Their Design Data Exchange enables designers to track embodied carbon. The organization offers a series of "Embodied Carbon 101" training courses to help members understand and take action on reducing embodied carbon.

https://www.aia.org/resources/202041-the-2030-commitment

Structural Engineering Institute (SEI). The mission of the SE 2050 Commitment is "to support the SE 2050 Challenge and transform the practice of structural engineering in a way that is holistic, firm-wide, project based, and data-driven. By prioritizing reduction of embodied carbon, through the use of less and/or less impactful structural materials, participating firms can more easily work toward net zero embodied carbon structural systems by 2050." Conceived and incubated at the Carbon Leadership Forum, the program's leading aim is education on the best practices of sustainable structural design and construction that will lead to net zero embodied carbon by 2050. More than thirty firms are currently signatories to the SE 2050 Commitment Program.

https://se2050.org/

World Green Building Council (WGBC). The Net Zero Carbon Buildings Commitment was issued by the WGBC in 2018 and "calls upon business, organisations, cities, states and regions to take urgent, ambitious and immediate climate action towards decarbonising the built environment." This commitment focuses on operational emissions, but their report *Bringing Embodied Carbon Upfront* calls for a 40 percent reduction in embodied carbon by 2030 and net zero embodied carbon by 2050. They have received more than eighty endorsements of their embodied carbon targets from large architecture and construction firms and cities worldwide.

https://worldgbc.org/news-media/bringing-embodied-carbon-upfront

Canada's Architects Declare. More than 200 Canadian firms are signatories to the Canada's Architects Declare initiative since it was launched in 2019, holistically committing to "raise awareness of the impact the built environment has on climate breakdown, ecological degradation, and societal inequity, with our clients and colleagues and to take immediate action through our projects, and in our capacities as advisors, advocates, educators, and enablers within our communities, cities, and supply chains." The declaration does not distinguish between operational and embodied carbon emissions but calls for "reductions in greenhouse gas emissions, and advocates for investments in a rapid transition to resilient climate-positive alternatives." Through not setting any measurable goals or targets for greenhouse gas reductions, the declaration is unique in its broad focus on political activism and its recognition of respect for Indigenous peoples, circular economy, regenerative design, and social equity as key aspects of climate action.

US Architects Declare has published a similar manifesto and has more than 350 signatories to date.
https://ca.architectsdeclare.com/
https://us.architectsdeclare.com/

Architects Climate Action Networks (Architects CAN!). In the United Kingdom, Architects CAN! is "a network of individuals within architecture and related built environment professions taking action to address the twin crises of climate and ecological breakdown." The group seeks to radically transform the regulatory, economic, and cultural landscape in which our built environment is made, operated, and renewed in order to facilitate rapid decarbonization of the built environment while challenging and redefining the value systems at the heart of our industry and education system. Their public campaigns to change regulations and keep political leaders accountable for measurable climate goals in the built environment have generated more than 700 signatories.

Education is a central activity of Architects CAN!, with regular courses and events aimed at raising the understanding of climate issues within the profession.
https://www.architectscan.org/

forward to new rules that help to ensure the future of the climate crisis is mitigated to the best degree possible. Chapter 11 covers the types of interventions we believe are needed at the policy and regulation levels. But we will not be able to formulate and enact them if the people who are responsible are not adequately prepared and trained. Climate literacy, climate science, and cooperation and collaboration with all levels of government and between different governments will advance the movement toward a regulatory environment that encourages and demands the kind of climate mitigation needed to meet existing targets.

Financiers and Insurers

The growing understanding of the impacts of building on the climate and the many climate-positive interventions that are both necessary and achievable within the building sector need to be matched by those in the finance and insurance sectors. At the very least, lenders and insurers must eliminate barriers that currently exist for climate-positive building projects, whether intentional or not. At best, these sectors can take a leading role in empowering climate-positive design and construction. As with other sectors, such initiatives will come from people who are well educated and able to understand the climate impacts of decisions that reverberate across the built environment.

Material Scientists

Here, too, an understanding of climate science and the direct climate impacts of material research and development are critical. It is no longer enough to explore materials based on physical performance requirements alone. Climate impact must take a place as a central guiding principle. We can't afford to develop new materials that meet all our existing criteria but are detrimental to the climate. Climate positivity must be the first criterion, after which all other criteria may be applied. Yes, material scientists too must be well versed in climate science.

Connecting Silos

The advice in this chapter can sound repetitive: Everybody needs to be educated about the climate, and everybody needs to be empowered to achieve climate-positive results from their work. It would certainly be a success if each profession that makes up the building sector were to pivot and make climate understanding and performance central to its educational efforts.

It would be exponentially more impactful if education included collaboration between these different professions. Cross-sector learning would speed up

Box 9.3   Architecture Students Take Matters into Their Own Hands

When architecture schools don't teach students how to design for a sustainable climate, some students are taking matters into their own hands. At Dalhousie University's School of Architecture in Halifax, Nova Scotia, student Laure Nolte felt that "sustainability seems like an optional choice instead of being integrated from the very beginning of the design process. I don't think we have an option to choose whether we want to be sustainable or not. We need to be demanding and advocating for architectural projects that weave regeneration and ecological design into projects from the beginning."

She and other classmates created the Supernatural Design Collective to "advocate for architecture and design communities to move beyond damage limitation (sustainability) and toward a regenerative perspective." Their mandate statement is a beacon of hope that the current generation of students is intent on holistically addressing both the immediate impacts of architecture on the climate and its underlying causes:

> Supernatural's mandate is to create a platform for architectural communities (including students, interns, researchers, faculty, and professionals) to actively shift education, research, and practice in response to Climate Change. We aim to move beyond what is taught as best practice and challenge the current state of architectural conventions by encouraging critical inquiry into all scales of the design process. This includes but is not limited to extraction and transportation of materials, biogeophysical origin of materials, built and supporting environment, carbon reduction and decarbonization strategies, occupant experience and health, passive design principles and building life cycle analysis.

Supernatural works to stay informed of research and data that has already been generated, and continue to build upon this body of knowledge. Additionally, we acknowledge that Climate Change and environmental degradation is both a symptom and a propeller of underlying social inequity, and we believe that environmental action offers opportunities to identify and disrupt systemic forms of oppression. Supernatural provides a flexible platform for socially-engaged programming, as well as cultivates relationships within an interdisciplinary framework that engages architectural design, research, experimentation, education and dissemination.

The Supernatural Collective, now over 100 strong, is not alone in attempting to take charge of their own education when they feel it is not up to the task of addressing climate change. The Students Climate Action Network (Students CAN!) asks the question, "The climate is changing, so why isn't the curriculum?" The group seeks to challenge their institutions to act on the climate crisis now and increase climate literacy at all levels of higher education in the built environment and has active groups in eleven design schools across the United Kingdom.

A survey of design students undertaken by the group showed that students feel let down by their education when it comes to climate change: 77 percent of respondents felt that their courses were not preparing them for their future work, and 69 percent felt their teachers were not responding appropriately to the scale of the climate emergency (figure 9.2).

continued

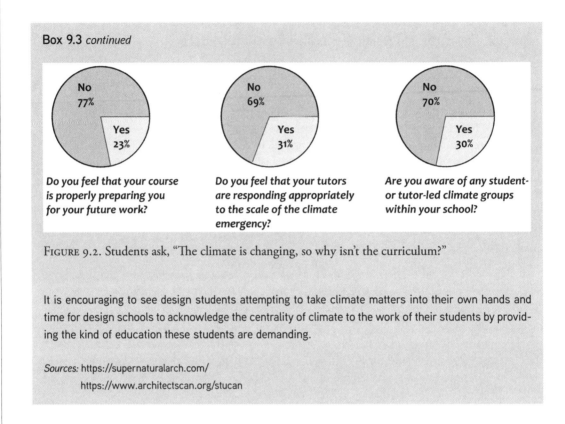

Box 9.3 *continued*

Do you feel that your course is properly preparing you for your future work?
No 77%
Yes 23%

Do you feel that your tutors are responding appropriately to the scale of the climate emergency?
No 69%
Yes 31%

Are you aware of any student- or tutor-led climate groups within your school?
No 70%
Yes 30%

FIGURE 9.2. Students ask, "The climate is changing, so why isn't the curriculum?"

It is encouraging to see design students attempting to take climate matters into their own hands and time for design schools to acknowledge the centrality of climate to the work of their students by providing the kind of education these students are demanding.

Sources: https://supernaturalarch.com/
https://www.architectscan.org/stucan

improvements in any one part of the larger industry. If students and practitioners were learning a bit about what goes on in other parts of the industry—architects learning about the trades, the trades learning about material science, and so on—and learning how to communicate across the industry, we could see change and improvement greatly amplified.

Making buildings is a complex dance that all too often amounts to a series of consecutive solos choreographed by siloed professionals. Building beyond zero requires group choreography based on training and education that maintains and improves the skills of each participant while adding the collaborative effort that improves the whole.

10. Circular Economy: Extending the Lifespan of Captured Carbon

We could defensibly say that the main product of the building sector is garbage—garbage that temporarily fills a useful role as buildings. We may not want to think of ourselves as generators of trash, but it is difficult to deny that our buildings are anything but a blip on the planetary time scale and that all the raw materials we conjure into place will spend less time assembled as we designed and installed them than they will as solid waste or emissions. The more we learn about the energy and emissions that are expended to make our buildings, the greater the urgency to transform our sector from makers of garbage to designers and installers of reusable components, intentionally placing well-designed assemblies of materials into buildings that are no longer the last stop before the landfill but rather long-term residencies for valuable resources that will go on to serve multiple functions beyond their time in a single building. In other words, it's time for us to get circular.

Architecture is no different from any other sector of our current economy in its linearity: We take, make, use, dispose, just like everyone else. Nearly every element of a building is destined for landfill or incineration not all that long after it is created, and although we ask many questions about the cost, performance, durability and now greenhouse gas emissions of those elements while they are on this linear path, there is an underlying assumption that the path leads directly from cradle to grave.

Circular systems "employ reuse, sharing, repair, refurbishment, remanufacturing and recycling to create a closed-loop system, minimizing the use of resource inputs and the creation of waste, pollution and carbon emissions."[1] The building sector has an opportunity to lead the way to a circular economy. Our designs, building techniques, and materials are all ripe for innovation in circularity that will help greatly to mitigate climate change while reducing building costs and construction and demolition waste.

Currently, each of us tends to play a very singular role in our assembly-line economy—harvesters of raw materials, manufacturers of products, designers, builders, demolitionists—and it has been easy to ignore the destructiveness and waste inherent in this model of behavior because nobody is fully responsible for what happens across the rest of the chain. Forming circular systems requires us to see our place in the linear economy and begin to bend that straight line and connect it to others in the system. Closed-loop systems require the full participation of everyone connected by the loop, and we will need to actively form and develop these connections in order to achieve circularity.

Circularity = Design for Disassembly

Building is all about assembling; we've done a remarkable job of figuring out how to put materials together. The safety, speed, and accuracy with which we're able to assemble buildings is impressive. Now we have to figure out how to design every part of a building so that it can be taken apart just as safely, quickly, and precisely. In doing so, we can extend the value of materials so that emissions generated can be "amortized" over a much longer time frame and carbon stored can be kept out of the atmosphere beyond the lifespan of a single building.

Currently, we design and build in a way that leaves us no option but to ruin materials in order to remove them, whether undertaking minor repairs and renovations, refitting interiors, or dealing with the end of a building's life. Our key building materials—reinforced concrete, structural steel, and masonry (blocks and bricks)—are almost exclusively single-use products (see chapter 8). Some effort is made to recycle steel from demolished buildings and to crush old concrete to use as aggregate and fill, but for the most part our buildings are impossible to dismantle in a way that preserves any of the value of the original materials. This isn't inevitable: Buildings are designed this way. They can be designed differently to achieve very different outcomes.

From the very start of a building design, we should be thinking about how each material in the building is going to be able to be removed and be reusable. We need to design as if the renovator's tools are not the wrecking bar and sledgehammer but the wrench and the screwgun. It must be the designer's responsibility to enable the demolitionist to forgo the wrecking ball and high hoe for the ratchet and the crane.

We know how to reuse almost every common building material save one: plastics. We say more about plastics, or more exactly petrochemical polymers, in chapter 7, but it bears mentioning here in a discussion of circularity.

To achieve circularity, we need to reimagine every part of a building, from structural frames to final finishes. We will need wall and ceiling sheets or panels that can be removed and reinstalled, interior partitions that can be unfastened and relocated, enclosure panels that are easy to bolt on and take off, glazing units that can be repaired or replaced without destroying trim and flashings, and structural frames that can be taken apart piece by piece. This is not a major leap: Most of our materials and systems are easily adaptable to this approach. But we will need to embrace a new aesthetic, one in which seamless surfaces and hidden fasteners are replaced by visible joints with exposed—and attractive—fasteners, one in which buried services become surface mounted or run in channels that are easy to access. This kind of building will tell a visible story about how it was made and how it can be unmade. All of its parts will be able to be removed and put to use in another place—in the same building or another one—without destroying integrity or value.

The automobile sector has always provided users with functional and visually appealing products that are designed to enable mechanics to remove, access, repair, and replace every single component. If cars were made like buildings, we'd have to smash out the door panel and throw it away in order to repair the latch and saw out the engine to fix the transmission.

Buildings may be a lot more bespoke and difficult to standardize than cars, but that doesn't mean we can't apply the same logic of necessity when it comes to removal, repair, and replacement: What type of fastener is being used, and where is it located? If we can find the fasteners, as we can on a car, then we can take that building apart.

Design for disassembly creates many potential layers of additional value through a building's life cycle. At the initial construction stage, buildings should be able to go up faster because we spend an inordinate amount of time and money trying to hide services, joints, and fasteners. Repairs to the building would be simpler and cheaper with removable finishes and accessible services. Replacement of damaged or defective components could be kept to affected areas and performed with minimal disruption. Refurbishments would involve removing—and selling!—any partitions, finishes, lighting, and other components that are no longer needed and easily installing new components. Need to expand your building? Unbolt the appropriate enclosure panels, fasten in new structural members, and reattach the enclosure panels. Finally, if the building really is no longer needed or wanted, all the parts can be dismantled and either reassembled in a new location or sold and redistributed to be used in other buildings. Even if climate mitigation weren't a compelling reason to get serious about design for disassembly, the economics alone should make it worth pursuing.

The tech sector can be an important partner in a comprehensive approach to design for disassembly (we can even call it DfD to make it tech-friendly). Software programs used to design buildings could be used to create databases of building components currently in use (locally, regionally, and even internationally). Over the lifespan of a building any parts being removed can be listed as available and the design information for those components uploaded directly into a new design. The dimensions, fastening method, and surface finishes would be documented and make such materials easier to reuse in another building. Documentation of all the components and fasteners used in a building would also become "repair and refurbishment manuals" to simplify all future work.

Building designers are a creative bunch; let loose on a concept like design-for-disassembly there would seem to be no limits to the creativity they could bring to its implementation. There are no technical hurdles that prevent us from designing for disassembly immediately. Although materials can be configured to better support this approach, the entire material palette available to designers and builders can be put together with existing hardware options. There is a growing move toward panelization and prefabrication of building components, which can lend momentum to design for disassembly because these components are already designed to go together quickly and could easily incorporate straightforward removal (see chapter 8). We should be able to quickly get to the point where "no material is left behind" and buildings become assemblies of parts that can be removed, replaced, and rebuilt quickly and waste-free (box 10.1).

Circularity at All Levels

Design for disassembly is one important way to close the loop and bring circularity to architecture, but a movement toward a comprehensive circular economy doesn't end with a design strategy. A circular economy isn't just one big loop; small circular systems can be nested within larger ones. There are roles for everybody in the system. While designers work on creating a circularity for components, these principles can be brought into the harvesting of raw materials and product manufacturing. The work to create circularity can start within individual enterprises and scale outward, picking up additional nodes as the circles widen.

Box 10.1   The Three Lives of Zero House

In 2017, the small building school where Chris works partnered with a group of faculty and students from Ryerson University to examine the potential for panelized construction of bio-based materials. Working from a design developed by Ryerson, the team at Endeavour put their minds to solving two issues at once: how to effectively use carbon-storing building materials in a way that exemplifies the principles of design for disassembly.

Endeavour has focused a lot of time and energy on refining the use of bio-based building materials, and often this has resulted in the panelization of wall systems. They built the first panelized straw bale walls for both public assembly buildings and residential use, but they had never assembled the panels with a plan for being able to take them apart and reuse them.

With Zero House, they had the perfect opportunity to try this out. They knew that they wanted to make the building at their home base in Peterborough, Ontario and had a great offer to show the building at the EDIT DX expo in Toronto. They also had a client who wanted to buy the building from them, which meant it would ultimately live in the small town of Thornbury. Thus began the three lives of Zero House.

The buildings at Endeavour always conform to a few basic principles: net zero energy, zero toxic materials, zero construction waste, and zero carbon footprint (which typically means net carbon storage). How hard could it be to combine these goals with design for disassembly? Oh, and to do it with zero R&D budget, at going market rates and on a tight timeline?

They were determined that every element of Zero House would be dismountable, from the structural panels to the final finishes. The design began with simple "boxes" that used dimensional lumber, structural sheathing, and bio-based insulation in various forms. The floor and roof boxes were made from wood trusses enclosed in zero-formaldehyde plywood filled with cellulose insulation and finished with locally harvested ash flooring. The walls were double stud frames with wood fiberboard insulated sheathing on the exterior (with a couple panels replacing this with mycofoam or cork sheathing) and ReWall (compressed, recycled drinking boxes) sheathing on the interior. Some walls were insulated with straw bales and some with cellulose. The walls and ceilings were finished with Forest Stewardship Council–certified plywood on the interior and metal panels on the exterior.

The design for disassembly extended to the energy systems. Adhesive solar panels applied directly to the snap-together standing seam metal roofing meant we avoided conventional racks and panels. A mini-split heat pump meant and through-wall ventilation, so they could quickly dismount the mechanical systems and avoid ductwork that would need to be taken apart and reassembled.

The house took 3 months to fabricate in a "flying factory" and another month to assemble and finish for the first time. It was dismantled and loaded onto two flatbed trucks over a week and reconstructed in downtown Toronto in 5 days, where it was visited by more than 5,000 show attendees. The second dismantling took just 3 days.

The home now lives on its permanent site, where it far exceeded the code minimum for air tightness (at 1.0 ACH50). It is unclear how long it will stand at its current location, but the team is very certain that it has the ability to be taken down and reassembled again.

continued

Box 10.1 *continued*

Design for disassembly in practice. The floor, wall, and roof panels of Zero House are reconstructed for the second time (top). The final—for now—assembly of the house sits in a small Ontario town, but it's ready to be taken apart and reassembled again if need be. (Photos courtesy of Endeavour Centre)

Raw Materials

Buildings start as raw materials, and a circular approach begins with acquisition of these raw materials. Currently, most building materials are based on extractive resources that cannot be replaced on a human time scale. Our utter reliance on extractive practices and their central role in our economy make it very difficult to imagine retreating from this approach toward circularity. But retreat from it we must if we are going to mitigate climate change and prevent the increasing destruction of ecosystems and species that increasingly threatens our own survival. The movement away from extraction and toward circularity for raw materials will have these characteristics:

- **Minimize extractive sources for raw materials.** We need to be able to identify which raw materials for our buildings come from extractive sources and, of these, which rely on the most destructive practices or extract materials on the brink of depletion. We need to advocate for corporate responsibility and transparency in supply chains, so we are able to understand and assess these impacts and make choices accordingly. Although we are not going to completely wean ourselves from extractive resources, we can do our best to ensure that the impacts are minimized.

- **Seek best uses of extractive resources and full use of co-products.** When we do extract raw materials, we must endeavor to minimize waste by prioritizing co-products and complete use of extracted materials. A key principle of circular systems is to view nothing as waste, rather as a potential raw material or input for another process. Many of our extractive industries currently pursue a single element or substance and throw away everything else. Cooperation between industries can help us identify where valuable co-products may exist and where co-location of processing facilities may be beneficial.

- **Rehabilitate extraction sites.** The world is full of extractive sites that are no longer being used. There are estimated to be more than 1 million abandoned mine sites globally, occupying tens of millions of hectares of land.[2] These sites can be rehabilitated in a way that can create billions of tons of potential carbon storage in biomass (through reforestation or biomass crops), in the soil, and in some cases by CO_2 capture through carbonation reactions with mining tailings and in mine shafts. In many cases, our most damaged sites can provide surprising opportunities for the most climate beneficial rehabilitations.

- **Use recycled replacements for extractive materials.** Substitution of recycled materials in place of virgin extractive materials is an important path to circularity.

Currently, we are awash with the waste that has been generated by our linear economy. Much of that waste could be used to reduce the demand for virgin materials. In pursuing recycled materials, it is important to ensure that we are achieving our goals of reduced emissions and impacts. Much postconsumer recycling requires the rounding up of small amounts of dispersed materials (often mixed with other materials or in composites) and can generate lots of emissions from collection, sorting, warehousing, cleaning, and remanufacturing. We must be clear about the impacts of recycling and ensure that they don't outweigh those of harvesting raw materials and do all we can to clear the path to beneficial recycling.

- **Maximize renewable sources.** Much of this book is dedicated to identifying renewable resources for building materials and to considering the impacts of adopting renewable materials. A short summary of the key considerations includes ensuring that renewable resources generate multiple co-benefits (food, medicine, soil health, biodiversity, just employment) and do not involve destructive processes (deforestation, herbicide and pesticide use, irresponsible water use).

Raw material acquisition is a critical component of the circular economy. The building sector uses an awful lot of raw materials, and our circularity successes will be closely tied to a successful transition of raw material suppliers from an extractive to a regenerative model.

Manufacturing

Very few raw materials make it directly into a building; they are transformed, combined, and manufactured into products. Product manufacturers play a critical role in the sector as the link between designers, builders, owners, and regulators, and they can bring advancements that respond to the needs of all stakeholders. Manufacturers also face significant economic pressures that are unique to the sector. New products require extensive R&D and testing and expensive manufacturing infrastructure in order to be brought into a highly regulated marketplace in which there are significant pricing pressures and a default bias for "proven" solutions; this is not an easy market for introducing change and innovation. Building owners, designers, occupants, and regulators must all encourage efforts by manufacturers to create products that support climate-positive, circular building. Those efforts need to include the following:

- **Promote transparency throughout the supply chain.** Circularity at the level of product manufacturing starts with transparency throughout the supply chain. Currently, there are numerous means to try to provide transparency. Environmental Product Declarations (see chapter 3) shed light on the inputs and outputs (including greenhouse gas emissions) of the product but often do not include detailed information about upstream raw materials and processes and do not include any social or human health impacts. Health Product Declarations (HPDs) and programs such as Declare (from the International Living Future Institute) focus entirely on human health impacts of material ingredients. Programs such as Cradle-to-Cradle attempt to provide transparency on several criteria but lack widespread adoption by industry and can be difficult for users to understand. Serious transparency requires an industry-wide standard for assessment and reporting rather than today's scattershot mix of reporting mechanisms.

- **Store carbon in materials wherever possible.** If a carbon-storing option exists for a product, we need to start making that product now. And if a product is responsible for excessive emissions, we need to stop making that product very soon. Manufacturers with product lines that all produce rather than store emissions will need to begin to diversify into carbon-storing materials, just as auto makers are having to pivot into electric vehicle production.

- **Avoid composites that cannot be separated.** Every time we combine materials—whether it be structural steel in concrete or wood fibers and glue in oriented strand board or the multiple layers in carpet—we are creating a material that will be difficult to deal with at the end of its lifespan. Every composite material we make must require a feasible end-of-life strategy besides landfill. If we're going to mix things together, it has to be with a full understanding and plan for getting them apart or reusing them. As we explore new biogenic products, we should consciously avoid single-use composites even if their carbon numbers look attractive.

- **Take full responsibility for waste, recycling, and reuse.** Product manufacturers are currently able to externalize the social and environmental costs of waste created by their products. Companies and industry associations must be mandated to own the costs of disposal or the collection and recycling and reuse of their products. To date, the small number of recycling programs have been limited in scope and availability and have made very little impact on construction waste. Designers, builders, and owners should also be involved in this circular responsibility.

- **Plan products for disassembly.** As this chapter attempts to establish, products and buildings need to have circularity built in at the design level. The work of designers and builders to make buildings circular will be easier if the products themselves have both assembly and disassembly instructions, and the ease of both can become a key sales feature.

Extending Carbon Storage Value

The question that hangs over this book is, How long can we store carbon in buildings? We think a strong case exists for short-term storage of 30–60 years—often the assumed lifespan of buildings and materials—which can play an important role in climate mitigation. But if we take design for disassembly seriously, the case for carbon-storing materials gets a whole lot better. The longer biogenic carbon can be kept out of the atmosphere, the greater the positive impact on the climate. Biogenic building materials—whether they be timber or bamboo structural frames, insulation boards made from recycled fibers, sheathing panels made from agricultural residue, or cladding made from cork—rarely wear out. Most building materials become waste because we just don't want them anymore, whether for aesthetic or programmatic reasons. The ability to remove those materials while preserving their usefulness can extend the lifespan of the material and therefore the carbon it contains. As material lifespan increases from 50 to 100 to 200 years, as is quite feasible for materials that can be removed and reassembled, the stored carbon remains out of the atmosphere until we have done all we can to mitigate the crisis. Future generations, having learned how critical it is to monitor and respond to climate concerns, will have ample time to decide how to wisely handle the carbon we thoughtfully put aside for a few centuries in the buildings they've been inhabiting.

11. Policy and Governance: Twenty-First-Century Cat Herding

The real problem of humanity is the following: we have paleolithic emotions, medieval institutions, and god-like technology.

—E. O. Wilson

"Governing is simple," said a friend, who is qualified to say that because he has been a county building official in California for years. To protect him from possible recrimination for his clarity of thought, we'll call him "George Clooney." "Everybody only wants two simple things from government," said George. I don't recall the precise wording, but he went on to explain those two simple things that each and every one of us wants from the various forms of polity around or above us: Leave me the hell alone, and protect me.

Leave Me the Hell Alone

Don't tell me what I can or cannot do. Don't make me ask for permission or permits or licenses. Don't make me fill out any paperwork or try to navigate some twisted, byzantine offices or website. And most certainly, don't charge me any taxes or fees.

This attitude is perhaps most pronounced in the United States, where citizens are supercharged with the spirit of hyperindividualism, which nonetheless doesn't stop them, like 3-year-olds everywhere, from adding:

Protect Me

Start with the obvious things: Provide defense, police, and fire protection. But I also mean, don't let anyone around or near me do anything I might not like. Don't let anybody play loud music, test explosives, work with weird chemicals, or build a car factory where their house used to be. Certainly, don't let them build an unsafe, oversized, or ugly house next to mine (or, God forbid, multifamily housing). Don't let anybody poison the water or compete unfairly with my business; make them play by the rules! Also, make sure they don't do anything else I might not like but maybe can't think of right now.

"And there you go!," said George, "It's just as simple as that: Leave me alone and protect me!" A stunningly simple assessment, and simple advice for all of you in government. 'Nuff said!

Still Medieval After All These Years
Note, however, that George never said "easy." In case you hadn't heard, governing is hard. Very, very hard. Excruciatingly hard. If you don't think so, just try it some time. We all complain to our school board, building department, town council, state, country, all the way up to the United Nations. Did you ever meet somebody who was completely satisfied with the way they were being governed? We even complain about God; we don't like the way the Universe is being run. It is so easy and satisfying to complain and so fantastically difficult to sit on the other side of that table.

Have we always been so unruly?

Meanwhile, Back in the Paleolithic
The emerging picture in addressing embodied carbon in buildings is one of more local governance driving the change we need. Somewhat like the emerging trends of localization of energy (let's get solar panels on every roof, microgrids in every neighborhood), water (collect and live within the constraints of what lands in your watershed), economy (buy from your local merchants), and food (buy from your local farmer), many of the most promising efforts to rein in building carbon emissions are local: businesses, individuals, and underappreciated, unsung county staffers developing policy to shift behavior. Or, we submit, craft policies to accept and foster locally based building solutions. Local governance is in many ways proving to be the best chance of enacting policy to protect the commons; we can still see and know each other and argue things out face to face. Unfortunately, local governance doesn't affect what happens in the next county; just as individuals cry out "Leave me alone and protect me!," so do cities and counties to states and provinces, as do they in turn to nations. National leadership would of course be more impactful, but to

date, and with very few exceptions, there have been very few effective advocates for climate action at any national level.

The clever bumper sticker "Think globally, act locally" is concise and to an essential point, but unfortunately it is lost on those who are too busy struggling to buy groceries, pay the bills, and raise the children to be much concerned beyond immediate family. Hungry people don't—can't—care about the environment. If anything, we think tribally and act tribally, which makes things even trickier because here in the twenty-first century, our "tribes" are typically neither geographically local nor global in scope or interest. Our tribes are religious (I'm a Christian, you're not), or political (you're red or you're blue), or cultural (I live in London, but my heart and family are in Bangalore). A well-honed and biologically useful instinct to band together under threat of wildfire or grizzly has morphed tragically into the racism, xenophobia, and a distrust of neighbors and government increasingly rampant today. (See also chapter 1.)

Which brings us to highlight another somewhat new trend needing attention here, one that augments the second item in George Clooney's rules of governing, "protect me." Starting with the Industrial Revolution but especially accelerating in concert with an exploding human population, ubiquitous technology, and climate change, we need to add:

Protect Everything from Us
Protect us from ourselves, and especially protect our descendants and the other species—who are more important to us than we yet recognize—from us! If we wipe out the bees, we don't get the honey; there's plenty of plain old self-interest underlying most environmental (not to mention social) legislation, because we're all in this together.

To one degree or another we all recognize that we count on our government at every level to set policy: to have and foster a vision bigger than the confines of one neighborhood, longer than the frenzy of the moment. Whether we realize it or not, we rely on governments to guide and protect us in ways that we cannot on our own—and neither can the "invisible hand" of the marketplace. And there's the dilemma of our times, the classic tragedy of the commons extended not just worldwide but across generations yet to come: All those other beings in the fabric of life have no voice in our council halls and senate chambers; they have no "standing" as the lawyers would say. If I live in a village, to borrow the classic example, and graze my goats too much on the common green, taking more than my fair share, everyone will see, everyone will know. The village will soon find a way to correct my abuse of a common resource. But if I live in a globalized world of eight billion people, I can abuse the commons more or less anonymously: spew poisons into air and water from my company's factory, pump water from aquifers, and threaten anybody anywhere, cloaked by the internet. What will future generations do, sue me? I can build any damn thing I want and drive on any damn side of the road I want.

Except to the extent that I am effectively governed otherwise. You can already hear those generations yet to come calling us to account, calling on us to govern ourselves quickly, systemically, and effectively.

> *This is all wrong. I shouldn't be up here. I should be back in school on the other side of the ocean. Yet you all come to us young people for hope. How dare you! You have stolen my dreams and my childhood with your empty words. And yet I'm one of the lucky ones. People are suffering. People are dying. Entire ecosystems are collapsing. We are in the beginning of a mass extinction, and all you can talk about is money and fairy tales of eternal economic growth. How dare you! For more than 30 years, the science has been crystal clear. How dare you continue to look away and come here saying that you're doing enough, when the politics and solutions needed are still nowhere in sight.*
>
> *How dare you!*
>
> —Greta Thunberg, September 23, 2019 at the U.N. Climate Action Summit

Maybe, when the ancient Romans figured out that people served by lead water pipes tended to go crazy and die, they outlawed lead water pipes and that was that. But just as likely, a few senators whose wealth was based on lead pipe manufacture delayed that process for as long as they could ("What, you want to take away people's water supply? Kill jobs?"). Even today, there are still lead water pipes serving much of the world, typically in the poorest neighborhoods because it costs a lot to replace them.

"Mad as a hatter" is an expression that still lives on, not so much from Lewis Carrol's *Alice in Wonderland* but from the common knowledge that the nineteenth-century people who turned animal fur into hats were typically eccentric and sickly. It took until the 1880s for them to figure out that mercury, commonly used to process the fur, was the reason why. Yet it took a few more decades for the use of mercury to be controlled in England and France, and several more again for mercury to be regulated in the United States.

Witness the killer smogs of the past century, in London, in Los Angeles, in Beijing, in New Delhi, and in just about every large, industrialized city on Earth. Yet we're still only just beginning to regulate those emissions ("What, you want to take away people's cars? Take away our TV and air conditioners? Kill jobs?"). There are plenty of examples of inadvertently destructive behavior that, even when known and visibly hurting people, didn't come under control for some time. As a species, we don't have a great track record in collectively managing diffuse risk, which makes for a sobering assessment at a time when the unprecedented and global impact of climate change is already upon us.

We are in a tale of two possible futures, the best and the worst. Stephen Pinker catalogues the best, but he leaves out the worst. According to the Bulletin of the Atomic Scientists' Doomsday Clock, we are 100 seconds to midnight, when the world wipes itself out because of nuclear blunder, climate change and other disruptive technologies. This is where planetary realism comes in. Instead of just "national interests," Russia, China and the United States—and other countries too—have to start accepting our common vulnerability and therefore our common interest.

—Jerry Brown[1]

Say, Anyone Know How to Operate This God-Like Technology?

Stupendous wealth and power are concentrated in people and entities that use it to influence or simply write the rules and control the narrative. Most relevant here, we all now know that Exxon and the other oil companies knew of climate change (it wasn't yet an emergency) more than 30 years ago, yet they spent that time obscuring their own findings, blocking valuable legislation, and effectively obfuscating the ever-clearer scientific consensus about climate disruption. Now more than ever, the wealthy write the rules and reap the profits, but our grandchildren will pay the price.

To be sure, wealth has always had its heavy hand on the wheels of governance, but until recently that didn't have global implications and was mostly by simple, local brute force: You cross the Emperor, you die. Exxon didn't have to assassinate anyone to avoid climate-protecting regulations. It didn't even have to persuade too many people of anything. It only had to sow enough doubt in the media and now the internet to maintain a sense of confusion: "This is still being debated by scientists on both sides!," and other seemingly innocuous nonsense. Even politicians who must know better go along with the ruse out of willful ignorance (or, less charitably, because it brings in the paycheck that keeps them in power), and they are thus complicit in the most massive and deadly abuse of the commons in history. The "might makes right" dynamic becomes further ensconced as climate disruption exacerbates local and global wealth inequality.

On top of all that, or underlying it, is Ayn Rand and the freakish cult of hyper-individualism here in the United States that spawns the fervid attacks by "conservatives" not just on regulations but on the government institutions that issue and enforce them.

> *The unceasing propaganda in our time for "the individual" seems to me deeply suspect, as "individuality" itself becomes more and more a synonym for selfishness. A capitalist society comes to have a vested interest in praising "individuality" and "freedom"—which may mean little more than the right to the perpetual aggrandizement of the self, and the freedom to shop, to acquire, to use up, to consume, to render obsolete.*
>
> —Susan Sontag[2]

With the coordination of massive wealth with a few key media and political powers, it has been sadly easy to play to the worst fears and angered frustration of many, leading to a distrust and visceral hatred of the institutions of governance. Or, in the case of technology-empowered authoritarian governments such as those in Russia, North Korea, and especially China, it's simply too hard and too risky to freely develop and exchange ideas.

As we said, governing isn't easy. We offer this preface to a chapter on policy and governance with an apology, for we have just run simplistic roughshod over a number of important, complex topics of the day. We claim no expertise other than being citizens of the times, but we had to provide some sort of context.

Let's now look at the growing array of climate-restoring rules and policies to govern a population that, to a great extent, still doesn't see the problem or even actively denies its existence. There are already some market drivers in place to cause positive change, as when mass timber structures are sometimes cheaper and faster to build than their alternatives of concrete and steel, or when a region can supply the insulation for buildings by skillfully using farm byproducts such as straw rather than products made from imported oil. But, mostly, the invisible hand of the market is taking us nowhere good; we need to guide and accelerate a massive carbon drawdown.

It's Elementary, Watson

The big picture is elementary. That is, we need to pay attention to two essential elements: carbon and hydrogen. But before we look at those two, we need to look at a third element overarching the effort: *knowledge*, and access to knowledge.

> *The only reason we ship raw materials across the planet is that we lack the knowledge to convert local materials into usable substitutes. . . . In short, knowledge is a substitute for both resources and shipping.*
>
> —Alvin Toffler, 1990[3]

If you want to write a tax, you need an accountant; if you want to build a bridge, you need an engineer; if you want to restore a forest, you need an ecologist. If you want to write effective climate policy—for buildings or anything else—you need people who can measure and track the flow of carbon around the biosphere and especially human economy; you need climate scientists, life cycle assessment (LCA), and people who can practice and teach it (see chapter 3). LCA as a science is still developing, but in the spirit of "laying the track while you drive the train," the building community is charging ahead and developing both the system, databases, and practitioners at a stunning pace. We have accuracy now, in our picture of greenhouse gas emissions, even if not always precision. But the effort needs much, much more support. LCA technical infrastructure depends on developing standards, data and methods, software tools, performance datums (benchmarks and baselines), guidelines, and education (see chapter 9). These cannot grow and mature properly piecemeal; they—we—need support at the national if not international level.

For more detailed policy suggestions, and to meet the first generation of pioneers in this new science of LCA, see box 11.1. As we develop a workable and robust system of carbon accounting, we'll be better able to track and manage those two elements so essential to our well-being: carbon and hydrogen.

Carbon

> *Governments raised more than $45 billion from carbon pricing in 2019. . . . Despite carbon prices increasing in many jurisdictions, they remain substantially lower than those needed to be consistent with the Paris Agreement.*[4]
>
> *Economists are nearly unanimous in their belief that a carbon tax is the most efficient and effective way to reduce carbon emissions. . . . Carbon dividends would*

*accelerate the transition to a low-carbon global economy and domestic energy inde-
pendence. Not only would this help prevent the destabilizing consequences of climate
change, it would also reduce the need to protect or seek to influence politically vulnerable oil-producing regions. With our electric grids susceptible to cyber-attacks, a
transition to cleaner power sources combined with new distributed storage technologies could also strengthen national security.*[5]

Put a Damn Price on Carbon!
To date, there are two basic mechanisms by which policymakers at state and national levels have priced carbon: with an emissions trading system (ETS, also called
cap and trade) or with a carbon tax. ETSs are falling out of favor for many reasons,
mainly that they haven't worked well because they are easily gamed, and sometimes
they create perverse incentives *not* to innovate or otherwise reduce our carbon footprint. By contrast, carbon taxes are proliferating because they are simpler, send
clearer price signals to industry, and can be established in a way that returns some
revenue to low-income people, eliminating the "poverty tax" effect. Good to know,
but tough to sell, especially in countries like the United States, where tax hating has
risen to the level of a religion and a political movement (TEA Party, a backronym
for "Taxed Enough Already"). Fortunately, there are plenty of mechanisms that
price emissions much like taxes without so much political fuss or administrative
work. These are the array of initiatives that are fast spreading at the local, regional,
and state levels, which we'll look at later in the chapter.

Did we mention? Put a damn price on carbon! Make emitting carbon expensive
and make sequestering it pay. We need to put the emissions engine in reverse, in every way possible, to draw the carbon down.[6] This is true conservatism: Make Earth
Great Again!

It bears reiterating the basic premise of this book here because many carbon
policy efforts to date are focused only on reducing emissions, not bringing them
back from the sky. Any new initiatives to address climate disruption, be they local,
regional, national, or international (or for that matter within startups and Fortune
500 corporations), should be crafted with intent to do both. Which makes this a
good place to look briefly at the fast-growing world of carbon capture, utilization
and storage (CCUS).

Carbon Capture, Utilization and Storage
If you do an online search for "carbon capture," you will probably come across
one or several pictures of big steel machines that look like enormous trees or walls,

accompanied by excited (or critical) discussion of capturing atmospheric carbon dioxide. These pictures sometimes engender sarcastic comments suggesting that the inventors haven't figured out that trees and grasses are doing that all the time, in massive collective quantity, using only solar power. Hah, Nature wins again, tech bro!

Well, right, but trees and grasses don't then deliver to us pure gaseous carbon dioxide, which is rapidly emerging as a crucial material to fuel a truly circular, sustainable economy. Many of the technologies described in this book, particularly for concrete, algae, and bioplastics, depend on a supply of gaseous carbon as feedstock, and you just can't get that from a Douglas fir. (Well, you could if you really wanted to, but it wouldn't be worth the effort.)

Much better than steel trees and walls dotting the landscape are the devices clamped over the smokestacks of power plants and heavy industrial plants such as steel and cement, where the exhaust gas is much richer in carbon dioxide. That is where the emissions are, and where the circular economy rubber meets the road.

> *Achieving deep emissions reductions in heavy industry (cement, steel and chemicals production) can be challenging for several reasons. But CCUS is a relatively advanced and cost-competitive option for dramatically cutting the CO_2 emitted during the production of these essential materials. It can also be more cost-effective to retrofit CCUS to existing facilities than building new capacity with alternative technologies. . . . Experience indicates that CCUS should become cheaper as the market grows, the technology develops, finance costs fall, economies of scale are reached, and experience of building and operating CCUS facilities accumulates. This pattern has already been seen for renewable energy technologies over recent decades.[7]*

We have already begun a transition off of fossil fuels, but that transition unavoidably includes continuing to burn them for a while longer. Carbon capture, essential to provide feedstock to many new industries, also provides a means to decarbonize existing heavy industry, or at least catch their emissions at the source. It's not exactly "clean coal" as has been disingenuously marketed, but it's a great and essential transition tool.

But then, once you've captured carbon dioxide, what will you do with it? That brings us to the "utilization and storage" part of the story, where things get more interesting.

> *At first glance, it sounds like something cooked up after too many martinis by a K Street lobbyist for the fossil fuel industry: Take legislation making it more profitable*

for oil companies to pump oil, and easier for coal-fired power plants to continue to operate—and then sell it as a climate change remedy. Calling it "counterintuitive" might sound like an understatement. . . .

"Proponents argue that the new federal incentives will help to close that gap and kick-start carbon capture and storage as existing federal and state incentives have done for renewable energy" said Bob Perciasepe, a deputy administrator of the Obama-era Environmental Protection Agency and now president of the Center for Climate and Energy Solutions. Tax incentives, he added, enabled "even the wind industry to drop the cost to the point where it can now almost compete straight up" with conventional power sources. Developing cheaper carbon capture and storage technologies will be particularly critical, he said, as India, China, and sub-Saharan Africa continue to build new coal-fired power plants.[8]

At present in the United States, the primary use of captured CO_2 (typically collected at coal and gas power plants) is to pump it deep underground beneath aging oil fields, thus giving new pressure and pep to the fluids in the rock above (oil and gas), enabling further profitable extraction. The various entities involved receive carbon tax credits from the U.S. taxpayer, and they can call it carbon burial for all the climate virtue that it seems to be. Problematic and troubling as this scenario may be, it does have value in jump starting the technology of capture.

CO_2-based enhanced oil recovery (CO_2-EOR) is by far the most well-understood form of CO_2U. There is a well-established body of practice, commerce and law around CO_2-EOR, and the technology is mature. Today, roughly 17 million tons/ year of anthropogenic CO_2 are used for EOR. While there remains debate over the use of CO_2-EOR as a climate mitigation option, various analyses have shown that it could be beneficial, and it is represented in economic and analytical models. Many governments, companies and investors see CO_2-EOR as a critical path for early CCS adoption since it provides revenues, tax receipts, jobs and large-volume offtakes.[9]

There are other problems with EOR, mainly that we don't know for sure that the CO_2 will stay down there in the ground. If it escapes to the surface in sufficient quantity, it can be toxic to all air-breathing life, so it's not a trivial risk. Fortunately, a huge array of economically viable products are already well in development that can store that carbon, albeit with varying degrees of durability, in commercial products and processes.

The carbon-based products industry (CBPI) can significantly contribute to reducing carbon emissions. Our initial estimate is that over 10% of annual CO$_2$ emissions can be captured in these products, representing an annual revenue opportunity of $800 billion to $1.1 trillion.[10]

This carbon-based product Industry includes a truly vast array of things, such as food, pharmaceuticals, polymers, chemicals, fuel, and fertilizer. Of interest to us here are the many construction products discussed in this book, such as artificial limestone aggregate, carbonated concrete, and algae concretes and plastics, which depend on a supply of carbon or carbon dioxide. At present, they must source much of those feedstocks from suppliers using fossil fuel energy to make the gases—carbon with a high carbon footprint! Obviously, the preference is to develop the carbon capture and supply infrastructure as fast as possible so that we're truly capturing emissions and durably storing them in buildings and everywhere else we can find. This, along with plants, will be how we bring the carbon home.

Hydrogen

There are some parts of the economy that electricity will not be able to decarbonize—some of the largest users of fossil fuels such as steel, heavy-duty trucks, shipping and cement. However, hydrogen is starting to emerge as a promising route to addressing the toughest third of global greenhouse gas (GHG) emissions by 2050 as its costs start to fall, according to new research from BloombergNEF. In its Hydrogen Economy Outlook, BNEF finds that clean hydrogen could cut up to 34% of global GHG emissions from fossil fuels and industry—at a manageable cost. However, this will only be possible if policies are put in place to help scale up technology and drive down costs.[11]

2020 has been notable for the rush of activity in the green hydrogen space. . . . Using renewable-powered electrolyzers to create low-carbon hydrogen can squeeze emissions out of sectors where direct electrification isn't going to cut it. Green hydrogen could replace methane [aka natural gas] to generate heat or power. It could replace high-carbon, or gray, hydrogen in a number of industrial and chemical processes. It could even be used as a fuel in heavy transport. As 2020 unfurled and then unraveled, climate change mitigation ambition ramped up. "Green recovery" emerged as a favored approach to stoking flagging economies—tackling the unparalleled challenge of climate change to invest our way out of an unrivaled economic test. Even prior to the coronavirus pandemic, there were clues that green hydrogen might shift up the agenda. . . . Wood Mackenzie declared the 2020s the decade of hydrogen.[12]

Hydrogen gas stands poised to supplant fossil fuels as a primary storage and transportation medium for energy. It has almost three times the energy density of gasoline or diesel fuel, as measured in megajoules per kilogram, and it can be made from water by electrolysis, with oxygen as a byproduct. Like most things, it can be made much less expensively at industrial scale, but unlike gasoline it can also be made in a backyard, or at a regional scale coupled, for example, with microgrids and wind farms. When it is burned in a fuel cell (as for motors) or as fuel (as for heavy industry), the waste product is water. The technology for making it is young and not yet cost-competitive with fossil carbon energy, but with time and the right policy guidelines it can be cheaply available and manufactured with renewable energy. Perhaps best of all, we already have the infrastructure in place, needing only modest adaptations of existing methane (natural) gas storage and pipelines. And we have a century of experience in dealing with highly flammable gases and liquids at every scale of modern society, so safety issues are largely known and resolved.

Another solution to transportation and storage challenges has been to focus on localized production. Nikola has partnered with Nel and Bosch to deliver a network of local hydrogen production stations that utilize renewable energy sources and electrolyzers, thus cutting out the logistics chain of conventional diesel and gasoline supply. . . . Even though there are challenges, the time for hydrogen is now, and here's why:

We are seeing increased regulatory pressure and industry demand. The European Union has committed to removing gasoline and diesel vehicles by 2030. At the same time, clean fuel standards and associated investment in California and Canada are creating the policy basis for change. Hyundai is planning for the production of up to 700,000 Fuel Cell Electric Vehicles per year by 2030, and Japan is targeting 800,000 FCEVs by 2030. . . . The more projects that increasingly use fuel cell technologies, the more potential for cost reduction and investment in the technology. China's commitment to get 1 million fuel cell vehicles onto the roads by 2030 offers huge potential for significant advancements in the efficiency and cost points for fuel cell vehicles. . . . Hydrogen has seen false dawns before, but this low-carbon alternative is being pushed by some of the largest companies on the planet across multiple sectors.[13]

Hydrogen gas stands poised to fill a crucial role in the renewable energy economy, but it needs fostering and support at the national and international levels—just as did fossil fuels over the past century.

Enhance the international knowledge infrastructure, put a price on carbon, and foster the emerging carbon capture and hydrogen economy. That's what nations can and must do. Now let's get more granular and look at the blizzard of initiatives to address embodied carbon, existing and developing, at more local levels.

Thinking Globally, Acting Locally

Policy initiatives are fast proliferating at the local (city, county, and sometimes state or province) levels worldwide, and globally they are distributed by type, somewhat like what is shown in figure 11.1.

Urban planning and land use policies, which determine what can be built, often in terms of use and density; and zoning policies determining where things can be built.

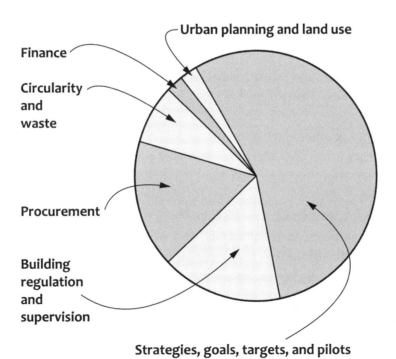

FIGURE 11.1

Building regulation and supervision policies affect how buildings and infrastructure are constructed.

Procurement policies direct how and what kind of materials, services, and projects are purchased by the governing entity.

Circularity and waste policies affect material life cycles and end of life use.

Finance policies use financial means such as taxation, fees, incentives, and commercial (dis)advantages to drive action on clean construction.

Strategies, goals, targets, and pilots are city actions that, though not enforceable policy, can be powerful steps on the way to a net zero construction sector.

Following is a summary description of these six policy categories along with commentary on each's effectiveness. The reader is urged to look up the policy resources in box 11.1 for more detailed explication and cross-referencing.

Urban Planning and Land Use
Amending zoning and land use laws is one the most effective ways to reduce emissions, just starting in a few places, but is lightly populated in figure 11.1 mostly because these are very hard levers to push. Land use patterns in most of the developed world are intractably well established so that, to use a common example, amending suburban zoning laws to allow some commercial use or denser housing will typically spark a flurry of protest and lawsuits. Suburban development seemed like a great idea during the boom after World War II, at least to white people in affluent areas, but it has been a heavy weight on both people of color and the climate.

Building Regulation and Supervision
There have been a number of efforts to govern emissions at the building scale. Although it's too soon to gauge, they hold great promise not just to drive a carbon-neutral and then carbon-storing palette of building materials but to establish a price advantage for climate-friendly products and practices down the value chain. There are essentially two types: material specific and whole building regulation.

   Material-specific regulations constraining embodied carbon are easy to write and enforce, and they usually start with concrete because it's the proverbial 800-pound gorilla in the room: a widely used material with a huge carbon footprint that's comparatively easy to reduce. Other "big footprint" materials, such as steel and plastic foam insulation, are far more difficult to affect with local regulations (see also chapter 6). Marin County, California, enacted the first low-carbon concrete code amendment[14] in late 2019 that provides both prescriptive (cement limits) and

Box 11.1   Policy Resources

They're easy to find online if you want to dig deeper.

Embodied Carbon Policy Toolkit
The Carbon Leadership Forum (CLF) has grown in a decade to become the international center of the burgeoning movement to address embodied carbon in the built environment. Besides the referenced Policy Toolkit, CLF and its adjunct the Embodied Carbon Network are the best places to find current knowledge and also find active people from academia, construction, development, industry, and government. Your go-to resource; all the organizations listed below are active members.
    https://carbonleadershipforum.org/clf-policy-toolkit/

City Policy Framework for Dramatically Reducing Embodied Carbon
Report coordinated by the Carbon Neutral Cities Alliance, with Bionova Ltd. (aka One Click LCA), with contribution from Architecture 2030.
    https://www.embodiedcarbonpolicies.com (undated, released in late 2020)

Clean Construction Policy Explorer
C40 Cities Climate Leadership Group, October 2020
    A truly global survey of cities and their policy actions to address embodied carbon. Their work provided most of the basis for figure 11.1.
    https://www.c40knowledgehub.org/s/article/Clean-Construction-Policy-Explorer?language=en_US

Reducing Embodied Environmental Impacts of Buildings: Policy Options and Technical Infrastructure
Jennifer O'Connor and Matt Bowick, December 2019, Athena Sustainable Materials Institute
    An excellent white paper; Athena Sustainable Materials Institute was one of the first to develop tools, protocols, and databases for measuring embodied carbon.
    http://www.athenasmi.org/wp-content/uploads/2019/12/Policy_white_paper_December_2019.pdf

Bringing Embodied Carbon Upfront
A white paper and guidelines for coordinated action for the building and construction sector to tackle embodied carbon.
    World Green Building Council, September 2019
    https://www.worldgbc.org/news-media/bringing-embodied-carbon-upfront

performance (Environmental Product Declaration–verified global warming potential limits) compliance pathways. That code language is freely available for use by others, but actual limits must be tailored to the concrete market in any jurisdiction contemplating a similar measure. (At the time of this writing, efforts are under way to develop a national model code, based on the Marin County low-carbon concrete code, through ASHRAE 189.1 and then the International Building Code.)

A related issue with outsize importance belongs here in the discussion: the need to comprehensively rethink the way we standardize and regulate the production and use of materials in construction. In the past century, highly centralized standardization systems have evolved all over the world that are increasingly dominated by the industries and enterprises that are able and willing to spend a lot of money developing the technologies and protecting market share. Outdated systems and materials—those that are based on cheap fossil fuels and an "away" where we can throw things—got baked into the rules, and there's precious little room left for innovation, or for making use of the innumerable plant, mineral, and municipal waste resources that are available in any one place but often no other. Every locale has a unique palette of building resources that, at present, it must either discard or squeeze through the acceptance filters written mostly by distant people who don't much know or care. How might we localize standards? The concrete industry may offer some clues here, in that every ready mix concrete plant is of necessity a local business that delivers a construction material comprising a range of local and imported materials; although we nominally require that its constituent sand, gravel, water, and cement meet national standards, we mostly care that the finished concrete performs as needed. The implication, then, is that a robust set of national or international *performance* (as opposed to prescriptive) standards could be created to govern all aspects of building while remaining agnostic as to constituent ingredients. Simple in concept, tricky as always in execution, but a necessary step toward more localized, climate-friendly architecture.

Whole building regulation makes more sense conceptually, because it allows design and construction teams flexibility to optimize the dozens or hundreds of materials and systems in a building project to get the overall lowest carbon footprint. However, the nascent state of LCA (chapter 3) and industry knowledge in general of carbon accounting makes this problematic: How do I set a limit on your building's footprint? Compared to what do we set limits or verify your design? Recognizing this problem, green building rating systems offer flexible means to address the issue. The Living Building Challenge requires the purchase of an offset for a project's embodied carbon, whereas others such as LEED and Green Globes use a self-defined "baseline" building design as the performance target (but don't provide clear guidance on how to produce a meaningful baseline). For the immediate future, many policy initiatives must of necessity be limited to disclosure:

> *Whole-building LCA requires a whole ecosystem of technical resources . . . [but already] North America has what it needs to support "soft" LCA-based policy: green building policy and programs that simply require design teams to perform LCA and report the results. This is useful for pulling the community up the steep whole-building LCA learning curve and for identifying technical gaps and market hurdles that will get in the way of policy evolution. . . . The next step is policy with teeth.*[15]

Procurement

Government at every scale is a big consumer of construction services, and so it can and should throw its weight around by requiring, or at least favoring, climate-friendly products and services (same holds true for corporate clients; money talks). California's Global Warming Solutions Act (AB32) of 2006, better known as "Buy Clean California," was a first attempt to do exactly that: use California's size and influence to foster climate-friendlier construction. Other states and nations have enacted (or tried to enact) similar provisions, but they all suffer the same constraint, for now, as described above for whole building LCA: we don't yet have the data infrastructure to do much more than require Environmental Product Declarations and build awareness and knowledge. Concrete is an exception here; we do know enough to write policy with teeth. But, unfortunately, concrete is (in the Spring of 2021) exempted from the Buy Clean California provisions.

Circularity and Waste

The idea behind circularity (see also chapter 10) is to transform our human economy to work more like Nature, where all "waste" is food for something or someone; everything is endlessly recycled, and there's just no such thing as waste. In practice this often means policies that encourage recycling and favor products with high recycled content. It also translates to fairly simple measures to control and limit demolition (to encourage building renovation and reuse of both materials and whole buildings; see box 2.1 in chapter 2), and to add cost in various ways to throwing anything away. Many of these measures already have a long history as components of solid waste management; they mostly dovetail smoothly with climate goals and will become more common as cities lose or just can't find sites suitable for landfill. They do *not* dovetail so smoothly with climate goals when solid waste is used as fuel for power generation, as is increasingly common while the global recycling market remains erratic and undependable. Generally, burning waste helps with two problems—solid waste disposal and power generation—but exacerbates the third and far larger one: climate change. In the absence of tight pollution controls, burning wastes will also generate chemical and particulate pollution that you generally don't want to breathe. The overarching strategy must be to encourage recycling and reuse or to get better at capturing emissions at thermal power plants to produce carbon for reuse in products.

Finance

Money is a powerful driver of behavior, but adding taxes and fees is politically difficult (see rule 1 at the beginning of this chapter). That probably explains why, according to our pie chart in figure 11.1, not too many cities have tried it. Procurement and building regulation measures can have the same effect—making high-carbon products more expensive—without the unwanted optics of a new tax. One idea commonly floated is to reward low-carbon projects with reduced permit fees or fast-tracked permit review times, but both are highly problematic to enforce. Possibly that will become less true as LCA science advances and, for example, a project can present for building permit already certified by a recognized green building authority (e.g., LEED, Living Futures, Athena). Meanwhile, as with procurement, government pension and other funds can leverage their investment influence to favor climate-friendly enterprises.

Strategies, Goals, Targets, and Pilots

Judging from their dominant share of the pie chart, these must be the best tools for effecting positive change. More usually, however, these are common policy measures largely because they are politically easy because they are generally toothless. Declaring "climate emergency," or forming a county-wide Climate Action Plan, or generically declaring "Net Zero by 2050!" are all laudable actions, but too often they are little more than a metaphorical kicking of the can down the road, masking an underlying ignorance or lack of will to meaningful action. That grumpy note aside, such declarations do establish a sort of mission statement for the jurisdiction, important for justifying more substantive measures that might follow and providing goals to which citizens can hold their governments accountable. They are necessary starts to government-organized or sponsored action.

I write this chapter on policy and governance having just run a common bureaucratic gauntlet: trying to secure a building permit, garnering the sort of frustration that almost everyone experiences in one way or another as we all try to do simple things and encounter frustrating, bewildering, and expensive roadblocks from governments. This was a classic case of the sort that we architects, engineers, and builders endlessly trade eye-rolling stories about, this time made a bit more galling by the fact that it was a very simple design for affordable farmworker housing in an area that desperately needs some. My client wanted to develop the design—net carbon-absorbing cabins of wood framing and straw bale walls—so she could offer it for replication around California where affordable housing is needed almost everywhere. A lovely idea, and my client knew that the county and planning staff were completely supportive. But no one told the guy who was charged with checking the plans, and for no visible reason he dragged the design team through three rounds of petty backchecking, a year of delay, and added cost with little benefit.

In other words, governing is hard. Hard for the governed but also hard for those who must enforce the rules. Everyone groans at the introduction of new laws, and crafting policy to change behavior or move the market is always a daunting prospect. (Unless you have some version of dictatorship, in which case it's easy: you, the dictator, just dictate. But that system of governance has a few of its own special problems.) Still, we already have historical precedent for the stupendous scale of effort needed to address climate change in World War II and the space race, both of which quickly and effectively mobilized previously unimaginable physical, financial, human and scientific resources. Now the stakes are even bigger as all of humanity faces an imminent (and already immanent) global crisis with no precedent at all. We weren't ready for this. Yet we do have to rise to it.

What I see now is that human civilization is in the process of trying to become like Earth, in the sense of learning how to become a persistent system. In this century, we're going to get a lot of harsh lessons on how not to persist—and then we will either correct that, or we won't. . . . I see a chance in this century for civilization to get out of its adolescence, to become more mature, pragmatic, skeptical and solution-oriented (rather than story-oriented) so that we can reverse planetary degradation. This won't be like ending the Cold War. This is a new kind of problem, where people have to really connect in order to fix it. . . . In the introduction to the Whole Earth Catalog in 1968, I wrote, "We are as gods and might as well get good at it." More recently, in "Whole Earth Discipline" (2009), I wrote, "We are as gods and <u>have</u> to get good at it." What changed between those two statements is global warming, which changed the sense of who the "we" is. . . . We certainly have a global economy and a global communications network, but there is no global body politic. When you *look at climate change, nobody except nations can change tax laws or carbon taxes. Corporations can't do it. The U.N. can't do it. Nonprofits can't do it. Nations are the only ones that have enough control of their economic instruments to be able to say, OK, there's going to be a tax that relates to the externalities of climate issues. And thus nations, to my mind, are again the lead players in making things go right with climate.*

—Stewart Brand[16]

12. A Just Transition: Building a Better Society Means More than Capturing Carbon

What does climate justice have to do with architecture? It seems possible to discuss climate solutions within the boundaries of architecture and leave "the rest" of a just transition to a climate-stable world outside our lens. But in doing so, we risk repeating the same cycle of mistakes and missteps that have brought us to the brink of a climate disaster and left so many people impoverished and disenfranchised. If we blunder into another crisis—assuming we get the climate rebalanced—the planet will already be less resilient. All the tenets of the precautionary principle[1] at the heart of the green building movement suggest we need to do everything possible to end the escalating cycles of human and ecological damage by seriously asking ourselves, How did we get ourselves into this situation?

We know that architecture is central to all cultures. Our buildings define us in a way that is pervasive; our cultures inform our buildings, and in turn our buildings inform our culture. Physically occupying the central spaces of our civilizations and firmly in the middle of our economies, we *are* our architecture. And if we need to change our culture to solve climate change, our architecture needs to change. If the change we need is climate justice, then we need buildings that offer and express climate justice.

It is all too easy to frame the climate crisis as a technical problem: Too much CO_2 in the atmosphere is causing the climate to change dramatically. This is certainly the physical reality we now face, but to find adequate solutions we need to ask ourselves, How did all that carbon get into the atmosphere? It wasn't by mistake. All those greenhouse gases (GHGs) were dumped in the atmosphere in a 150-year binge of fossil fuel burning and deforestation around which we based our entire culture and economy. Plenty of warnings that these were bad ideas have gone unheeded, from the late 1800s to today.

The failure to rein in emissions has been a deliberate and conscious choice since at least the 1950s, when leading scientists began issuing direct warnings to politicians about the measurable upward trajectory of GHG emissions and the predictable effect on the planet's climate.[2] We find ourselves in this climate crisis because we have valued our pleasures and comforts while ignoring social and planetary health. This choice has been made throughout history: We have repeatedly deforested and desertified large tracts of the planet, devastating ecosystems while engaging in brutal treatment of other humans. Our moment in history is not unique in the collective unwillingness to value human and ecological well-being over economic gain, but it is unique in the rapid and planetary scale of the current devastation. Every strip mine, clear cut, and poisoned watershed has been a localized version of the impacts of destroying the ecosystems that sustain us. Our response to destruction we've wrought has been to move on and abandon what we've ruined, but global climate change doesn't allow us that option.

Climate justice is a recognition of this cycle and an understanding that we must do more than curb emissions and balance CO_2 levels in the atmosphere; we must end the pattern of destructive behavior that is bringing us to this existential brink and understand that this is not "just" an environmental issue but a civil rights issue. To do any less is to ensure that we will reach another deadly precipice in the not-so-distant future. It is all too easy to think of climate justice as a chance to accomplish some nice social goals while we invest in "green savior" technologies. But justice is not likely to be a bonus side effect of fixing climate change; climate change is much more likely to be fixed by creating a just world. When we can leave behind an extractive economy for a regenerative economy and undo the concentration of wealth and power in favor of ecological and social well-being, we will have mitigated climate change and the likelihood that another such crisis will be created in its wake.

Speaking about climate justice can be difficult. Collectively, we are only just starting to be able to talk about the literal, scientific aspects of climate change in a rational way; staring head-on into the underlying causes is a big leap, and it's frightening. It's no small ask to face the reality of an existential threat and simultaneously dig under the foundations of everything we have come to know as normal, especially if our "normal" is a position of relative privilege. If this topic causes you anxiety, please don't turn away. The first step toward a just transition is simply taking the time to listen to people whose ideas about solutions to the climate crisis are different from our own and to give serious consideration to those ideas. Engaged listening costs us nothing, commits us to nothing, gives up nothing, but does so much to make change possible. Justice does not seek to raise some at the expense of others, it seeks to offer every person the dignity of life's basics and the opportunities to explore, create, enjoy, and share in rich and rewarding lives. That seems like a reasonable basis for starting a discussion.

There is a lot to say about climate justice, and this book is not intended to be a comprehensive exploration of the topic. We encourage our readers to explore the resources such as "The Case for Climate Justice" by Global Justice Now[3] to begin to explore the issue and understand the premise. The desire to reverse climate change through creative solutions that brought you to this book is an important step toward climate justice: We do need to fix this problem, and everybody actively working on climate mitigation must actively be working for climate justice. The real solutions to the climate crisis are intertwined with all aspects of a just transition and show up in every discussion in this book about materials, governance, accounting principles, design, and construction aimed at ambitiously addressing the climate. Our intent is to elaborate on key aspects of climate justice and offer some context and some definitive steps those of us in the building sector can take to help shape a just transition.

Climate Smarter

We can measure "climate smart" with numbers, focusing on tons of CO_2 emitted and stored, and many of us in the building sector are comfortable in this space. Although we've just made the case that these efforts in and of themselves may not be enough, they are certainly an important place to start.

In the building sector, carbon smart means adopting practices to quickly ensure that all our projects are responsible for as few emissions as possible. It must be our short-term goal to arrive at net zero emissions from all aspects of construction, from materials to construction to operations and demolition. Simultaneously, we need to start storing carbon in our buildings. That is the point of this book and an initial—and critical—stepping stone toward climate justice.

Climate smarter, you could say, extends beyond our core business of designing and making buildings. We need to make the buildings we work in, the vehicles we move around in, the internet we connect to—all these things and every other aspect of our operations that contribute to climate change—become part of our focus.

Addressing our own operations while committing to a climate-positive construction practice can seem overwhelming, but they can be mutually support-ive. Understanding the practical needs, concerns, and hurdles to achieving climate smarter in our own buildings and operations helps us to better plan and design systems that will work for our clients. We share the learning curve, experience the pitfalls, and build better solutions if our zero carbon buildings arise from zero car-bon operations.

Attending to the carbon numbers alone is not enough to address climate change, but it is certainly something we all must do. Adopting an unwavering commitment to understanding the practical, numbers-based, carbon accounting aspect of this work and wholeheartedly moving to absorbing rather than generating emissions will open many pathways for comprehensive climate justice. Emission reductions can be achieved without disrupting the kinds of activities that currently pollute, destroy ecosystems, expose workers to toxic materials, and in so many ways devalue the lives of people. A society that is focused on absorbing emissions will have the opportunity to think very differently about the complex ties between humans and the environment, people and the economy.

Regenerative Systems and the Case for Abundance
Immeasurable human effort and talent have been expended creating means by which capital can be grown. Turning a small amount of money into a bigger amount of money has been the core role of a modern entrepreneur; it's the boundless growth principle that has brought many widespread benefits and advances but also pro-pelled us headlong into a climate crisis.

Imagine even a fraction of that creativity and energy being put toward the creation of regenerative food, energy, and shelter systems that become real, long-term climate solutions. Instead of multiplying money, we could be multiplying opportunities to meet all our essential requirements in a mutually supportive and climate-positive way. Regenerative agriculture systems can provide healthy food while contributing to soil health and diverse ecosystems while also supplying raw materials for build-ings and meaningful employment to people. Energy systems based on renewable inputs can be connected to grids that reliably store, move, and share power when and where it's needed while ensuring that there is no waste in the form of emissions or heat. Regenerative buildings can be made from carbon-storing materials, can be production and storage hubs for renewable energy, can collect sunlight and water and provide space to grow food using water and wastes generated on site, and can provide soil carbon storage services and spaces for human activities and mutually supportive biosystems.

All this may seem overly optimistic and utopian. Skepticism about regenerative visions is understandable, but it also flies in the face of all the available evidence. Demonstrations of all these regenerative systems exist all around the world. Permaculture farms, desert reclamation projects, passive and renewable energy systems, and living buildings all exist today, and they have most often been built by committed individuals and groups on small budgets with minimal research and development support. If we can imagine investing human and financial capital in regenerative projects at the same scale as we invest in the extractive economy, then it is not difficult to imagine a regenerative transformation taking place quickly. Humans have overcome so many substantial technical challenges in our history; creating regenerative systems offers many fewer technical hurdles than our advancements in transportation, energy, medicine, and space travel, to name but a few.

Developing and maintaining regenerative systems is not a new undertaking. Indigenous cultures around the world successfully built regenerative food, energy, and shelter regimes that lasted for thousands of years. The degree to which we have dismissed and ignored this vast source of knowledge is astounding. For millennia, Indigenous peoples have intentionally aligned with natural systems to protect and enhance the abundance the natural world provided for them. It has been a grave error of colonizing cultures to dismiss these systems as crude and "savage," stealing their lands while attempting to delete their cultures. Instead, many of them provided a return of abundance for a minimum of input that far outperforms anything we've imposed on the landscape ever since. We don't need to replicate—nor can we—historic indigenous systems on our current landscape. However, we can learn a vast amount from the experience and success of indigenous knowledge and its respect for the forces of life and recognize its destruction as fundamentally destructive to our own best interests, and theirs.

In a convergence of indigenous knowledge and modern science, numerous scientific disciplines are emphasizing the importance of embracing living systems rather than defying or destroying them. From biological computing to advances in multi-omics in medicine (a "multi-omics" approach combines major fields such as genomics, transcriptomics, proteomics, and metabolomics, in addition to minor omics-based approaches in order to obtain elaborate knowledge of an entire biological system, in a single study[4]) to the use of mycelium and algae to grow building materials (see chapter 6), the exploration of the systems and mechanisms of life to further enhance our lives shares an inherent link to indigenous approaches to human betterment through natural abundance.

Expertise in building and maintaining regenerative systems is expanding.

However, it needs to become a central focus for all of us. The answer to every question and line of inquiry—about preventing climate change or any other human endeavor—must adhere to the principles of regeneration and enhancing life.

Regeneration must be at the foundation of our governing principles, and this includes eliminating waste as an acceptable outcome. We need to produce only byproducts and co-products and never "waste." Every activity must be mutually supportive of multiple activities.

Dreamy thinking, to be sure, yet we have precedent: Humans have figured out how to prosper, or anyway get by, under every set of rules that has ever been created. We can undoubtedly prosper in a new system that ends the notion of waste and enshrines the principles of regeneration.

For the building sector, embracing regenerative systems doesn't require an immediate leap into growing our buildings. We can start by understanding our current systems and supply chains, identifying where we encourage and create waste, and curbing those practices. We can ask ourselves and our suppliers to identify harmful ecological and human impacts and move to eliminate them. Then, going beyond harm reduction, we can begin to explore and create positive co-benefits across our operations, from product harvesting and manufacturing to community improvements spiraling from our buildings.

Waste issues provide one example of how to begin embracing regenerative approaches. We are so accustomed to the "necessity" of construction waste that even starting to consider the potential for its transformation to valuable co-product can dramatically alter our practices. As designers, we can design for circularity, making every piece of our buildings easy to put up, take down, and reuse (see chapter 10). We can collaborate with manufacturers to ensure that all products are easily reusable and recyclable. We can collaborate with builders to create systems for recycling collection and flow directly into our building plans, knowing where offcuts and leftovers are generated and enabling easy sorting and collection. We can directly support local efforts to establish markets for materials that will leave our project sites and invest in local sites to receive and transform these materials into useful products. Each new effort and new link between parties that don't conventionally see themselves as partners can spiral into wider and larger regenerative systems.

Cooperative Systems

Cooperation is essential to architecture. Although we may think of our business as being competitive (design firm vs. design firm, manufacturer vs. manufacturer), we collectively agree on codes and standards, contract language, common dimensions and material properties, assemblies and details, safety protocols, and so much more. The development of a building from initial concept to inhabited structure is a model of cooperation, requiring skills and input from multiple stakeholders and knowledge holders working together for a common goal, none of whom would be able to complete the project without the other team members. Architects, engineers, and tradespeople all contribute valuable skills and expertise and dance along with developers, bankers, and regulators in diverse forms of collaboration that have built every town and city across the planet. That dance needs to include the communities and individuals affected by these projects to be more fully cooperative.

Cooperative systems are also essential to climate justice. As with the making of buildings, the climate crisis will not be solved from within individual silos of knowledge but by interdisciplinary cooperation by stakeholders and knowledge holders from across society. With centuries of experience in tackling complex problems through cooperative approaches, architecture could be well positioned to lead in this area.

However, architecture has much to learn. Cooperation within project teams is essential and well understood in the sector, but the dominant economic model of architecture is deeply situated in exploitive practices. From land acquisition and development through hierarchical corporate structures to abusive labor practices in construction, the field is a microcosm of the issues that have led us into the climate crisis. We need to embrace cooperation across the full scope of our operations, and cooperative economics offers an opportunity to embed values of justice in the very structure of our businesses and also provide resilience in a sector that has a long history of boom-and-bust cycles.

A cooperative economic model has long existed alongside the more dominant competitive and exploitative model. The first western-style cooperative societies were born amid the industrial revolution in England in the mid-1700s, as exploitive economics were quickly ascending and wreaking havoc on people's lives. The Rochdale Society of Equitable Pioneers in Rochdale, United Kingdom, set out the "Rochdale Principles" in 1844, and versions of these principles still guide cooperative societies today (box 12.1). These tradespeople were facing increased poverty as factories displaced the need for their skilled labor, and, confronting hunger, they banded together to open a store to provide food and essentials to their members at reduced costs. As their cooperative grew, all members benefited from the proceeds of the increased sales. Furthermore, a legitimate form of economic organization was

> ## Box 12.1   Combining Carbon-Storing Building and Just Transition
>
> When the design/build firm New Frameworks decided to go into business producing prefabricated straw bale wall panels under the name Gryphon, addressing climate issues was central to their purpose. Having designed and built dozens of custom straw bale homes across the northeastern United States, the company principals were well aware that straw was an excellent way to store carbon in buildings.
>
> But New Frameworks has never been focused on climate alone. The worker-owned cooperative was founded on principles of social justice, and with their Gryphon panel business they are exemplifying what a just transition can look like. The company sources the straw for its panels from local organic grain farms and timber from small, sustainably managed forests to ensure that their materials contribute to the improvement of soil carbon stocks and regenerative agriculture and forestry systems.
>
> The company has also partnered with Migrant Justice, an organization that brings together Vermont's migrant dairy farm workers to improve their working and living conditions. This partnership has facilitated connections to the migrant worker community to help staff the growing Gryphon Panel team, bringing together the need for adequate housing and year-round well-paying work and cooperative ownership for migrant workers.
>
> The example of Gryphon at New Frameworks provides one possible roadmap for combining efforts to store carbon in the built environment while multiplying the impact with strong social and ecological outcomes.

born out of desperate need, supplying a community with its needs and returning the economic benefit to members of that same community.

Retail operations were not the only cooperatives that formed over the subsequent decades. By the mid-1800s, cooperative societies were providing insurance and banking services, electricity, and fair markets for farmers, among many examples.[5] At times, governments have promoted cooperatives as essential elements of economic development, especially in rural areas. Examples of cooperative architecture, construction, and material manufacturing firms, though less prevalent, have historical precedents and exist today in many forms.

The Rochdale Principles embed core aspects of climate justice into the foundational mission of a business. Cooperative principles could apply to firms that offer distinct services within architecture but could also be formed to include all the stakeholders and businesses needed to complete a project from start to finish. Housing cooperatives could include land acquisition, development planning, architecture, engineering, and construction firms as well as residents. Whether at the level of individual firms or entire sectors, cooperative structures can embody principles of climate justice in the fabric of the industry and extend the model of cooperation inherent in a project-by-project model of architecture to the underlying model of operation.

Democracy, Diversity, Inclusion, and Reconciliation
GHG emissions are produced by countries with a great many forms of government. From military dictatorships to communist states to democracies, the structure of a nation's government is not a determining factor of its total emissions. In theory, democracies should have reacted faster and done more to prevent climate change; after all, what informed citizenry would willingly choose to act in a way that would ruin the planet for their children?

The principles of climate justice contend that informed and empowered people will make choices that protect their futures and those of their families and that this would make it much less likely that GHG emissions would ever have been ignored and dismissed as long as they have been under our current forms of democracy (box 12.2). The fact that the world's democracies still generate emissions at current levels is less an indictment of the citizens who vote once every few years and more the fault of our current democratic structures that limit democracy to an occasional vote rather than a deep and ongoing participation in decision making.

The building sector need not tackle structural reform of our governing structures head on, but we can work to embed democratic principles deeply into our own practices. As we learn how participatory decision making really works, we often get hungrier to implement it everywhere. Architecture can lead by intentionally seeking democratic input from all stakeholders affected by our work. Developers and building owners are already at the table, and so are design team leads and sometimes municipal officials, but we need to consider adding the missing voices of building occupants, neighborhood residents, tradespeople, and service providers. Will this be messy? Yes, as we already know from the many times we've tried. Learning how to actively participate in a democracy isn't something many of us have learned, and when we begin to hear from people who have previously been missing, we may be told things we don't want to hear. But our solutions will be improved, despite not always pleasing everybody. And we will begin to develop conversations, understandings, and maybe even alliances that inform our work in constructive ways.

For example, the world's oldest and most powerful democracy, the United States, began as a distinctly noninclusive polity that recognized only the voices and votes of White, male landowners. Yet the United States is coming as a nation, however

---

Box 12.2   US Climate Action Network's Justice, Equity, Diversity, and Inclusion (JEDI) Statement

As our mission indicates, we are committed to fighting climate change in a just and equitable way.

We believe that we can accomplish far more together than alone. Our passion for a just and equitable world requires that we are inclusive, transparent and fair in all that we do, and that we act in solidarity and with appreciation for the work of our colleagues around the world, especially in the global south. We can only achieve our vision with full participation from a multitude of cultural and life experiences and communities.

Our commitment to building trust and alignments among our members requires that we build situations and relationships where all members are valued, heard, respected and empowered, so that our collective action is informed by a broad range of perspectives.

Our pursuit of justice, equity, diversity, and inclusion recognizes that the impacts of climate change disproportionately hurt the most vulnerable communities, including women, communities of color, income-challenged communities, and those who are not able to advocate for themselves.

Science and community input inform our work. We know that systems of racial and economic injustice must be dismantled and a new system created to bring justice to the marginalized communities that are most affected by climate change. We seek to address these historic inequities in our work.

We value justice, equity, democracy, inclusion, trust, relationships, optimism, wisdom, and perseverance. In order to fulfill our purpose and live our values, we aim to make our commitment to justice, diversity, equity and inclusion evident in our network structures, organizational structures, policies, board of directors, staff, mission, and vision. We are accountable to each other in our network, and transparent in our pursuit of equity. We embrace people of all backgrounds and seek to foster a culture where everyone is welcome, and historically marginalized voices are heard. We move collectively, taking leadership from frontline communities, marginalized communities, and communities of color. We act in accordance to the Environmental Justice Principles and the Jemez Principles for Democratic Organizing.

In summary, our commitment to justice, equity, diversity, and inclusion is essential to achieving our mission and vision.

Source: USCAN's Justice, Equity, Diversity, and Inclusion (JEDI) Statement, https://www.usclimatenetwork.org/justice_equity_diversity_and_inclusion

---

painfully and tumultuously, to recognize that strong democratic structures are diverse and inclusive, actively inviting and welcoming people who have not previously participated. Depending on where in the world a democratic initiative is being started, the reasons for past exclusion of participants may be based on race, gender, income, religion, language, and other factors. Inclusivity asks us to consider who is going to be affected by our decisions, who holds historical and relevant knowledge about our decisions, and whose interests could be served by our decisions and then seek to actively bring those voices into the process. Inclusivity is not consensus whereby any dissent derails a project, nor is it "information sessions" that tell stakeholders what's already been decided in their absence. Inclusivity lives in the untidy area between these extremes.

Reconciliation goes beyond active inclusion in decision-making structures and addresses past injustices. Canada's aboriginal Truth and Reconciliation Commission provides this definition:

> *Reconciliation is about establishing and maintaining a mutually respectful relationship between Aboriginal and non-Aboriginal peoples in this country. In order for that to happen, there has to be awareness of the past, an acknowledgement of the harm that has been inflicted, atonement for the causes, and action to change behaviour.*[6]

Inclusivity cannot be facilitated without the awareness, acknowledgment, and atonement elements of reconciliation. Here, we become active participants in a process that begins to address and heal past injustices through direct engagement and efforts to share power with affected groups and individuals. Reconciliation is often thought to be the work of governments, but it can be enacted at every level from federal governments to architecture firms to individuals, and it starts to be meaningful only when it is happening at all these levels.

Beyond Zero Goes Beyond the Building

Acting for climate justice starts with intent that leads to actions that spiral outward in a strengthening and expanding pattern of engagement, learning, sharing, and growth. Those who work in the building sector are used to sitting around large, well-populated tables, and we know that our projects are improved when stakeholders are active participants. Climate justice expands the size of that table and can bring benefits to a specific building that spill out well beyond the walls. Those who have not, in the past, been actively invited and heard must be full participants whose ideas, creativity, and community connections will complete a full complement of stakeholders.

Climate justice means making it our business to make a brilliant world for our brilliant buildings to stand in (box 12.3).

Box 12.3   A Manifesto for the Pivotal Decade
By Ann Edminster

Readers, whereas most of you are building professionals, you all *are members of the body politic. And although the bulk of solutions, prescriptions, and strategies presented herein are directed to you in the former capacity, I ask that you consider this proposition through the latter lens. For ultimately it is our government leaders who have the most power to effect change at the speed that is necessary to avert cataclysmic climate change, and it is we who must drive the critical decisions they will make that will determine our collective fate.*

* * *

In the words of Nancy Reagan, "Just say no." In this book and its antecedent, *The New Carbon Architecture*,[a] my colleagues have amply demonstrated that we can ill afford our addiction to embodied carbon, that its expenditure in buildings and infrastructure represents a staggering fraction of the overall climate impact—perhaps as much as 80 percent—within the first decade of life of newly built structures. Also well established by now is that we have a very short window—again, one decade (or less)—in which to avert devastating climate change. Thus every new construction project should be closely scrutinized through the macro lens—the lens focused on the years between now and 2030.

Furthermore, because buildings represent a very large wedge of the global greenhouse gas emissions pie, it inescapably follows that we have a moral obligation to provide unassailable justification for the embodied carbon expenditures entailed in any proposed construction projects.

These reflections led me inexorably to this conclusion:

We shouldn't be building ANYTHING. Full stop.

This assertion, from someone who makes her living in the building industry, may seem absurd—as well as being a completely untenable public stance. Growth is the loom on which the fabric of our western, capitalistic society is woven, and construction is one of the principal ways in which we grow.

Here in California, the state assigns municipal growth targets in the form of Regional Housing Needs Allocation goals—numbers of housing units that each city should provide to meet demand, parsed by income category. Yet within the state as a whole, and in many individual jurisdictions, we consistently build well beyond the demand for well-heeled demographic groups while utterly failing to meet the allocations for lower-income residents. In fact, the lower the income bracket, the more egregiously do we fall short of the Regional Housing Needs Allocation goals.[b] This phenomenon is far from unique to California; worldwide, the poorer you are, the more meager the supply of decent, affordable housing.

When affordable housing developers do manage, heroically, to scrape together sufficient funding to produce a paltry fraction of the grotesque shortfall of units needed for low-income households, their projects are often relegated to marginal sites, away from services, amenities, and public transit hubs. And perversely, when transportation is improved in a given locale, it seems to result, inevitably and tragically, in increases in housing costs in that locale.[c]

Perhaps—But Only When Justified
In my home territory, the San Francisco Bay Area, I have observed with increasing distress, year after year, burgeoning numbers of unhoused people drawn to the most inhospitable of shelters—their tents and shopping carts valiantly encrusting freeway interchanges like barnacles—making the most of the mean resources that the more fortunate have no desire to claim.

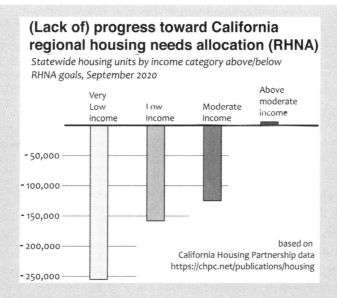

(Lack of) progress toward California regional housing needs allocation (RHNA)

Statewide housing units by income category above/below RHNA goals, September 2020

based on
California Housing Partnership data
https://chpc.net/publications/housing

I believe that everyone has a right to sound, clean, healthy, and affordable housing, including access to affordable transit modes—in other words, housing with dignity. And so, pre-COVID, I was prone to modify my proclamation above as follows:

We shouldn't build anything EXCEPT housing with dignity for those who lack it.

Now, though, we live in a different world; as a friend poignantly observed a few months into the pandemic, "I think our lifestyle just expired." It will be years before we fully understand all the fallout from this "expiration," but a few things are already crystallizing. The light has dawned for many large companies that their employees don't all need to congregate in downtown office towers for more than 40 hours every week. So even after the pandemic, hundreds of thousands (if not millions) of square feet of office space will languish, unwanted by the former occupants.

In recent decades, the "jobs–housing balance" has been a significant preoccupation of sustainability advocates, said balance being highly elusive because of a long history of poor land use and policy choices that hindsight reveals to have been misguided. To enumerate just a few:

- Sprawling, low-rise, low-density, car-centric suburbs devoid of significant work opportunities and lacking vibrant street life
- Disinvestment in city centers, fostering population flight to those very suburbs
- Evisceration of once-thriving transit systems
- Monoculture zoning, aptly dubbed "ghettoization" by New Urbanist architect and planner Andres Duany

So, irony of ironies, we now find ourselves with a wealth of unoccupied space (and more being built as I tap these keys) within the hearts of many of our cities—with a paucity of prospective tenants in the foreseeable future, yet where society's economic engines still churn. Indeed, precisely where, just one year ago, nary an affordable housing unit could be found, we now have an immense surfeit of housing

continued

Box 12.3 *continued*

potential—and with it, just maybe, an opportunity to make a positive adjustment in the jobs–housing balance and in the low-income housing shortage.

My Manifesto

Above I've set the table with an array of loosely related notions:

- We should be supremely parsimonious in our expenditures of embodied carbon.
- We should look upon (and respond to) housing "needs" with a jaundiced eye and with particular attention to *who* needs housing, of what kind, where, and at what price.
- We have a surplus of floor space in the hearts of our cities, where its value has plummeted since early 2020, with a very long recovery trajectory ahead.[d]
- The jobs–housing imbalance in our city centers needs to be corrected.

To these I add my grave misgivings, laid out in *The New Carbon Architecture*, about the disproportionately high climate impacts of building tall buildings (where by "tall" I mean above about fifteen or twenty stories) in our developed urban centers. All of which has led me to this manifesto:

We should focus our professional and civic efforts on using the existing building surplus in our urban centers to provide housing with dignity for those who lack it.

In this moment in U.S. history, I cannot believe that we need more buildings. What we need is to repurpose and refurbish buildings we already have, making them efficient, healthy, and habitable, at the lowest responsible carbon investment, for the members of our society we have so shamefully neglected.

Our Civic Responsibility: Exercising Local Control

We cannot achieve this transformation as private individuals; we need to work with government, impressing on our elected officials the imperative to cease and desist from spewing more greenhouse gases in the creation of more new structures—*unless and until* we can justify the expenditure of embodied carbon beyond the shadow of a doubt.

As a society, continuing to build without undertaking this carbon and social accounting is as shortsighted and self-destructive as compulsive gamblers spending their wages on lottery tickets. Worse, because the gambler has a chance to win.

One way we address addiction is by treating the addictive item as a controlled substance—so why not carbon? What if cities established a mechanism to control embodied carbon, allocating it according to a Climate and Equity Score (CES)?

A rough work plan for a city to implement this might proceed as follows.

1. Develop a 10-year and an annual embodied carbon (EC) budget based on the city's climate goals.
2. Allocate the EC budget across the city's operations, purchases, and development projects, including apportioning part of it to construction.
3. Enact policy establishing priority levels for different types of building projects, with housing for the unhoused being Priority 1, very low-income housing Priority 2, and so on.

4. Establish per-square-foot EC scales for multifamily housing and other building types of interest, bracketed by best practice (low) values for existing building refurbishment and representative (high) values for new construction.

5. Create a CES rubric for proposed projects, factoring in priority level, position on the EC scale, proximity to services and public transit, other applicable climate and equity criteria, and the city's available EC budget for the year and the decade.

6. Formalize the CES evaluation process (e.g., as part of the city's Objective Design Standards).[e]

This process would certainly encounter some political challenges—including the pace at which government operates—but the technical tasks are well within the reach of the green building and climate-concerned community. I encourage anyone who is interested in pursuing this approach to email me (ann@annedminster.com).

* * *

As building professionals we can create better, lower-impact buildings, even sequestering some carbon for a period of time. But as members of the body politic, we can do more—we can and *must* influence the institutions that ultimately control what is built (and where and how), to make existing buildings do a better job of meeting existing needs, and limit construction to only what is truly needed.

Without making a sharp pivot in our carbon-producing behaviors as a culture, we will unquestionably lose many things precious to us. Yet if we do make rapid and dramatic changes, we have a chance to preserve what remains of our planet's biodiversity and along with it our own safety, security, quality of life, and myriad sources of joy and inspiration.

Notes

a. Bruce King, *The New Carbon Architecture* (Gabriola, BC, Canada: New Society Publishers, 2017), for which Ann Edminster authored chapter 9, on optimal building height, and a couple of other bits.

b. California Housing Partnership, "New Data Underscores California's Failure to Meet Low-Income Housing Production Goals" September 24, 2020. https://chpc.net/new-data-underscores-californias-failure-to-meet-low-income-housing-production-goals-dashboard-series-3/

c. Emma G. Fitzsimmons, "Second Avenue Subway's Arrival Brings Fear that Rents Will Soar," *New York Times*, December 30, 2016. https://www.nytimes.com/2016/12/30/nyregion/second-avenue-subway-rent-worries.html

d. Joy Wiltermuth, "Distress Looms over U.S. Commercial Real Estate in 2021," *MarketWatch*, December 13, 2020. https://www.marketwatch.com/story/distress-looms-over-u-s-commercial-real-estate-in-2021-11607801514

e. In California, every local jurisdiction is required to establish Objective Design Standards, per SB35, which went into effect on January 1, 2018. https://leginfo.legislature.ca.gov/faces/billNavClient.xhtml?bill_id=201720180SB35

13. The Next Three Decades: Where Do We Go From Here?

The future ain't what it used to be.

—Yogi Berra

Everything we've presented in this book leads up to and begs the question, *How much?* Just how much carbon can we lock durably away into the fast-growing built environment? Predicting the future has always been a bit of a fool's errand, and as Yogi points out, that is truer than ever. In fact, it's even truer for us, now, than it was for Yogi a half century ago when he said that. We live in the age of hockey stick curves, some of which we've already shown: population growth, computing power, and global warming emissions, to name just the big ones. But here's the catch: If you're living in the inflection point of curves like these, you don't really know it. You will still predict the future based on past trends—based on your experience. Seems reasonable, and isn't. It's already trite to say that things are changing faster and faster, but we hardly know what to do about that. Who among us, 50 years ago, might have predicted Wi-Fi, Google, or the frightening rise of antidemocratic nationalist movements all over the world? Your life would be science fiction to your great grandmother.

Life on a hockey stick

You in the here and now can see left (into the past) with its nice, gentle curve, but not so clearly to the right (the future) with its sharp unpredictable uptick

A prescient or lucky few did successfully predict one or another trends, and some even made fortunes from doing so. Just as often, though, charismatic leaders in government or business made history simply by following the old dictum: *The best way to predict your future is to create it.*

So how much carbon can we lock durably away into buildings and infrastructure? You probably won't be shocked to hear that the answer is, in so many ways, "It depends!" We see anything from a pessimistic "zero" to a more optimistic "dozens of gigatons per year" in the growing body of literature on the subject. The safe bet is somewhere in between. We're pleased to see that knowledge about embodied carbon and its outsize time value has grown rapidly in just the past few years, yet that discussion has been almost entirely constrained to the "Getting to Zero" mentality—that is, to obsessing over how to do less harm. That's good, but it's inadequate to the challenge before us as a species and as an industry; we need to cease causing harm but concurrently begin repairing the damage we've done to the climate in the past century. Many are calling for a global, societal goal of removing a full teraton—a trillion tons—of carbon, which is roughly what we put up in the sky during the past 250 years of the Industrial Revolution. To do that we can and must find places to durably store it in the built environment—and in the rock, and in the soil, and any unharmful where else we can think of.

A lot, and soon.

We, a growing community of researchers, builders, architects, and engineers, are only beginning to formulate a comprehensive guess as to how much is possible. A number of studies focus either geographically (not globally), or by a particular industry (e.g., mass timber), or are limited by temporal, ecological, or economic system boundaries. Not a simple matter, and it isn't helped by the silo effect: To a great extent, the timber people aren't talking to the agricultural byproduct people, who aren't talking to the hemp or bamboo people, who aren't talking to the concrete people, who aren't talking to the biomaterial people. Furthermore, we rarely if ever pause to consider a wider view of the built environment or such seemingly irrelevant trends at play such as women's rights and early education for girls (clearly predominant in Paul Hawken's *Drawdown* as levers for climate healing); the hockey stick growth of robotics, machine learning, and artificial intelligence; or changes in farming, manufacturing, transportation, and governance—not to mention construction.

There are also many considerations here around time, many of which have been discussed earlier in this book. Primarily, though so very hard to change, is the ever-increasing need to hurry, the "time is money" mentality driving nearly every modern business. In a very great many ways, up and down every value chain, emissions can be reduced by simply allowing more time. That is of course impractical (or expensive) in most cases, but we also see examples where "hurry" is more a matter of habit than real need. Also, when do emissions occur, and how long-lasting are the gases? For example, some greenhouse gases such as methane start out far more potent but degrade to lower heat-trapping potency. Also, how quickly does a replacement forest (e.g., of softwoods or bamboo) or a field crop (e.g., wheat, rice, or hemp) regrow after harvest—and how much water, energy, and fertilizer is involved? Furthermore, we should note the durability (or ephemerality) of the stored carbon: How long can we expect the buildings or building materials to last? As one example, light wood framing, as predominates in North America, is highly vulnerable to fire, and the massive wildfires of Australia and the American West are likely to get worse for the foreseeable future; this complicates the notion of sequestering carbon in light frame construction. Likewise, hurricanes are becoming stronger and more destructive, which along with rising seas foretell enormous losses for the coastal communities in their paths. Finally, note that we ourselves are often the most destructive agent on buildings, as when we (almost exclusively in the more affluent parts of the world) decide we no longer like a building and rip it down to be hauled "away" and replaced with something brand new and more to our fancy. Or, sometimes, we just goof up and a new building soon collapses, rots, or burns.

To some extent, these concerns can all be addressed with good design and good construction. Given the chance, we can completely screw up a "modern" steel or concrete building, and conversely we can make a lovely, long-lasting structure entirely out of cellulosic materials, in both cases depending mostly on how closely we pay attention. Quality of design and construction, along with the many temporal effects previously described, render somewhat fuzzy any attempt to predict carbon storage in buildings. We note them and proceed with our estimate by more or less assuming that we'll continue with the same mix of good and bad design, good and bad construction, and a somewhat flighty approach to building and urban planning. In a medical emergency you think about triage before long-term care, and you do immediately what most urgently needs doing. Our premise here is that we are analogously doing climate triage, which tells us to store the carbon as soon as possible in as great a bulk as possible with as much durability as possible—but not fuss so much over 40- versus 60- versus 100-year life expectancy.

What follows is a brief summary of the material addressed in the book, with numbers that are both an assessment of what is possible and goals to aim for in the near term (5 years), mid-term (15 years), and long term (30+ years). We use the best, latest, and most scientifically defensible numbers we have found. This might not pass proper academic review, but neither is it some fantastical guess; we've spent a lot of time thinking about and researching this in concert with our many colleagues around the world. Some will question the goals we set out here because they might seem too ambitious, but in fact a case could be made on the evidence (albeit less confidently) to aim even higher. To remove a trillion tons of carbon in the next few generations will require everyone pulling on their oars with all they've got. This is climate emergency; we have to aim as high as we can, move as fast as we can. Fortunately, the powerful force of business is turning, finally, in the right direction.

> *Climate change is the defining crisis of our time, and as it becomes more imminent, our efforts to address it will become the epicenter of the next entrepreneurial revolution. . . . Climate tech investment increased from $418 million per year in 2013 to $16.3 billion in 2019, growing at five times the venture capital market rate over the last seven years. Heating and cooling systems, agriculture, raw materials, and manufacturing are all overdue for reinvention as we strive for a greener future, creating the promise of even more innovation on the horizon. The climate will also reshape residential and office construction, insurance, finance, and agriculture, in regard to where and how food is produced. Massive climate migrations have only just begun; tens or hundreds of millions of people will need to be resettled. Will we offer them shantytowns, or will we help them become settlers building a new, better world? Experience teaches us that the best opportunities come when businesses solve urgent problems for their customers. What could be more urgent than this? . . .*
>
> *For investors and entrepreneurs, there is a clear call to action: Work on stuff that matters, invest in solving problems, and make a real difference in people's lives. There's no doubt that climate tech is the new frontier in venture investing, and solving a global crisis will require the best of what we have to offer.*[1]

All numbers that follow are global, per annum, in gigatons of CO_2e (the 12 percent difference between long metric or short tons washes out at this rough level of precision), and approximate, based on multiple sources.

Concrete
We can substantially lower concrete's immense footprint right now with available technology and materials; it is mostly a matter of paying attention, disseminating climate-friendly practices, and ending the habit of routinely making overly strong (high-carbon) concrete. As regulations and standards evolve and adapt, we can do even better, mainly by using performance-based standards and design, and partially calcined clay and ground limestone in multiple forms of blended cements.

As carbon sequestering technologies mature and disseminate (e.g., CarbonCure, Solidia, Blue Planet, Minus Materials, CarbonBuilt), the prospect of true, widespread, carbon-positive (net storage) concrete is within a generation. An industry that now accounts for about 8 percent of global emissions could be actively sequestering quadrillions of tons of CO_2e annually.

Goals
Near term (next 5 years): Current 4 gigatons (billion tons) emissions reduced to 3.
Mid-term (next 15 years): Emissions reduced to net zero.
Long term (next 30 years): Net carbon storage of 2 gigatons.

Steel and Other Metals
Metals can get to a zero footprint, mostly by societal transition to a hydrogen economy (and also renewable energy–based hydrogen production) but probably no better. They have few if any substitutes, for now, so we have to get better at preserving and recycling them. These numbers are for the total of all metals in buildings.

Goals
Near term (next 5 years): Current 5 gigatons emissions reduced to 4.
Mid-term (next 15 years): Emissions reduced to 1 gigaton.
Long term (next 30 years): Net zero emissions.

Straw and Other Agricultural Byproducts
There are huge opportunities here, only just starting to ramp up in the marketplace (e.g., Ecococon). Two billion tons per year just of cereal straw is 1 billion tons of carbon that could be turned into sheathing, insulation, and structural "straw lumber." Many residues can be turned into pozzolans for concrete or biochar to hasten rejuvenation and the recapture of carbon by soils everywhere.

Goals
Near term (next 5 years): Net carbon storage of 1 gigaton.
Mid-term (next 15 years): Net carbon storage of 2 gigatons.
Long term (next 30 years): Net carbon storage of 3 gigatons.

Wood
Mass timber remains a poster child for carbon-storing architecture but presents a very complicated picture; carbon storage claims are not credible that fail to account

for changes to forests and forest carbon. (Still, for as long as we're cutting trees, it is far better to use them in buildings, in *any* way, rather than for disposable paper cups and shipping cartons.) There are plenty of places near softwood forests to make skillful use of mass timber, in its various forms, as a climate-positive alternative to steel and concrete structures, thus deserving some credit for supplanting carbon-intensive alternatives. That said, there are probably a lot more places, such as China and India where growth is so fast right now, or Africa and South America where it soon will be, where mass timber just doesn't make much sense. We argue: Let the remaining natural forests grow, let them become ever more (re)established and mature so that they can store carbon at ever faster rates, not to mention support the many other plants and creatures that we've been depriving of viable habitat. Our goals and estimates that follow express our tempering of the cheery "Wood is good!" marketing tropes with the larger picture of ongoing loss of forest carbon, loss of growing trees, and inefficiencies in manufacture.

Goals
Near term (next 5 years): Emissions reduced to net zero.
Mid-term (next 15 years): Net carbon storage of 1 gigaton.
Long term (next 30 years): Net carbon storage of 2 gigatons.

Hemp, Bamboo, and Other Purpose-Grown Crops
Hemp and bamboo provide us with very high-quality fiber much faster, on a per-acre per-year basis, than softwoods. All we need are the right glues (cheap, nontoxic, strong enough, durable) and some clever innovations (e.g., Bamcore, Just BioFiber, Rizome). Cork forests, somewhat abandoned as the wine industry turns to plastic stoppers, can expand to supply a host of building products as are already available.

Goals
Near term (next 5 years): Net carbon storage of 1 gigaton.
Mid-term (next 15 years): Net carbon storage of 2 gigatons.
Long term (next 30 years): Net carbon storage of 3 gigatons.

Plastics and Adhesives
At present the plastics, adhesives, and thousands of other petrochemical substances enmeshed in our lives and buildings are, for the most part, both wonderful and terrible. Wonderful because they impart so much ease, waterproofing, sanitation, insulation, and many other properties; terrible because they all, to one degree or another, present us with intractable chemical and solid waste disposal problems. If we

can collect and make effective use of the plastic clogging the oceans and landscapes, and if we can develop ecologically benign replacement materials—almost surely from microbes and captured emissions (e.g., Mango Materials, Novoloop)—that will be a huge benefit to the other species and to our descendants.

Goals
Near term (next 5 years): Emissions reduced to net zero.
Mid-term (next 15 years): Net carbon storage of 1 gigaton.
Long term (next 30 years): Net carbon storage of 2 gigatons.

Micro-Biomaterials (e.g., Fungi, Bacteria, Algae)

This is our wildcard that makes us wild with anticipation. We have only just begun to explore the possibilities for making building materials (e.g., Ecovative, BioMason, Prometheus Materials) in partnership with the innumerable microscopic life forms whom we are just starting to know. If present, nascent trends and research go well, we can be growing concrete, insulation, flooring, and who knows what else (not to mention artificial meat and various low-carbon foods, materials, and textiles as a growing population will need). Furthermore, it will probably be microbes of one or several sorts that will help us clean up the landfills and aquatic pollution now proliferating everywhere and help us separate the useful metals and polymers back out of the complex assemblies such as electronic waste—all while absorbing atmospheric carbon.

Goals
Near term (next 5 years): Net carbon storage of 1 gigaton.
Mid-term (next 15 years): Net carbon storage of 2 gigatons.
Long term (next 30 years): Net carbon storage of 3 gigatons.

A few facts about where we are right now: Human activity is currently emitting about 40 to 50 billion tons of greenhouse gases annually (yes, estimates vary that much), and it looks like at least 12 percent of that—about 6 billion tons—is from making cement, steel, and the other metals, fibers, glasses, and plastics that make up the built environment. Our friends at Architecture 2030 have already announced a goal for embodied carbon[2]: reduce emissions by 65 percent by 2030 and to zero by 2040. The U.S.-based Structural Engineering Institute[3] declared a goal for structural engineers, now being adopted by more and more firms, that states, "All structural engineers shall understand, reduce and ultimately eliminate embodied carbon in their projects by 2050." More broadly, we see polities at every scale, as well as professional firms and industry associations, adopt some version of the "net zero by 2050" goal. (It bears adding, here at the end of 2021, that the most recent IPCC report says that net zero by 2050 still isn't good enough; the world needs to get to zero faster in order to hold temperature rise to 1.5°C.)

With all that in mind, we propose a goal for carbon storage in the built environment: 15 by 50, very much within technological reach.

This is an ambitious but realistic goal. We hope and expect that it will prompt debate and discussion, all held within the improbability of accurately predicting *anything* about the industry in 10 years, much less 30. We might be aiming too high, but we might just as easily be aiming too low. Either way, the goal is clear: Build beyond zero. And it's not just a goal, as the case study in box 13.1 makes clear. This is something we can start to achieve today and just get better from there.

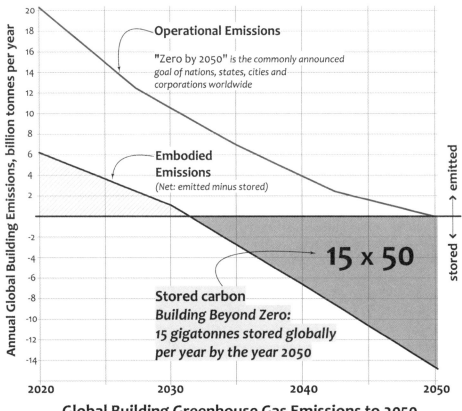

Global Building Greenhouse Gas Emissions to 2050
achievable goals

Box 13.1   Building Beyond Zero, for Real: Trent University's Forensic Science Building

If we're going to store 15 gigatons/year of CO_2 in buildings by 2050, we need to start today. Immediately. We need carbon-storing designs from licensed professionals and permits from our municipalities under existing code regimes. We need to use materials that exist today, and the buildings have to be assembled by our current workforce. Can we actually do this?

We know the answer is yes. We see evidence of buildings at all scales that use carbon-storing materials to an extent that *probably* results in net zero emissions from the materials and perhaps even net storage. But what if we want measured proof that we can build beyond zero today? A project would need to meet a few key criteria to stand as a real case study, including net zero carbon emissions from the building's operations over its lifetime and net carbon storage from its materials.

Trent University's Forensic Crime Scene Facility on its campus in Peterborough, Ontario, provides just such an example. Built in 2020, the building was intended to "combine Trent's renowned forensics leadership with its reputation as one of Canada's top environmental teaching and research universities."[a] In order to do more than claim vague green credentials, the Trent team (of which Chris was a member) chose to meet the International Living Future Institute's Zero Carbon Certification, the first worldwide Zero Carbon third-party certified standard. This program recognizes the growing interest and focus on a broad-based tool for highlighting super energy-efficient buildings, which are designed and operated to fully account for their carbon emission impacts. Although the International Living Future Institute Zero Carbon Certification includes accounting for the embodied carbon emissions of the building's materials, the university set an ambitious goal to far exceed the requirements of the program and aim to store more carbon in the building's materials than were emitted in manufacturing them. To do this, they used the Building Emissions Accounting for Materials tool, which uses Environmental Product Declaration data and carbon-storing metrics for all biogenic materials to give a comprehensive estimation of the material carbon footprint of the building.

The requirements of the Zero Carbon Certification demand a high-performance building enclosure, particularly for a building in a climate zone that includes both high heating and cooling demands at different times of the year. The way to achieve this level of performance is well understood in the industry, and the team used proven strategies for super-insulation, air tightness, and efficient, electrified mechanical equipment to reduce the building's energy demands to the absolute minimum. A roof-mounted solar array with 43 kilowatts of peak production capacity was installed to offset carbon emissions from any energy the building consumes from the local utility grid (which is relatively clean in Ontario).

Rather than stopping at net zero operational emissions, the team selected materials for the building by prioritizing the lowest-emitting materials in all parts of the building and specifying biogenic, carbon-storing materials wherever possible with the intent of far surpassing the 500 $kgCO_2e/m^2$ embodied carbon target required by the certification.

All the team's material selections were commercially available, though often from small manufacturers with limited distribution. This highlights a pinch-point for projects aiming to build beyond zero: More than the actual cost of carbon storing materials, it is the effort to find and source the best materials that can improve design and project management timelines and budgets. Here in 2021 the right stuff is out there and affordable, but it's not always obvious or easy to go out and get it.

continued

Box 13.1 *continued*

But this team did. After studying the carbon footprint of each material that would have been used in a baseline building with conventional construction for the area, the team addressed the main hotspots for material emissions, including foundation and slab floor, insulation, and cladding. Some of the key materials substitutions included:

- Sub-slab: Foam glass aggregate replaced gravel and foam insulation.
- Foundation walls and slab: Concrete with the highest possible cement replacement.
- Exterior walls: Hempcrete blocks and wood frame walls with hemp fiber and wood fiberboard insulation replaced concrete masonry units and foam insulation.
- Interior walls: Hemp fiber insulation replaced mineral wool.
- Roof insulation: Cellulose insulation replaced either mineral wool or spray foam.
- Cladding: Charred wood siding from a local mill replaced some of the metal siding.

These straightforward material choices had a dramatic impact on the carbon footprint of the building. The baseline building would have just squeaked under the carbon footprint intensity required by the Zero Carbon Certification, at 498 $kgCO_2e/m^2$ (figure 13.3).

Trent University Forensic Building   Embodied Carbon

Base Case

Part of Building	Embodied Carbon (kg. CO2e)
Footings & slabs	29,516
Foundation walls	13,108
Exterior walls	123,900
Exterior cladding	11,327
Windows & doors	3,378
Interior walls	6,968
Floors	858
Ceilings	963
Roof	21,138
Net total	211,156
Carbon intensity kg. CO2e/m³	498

As Built

Part of Building	Embodied Carbon (kg. CO2e)
Footings & slabs	13,503
Foundation walls	9,866
Exterior walls	- 6,967
Exterior cladding	6,263
Windows & doors	3,378
Interior walls	- 4,900
Floors	- 15
Ceilings	227
Roof	4,130
Net total	25,484
Carbon intensity kg. CO2e/m²	60

As Built including lumber

Part of Building	Embodied Carbon (kg. CO2e)
Footings & slabs	13,503
Foundation walls	1,128
Exterior walls	- 18,043
Exterior cladding	2,861
Windows & doors	3,378
Interior walls	- 3,580
Floors	- 679
Ceilings	227
Roof	- 5,624
Net total	- 6,829
Carbon intensity kg. CO2e/m²	- 16

carbon reduction   *carbon storage*

FIGURE 13.3. **Net carbon storage.** More than 200 tonnes of emissions were eliminated from the base case building through material substitution, getting this building close to zero embodied emissions without counting on carbon storage in wood products and moving into net storage if a portion of the wood sequestration is included.

Two sets of results were generated for the as-built version, one that ignores the carbon storage in all timber products (see chapter 6 for a discussion of the complexities of accounting for carbon storage in timber products) and the other that recognizes this storage.

These results indicate that, for a building of this size and type, it is possible to get the carbon footprint of a building very close to zero without relying on storage from timber products. The result of 60 kgCO$_2$e/m^2 is a 88 percent reduction from the baseline building, all but eliminating the material emissions and getting close to zero.

Counting the carbon storage of timber products used in the building, the results arrive in net carbon storage territory at –16 kgCO$_2$/m^2. The project team made every effort to ensure that timber products were sourced from local and sustainably harvested forests, as this is currently the best proxy for carbon storage potential in timber products.

As we pointed out in Chapter 4, concrete stands out as the material most in need of attention in this design (as is so often the case). By reducing the amount of concrete needed and the specifications of lower-carbon concrete mixes, the team was able to get the footprint of the concrete down from 32 tonnes to 14 tonnes. If the remainder of that carbon footprint were to disappear—or better yet, become carbon storing—then much deeper levels of carbon storage could be achieved.

FIGURE 13.4. **Hempcrete blocks add carbon storage.** The innovative product from Just Biofiber combines insulation and structure and provides a significant amount of the building's carbon storage.

FIGURE 13.5. **Net carbon storage doesn't look so different.** The completed building doesn't necessarily look so different from other buildings on campus, but the climate impact is radically different: It doesn't really have one!

continued

Box 13.1 *continued*

The building was designed and built with a cost premium, most of which resides in the large solar array needed to meet net zero operational performance. The cost to upgrade the materials to achieve net carbon storage was less than the cost of the solar array. As energy grids become less carbon intensive, this points to the cost-efficiency of reducing emissions at the material level where building owners can absorb it and to collectively address the move to more renewable energy grid sources.

Trent Forensic Crime Scene Facility is just one building. The 200 tonnes of emissions averted—and perhaps 16 tonnes stored—is the smallest of drops in the biggest of buckets. But as an example of what we can achieve if we start measuring material emissions and taking storage seriously, starting right now with the skills and materials we already have, it suggests that 15 by 50 is quite achievable.

Note

a. "New Forensics Crime Scene Facility at Trent University an Environmental and Academic First for Canada," Trent University, February 14, 2020. https://www.trentu.ca/news/story/26383

14. What's Next? *Wow. Just Wow.*

You can short civilization if you want. Not a bad bet really. But no one to pay you if you win. Whereas if you go long on civilization, and civilization (therefore) survives, you win big. So the smart move is to go long.

—Kim Stanley Robinson, *The Ministry for the Future*

Perhaps like us, you have once or twice found yourself being asked, or asking a friend or colleague, something along the lines of "*Is it too late? Can we still fix this?*" These questions usually elicit a shrug of the shoulders, or some peppy, can-do optimism, or else glum foreboding and despair. On any given day, we will feel any and all of these things, all while wondering more than a little bit about the world our children will inherit. If you never experience rage, despair, and grief, you haven't been paying attention or else have become thoroughly numbed. If you never experience joy and hope, you haven't noticed that, as we have mentioned, human beings (not to mention the stunning tapestry of life of which we are but part) can be cool. Sometimes really, really cool.

But here's the thing: We don't know. You don't know and I don't know what will be. Prognostication is perpetually perilous, at least if you treat it as other than speculation. This has always been the condition of life, of course—the dinosaurs didn't see that asteroid coming, no one expected the *Titanic* to sink on its maiden voyage, almost no one in 1985 would have predicted the dissolution of the mighty Soviet Union, and *almost* no one expected the attack on the United States on 9/11, nor the COVID-19 pandemic.

243

But it's not just the bad stuff that catches us by surprise. Few could imagine, 60 years ago, save for a few sci-fi propeller-heads, a man walking on the moon, the World Wide Web, Google, smartphones, or the end of polio. Nor, for that matter, did the wealthiest people in the world imagine, up until 120 or so years ago, that luxuries unavailable to them at any price would become common all over the world. Indoor plumbing, telephones, electric lighting, motorized individual mobility, the power grid, air travel, refrigeration, and Wi-Fi access have each and all massively transformed our lives. There is still plenty of work to be done making those services available to everyone everywhere, for sure, but it is astonishing to consider how quickly they have evolved and become both ubiquitous and taken for granted. We don't even notice any more, most of us, as we try to keep our balance on these many wild hockey stick curves of change rocketing up around us. Your life would indeed be science fiction to your great grandmother, and it would maybe have been like science fiction to you yourself 30 years ago.

You don't know and I don't know what will be. This is profoundly frightening, in that every generation until modern ones has always had a pretty clear sense of what the world would be like for their children. It might have been a pretty tough world, and it did get disrupted by the occasional war, volcano, or plague, but humans could generally know what to expect. You and I don't, no matter how well educated, traveled, and imaginative we may be. We don't know what's next, not even in five years, much less thirty or a hundred, and it's freaking us out on top of everything else that's freaking us out.

At the same time, we don't know what's next, and that's the best part—it's a wide-open field ahead. That doesn't let us off the hook to try and move things in the right direction, but it does allow some relaxation and even humor in the face of our profound not knowing.

One of the most common themes among future predictors and science fiction writers is artificial intelligence; sooner or later, it seems, our machines will become as smart as we are, by whatever definition of "smart" you like. The future predictors then speculate with confidence that the machines will keep on getting smarter at an ever-faster pace (another hockey stick curve!) and soon evolve far beyond us. Perhaps that is so, and it certainly makes for lots of great sci-fi both dark (*Terminator*, *Ex Machina*) and positive (*Star Trek*). But here's an interesting implication: We can imagine an AI that is so extremely smart that, when we ask it what to do to restore climate stability, it thinks for all of a few microseconds and then prints out a list of the ten or twenty things humanity needs to do. *Problem solved!*

Except: We already have that list. There is plenty of interesting and disruptive technology yet to come, for sure, but we largely have, already, the tech we need to restore the climate. We know how to grow food, transport and shelter ourselves, manage water and wastes, and harvest renewable energy in a way that doesn't ravage the ecosystems around us or the poor among us. We already have the list. What we don't have is the will to act, the maturity to respect and honor one another. A difficult situation, you might say.

> *We've never faced a challenge such as the climate crisis before. So we don't know what could happen if we took action—and that is also very hopeful. . . . If the media started treating the climate crisis like a crisis, that could change everything overnight.*
>
> —Greta Thunberg

"Getting to zero," to repeat one more time, is a lousy goal, or anyway incomplete. You make a mess, you clean it up, as my mother would say. You don't just stop messing, you also start cleaning. We've made a hell of a mess, and so far we haven't done much to even acknowledge it, much less clean it up. We dither and delay, posture and politicize, making it ever harder to act effectively. It seems pretty daunting, with some heavy odds stacked against us. We are human beings, and all too often we are stupid and short sighted, vicious and cruel. But sometimes, just sometimes, we can—not to boast—be really cool. It's a world of possibility.

> *One of the things that's long been curious about this crisis is that the amateurs and newcomers tend to be more alarmist and defeatist than the insiders and experts. What the climate journalist Emily Atkin calls "first-time climate dudes" put forth long, breathless magazine articles, bestselling books and films announcing that it's too late and we're doomed, which is another way to say we don't have to do a damned thing, which is a way to undermine the people who are doing those things and those who might be moved to do them. . . . The climate scientist Michael Mann takes these people on—he calls them inactivists and doomists—in his recent book "The New Climate Wars," which describes the defeatism that has succeeded outright climate denial as the great obstacle to addressing the crisis. He echoes what Carbon Tracker asserted, writing: "The solution is already here. We just need to deploy it rapidly and at a massive scale. It all comes down to political will and economic incentives." . . . The visionary organizer adrienne maree brown wrote not long ago: "I*

believe that all organizing is science fiction—that we are shaping the future we long for and have not yet experienced. I believe that we are in an imagination battle."

—Rebecca Solnit[1]

The story of carbon continues, and it is you. You and the allies you find and who find you. Do what you can, wherever you are, with what you have. And then imagine even beyond that. Imagine building beyond zero to a world that works for everyone.

All things are become new.

FIGURE 14.1. Pilgrim Holiness Church, Arthur, Nebraska. One of the oldest extant straw bale buildings in the world (1925).

Endnotes

Introduction

1. Paul Hawken, ed., *Drawdown: The Most Comprehensive Plan Ever Proposed to Reverse Global Warming* (New York: Penguin Books), April 18, 2017.

Chapter 1

1. Jerry Brown and Stewart Brand, "The Origins of 'Planetary Realism' and 'Whole Earth' Thinking", *Noema Magazine*, February 9, 2021, www.noemamag.com

Chapter 3

1. Liz Marshall and Alexia Kelly, "The Time Value of Carbon and Carbon Storage: Clarifying the Terms and the Policy Implications of the Debate," World Resources Institute, November 2010, MPRA paper no. 27326.

Chapter 4

1. International Energy Agency, "Iron and Steel Technology Roadmap," Technology report, October 2020. https://www.iea.org/reports/iron-and-steel-technology-roadmap

2. Caitlin Swalec and Christine Shearer, "Pedal to the Metal: No Time to Delay Decarbonizing the Global Steel Sector," *Global Energy Monitor*, 2021. https://globalenergymonitor.org/report/pedal-to-the-metal-no-time-for-delay-in-decarbonizing-global-steel-sector/

3. Jason Deign, Greentech Media, December 2008, "The soaring hype surrounding green hydrogen reached new heights this week, as a seven-company-strong consortium unveiled plans for a fiftyfold scale-up in production capacity by 2026. ACWA Power, CWP Renewables, Envision, Iberdrola, Ørsted, Snam, and Yara launched a coalition called the Green Hydrogen Catapult with the aim of deploying 25 gigawatts of renewable-based hydrogen production capacity

by 2026. The coalition, which is linked to the United Nations Framework Convention on Climate Change's Race to Zero campaign, is also hoping to halve the cost of green hydrogen production, cutting it to less than $2 per kilogram. A January 2020 report from industry group the Hydrogen Council suggested this price could be a tipping point for green hydrogen and derivatives such as ammonia to become 'the energy source of choice across multiple sectors,' according to a Race to Zero press release." 2020. https://www.greentechmedia.com/articles/read/coalition-aims-for-25-gw-of-green-hydrogen-by-2026?utm_medium=email&utm_source=Daily&utm_campaign=GTMDaily

4. Thomas Koch Blank, "Green Steel: A Multi-Billion Dollar Opportunity," Rocky Mountain Institute, September 29, 2020. https://rmi.org/green-steel-a-multi-billion-dollar-opportunity/

5. Swalec and Shearer, "Pedal to the Metal," p. 11.

6. World Green Building Council, "Bringing Embodied Carbon Upfront," n.d. https://www.worldgbc.org/embodied-carbon

Chapter 5

1. Modern concrete has yet to prove better than the much-lauded Roman concrete that lives on so well today after thousands of years. But that is because the Romans were lucky and smart, had plenty of cheap labor (slaves), and didn't put rustable iron or too much water in the concrete.

2. Global Cement and Concrete Association, https://gccassociation.org/climate-ambition/

3. See Karen L. Scrivener, Vanderley M. John, Ellis M. Gartner, *Eco-Efficient Cements: Potential, Economically Viable Solutions for a Low-CO₂ Cement-Based Materials Industry*, Paris, 2016. (For those who want more, this is an excellent, comprehensive and highly recommended resource.)

4. Duncan Brack/ Chatham House, *The Impacts of the Demand for Woody Biomass for Power and Heat on Climate and Forests*, The Royal Institute of International Affairs, 2017.

5. Scrivener et al., *Eco-Efficient Cements*.

6. Far better, we submit, than putting it in ponds that sometimes fail or, worse, just letting it fly into the sky for all to breathe. Some also contend that the presence of fly ash in concrete presents a health hazard, but all the evidence we've seen suggests otherwise; it is not much different from ordinary concrete. For more on fly ash, and pozzolans in general, see Bruce King, *Making Better Concrete*, Green Building Press, 2005.

7. See also Karen L. Scrivener, Vanderley M. John, and Ellis M. Gartner, "Eco-Efficient Cements: Potential Economically Viable Solutions for a Low-CO₂ Cement-Based Materials Industry," *Cement and Concrete Research*, 114, 2018.

8. Just to avoid any confusion: The abbreviation "AAC" is also used in this industry to denote *autoclaved, aerated concrete,* a very lightweight insulating concrete made by mixing powdered aluminum with portland cement and sand. The aluminum particles react with the cement in the presence of water to develop tiny air bubbles, resulting in a solid foam product. There have been various efforts to market such insulating blocks, but we don't treat this type

of AAC further here because the enormous carbon footprint of aluminum renders the concept dubious at best from an embodied carbon and climate perspective.

9. Minimum Cementitious Materials Content in Specifications ACI 329.1T-18 TechNote, American Concrete Institute, 2018.

10. As we write this, Bruce was just asked to review a mix design for a new house nearby (he is still a practicing engineer). The supplier showed 5,500-psi concrete, for no apparent reason, when 2,500 was all that was needed or specified. Bruce rejected their proposal, and they came back with a 2,500-psi mix that will save, just for one house, hundreds of pounds of emissions. But he had to ask in order for that to happen.

11. Section II: Marin County Code Chapter 19.07 Added to Marin County Code, Title 19. https://www.marincounty.org/-/media/files/departments/cd/planning/sustainability/low-carbon-concrete/12172019-update/low-carbon-concrete-code.pdf?la=en

12. County of Marin, "Low-Carbon Concrete Requirements." https://www.marincounty.org/depts/cd/divisions/sustainability/low-carbon-concrete

13. Substantial global carbon uptake by cement carbonation, multiple authors, *Nature Geoscience*, Nov. 2016.

Chapter 6

1. Galina Churkina, Alan Organschi, Christopher P. O. Reyer, Andrew Ruff, Kira Vinke, Zhu Liu, Barbara K. Reck, T. E. Graedel, and Hans Joachim Schellnhuber, "Buildings as a Global Carbon Sink," *Nature Sustainability*, https://doi.org/10.1038/s41893-019-0462-4

2. Food and Agriculture Organization of the United Nations, *World Food and Agriculture 2017 Statistical Pocketbook* 2018, Rome, Italy: Food & Agriculture Organization, 2019.

3. "Evaluation of the Environmental Benefits of the BamCore Prime Wall System: A Screening-Level Environmental Life Cycle Assessment with Comparisons to Wood Framing and SIPs," Quantis International, 2017.

4. Qiu, H., Xu, J., He, Z., Long, L., and Yue, X., "Bamboo as an Emerging Source of Raw Material for Household and Building Products," *BioRes*, 2019. 14(2), 2465–2467.

Chapter 7

1. Scott Carpenter, "Why the Oil Industry's $400 Billion Bet on Plastics Could Backfire," *Forbes*, September 5, 2020. https://www.forbes.com/sites/scottcarpenter/2020/09/05/why-the-oil-industrys-400-billion-bet-on-plastics-could-backfire/?sh=61d8adbb43fe

2. Judith Enck, president of Beyond Plastics, interviewed January 22, 2021 by Bill McKibbon in *The New Yorker*. https://www.newyorker.com/news/annals-of-a-warming-planet/to-counter-climate-change-we-need-to-stop-burning-things

3. Beth Gardiner, "The Plastics Pipeline: A Surge of New Production Is on the Way," *YaleEnvironment360*, December 19, 2019.

4. Lauren Phipps, "Algae Is the Plant-Based, Nontoxic Alternative to Plastic," April 7, 2020, BrinkNews.com.https://www.brinknews.com/algae-is-the-plant-based-nontoxic-alternative-to-plastic-sustainability-environment-climate/

5. Heather Clancy, "What's My Carbon Date?," *Verge Weekly*, February 17, 2021, www.green biz.com

6. Dewey Johnson and Robin Waters, "Plastics Sustainability: Risks and Strategy Implications," IHS Markit, May 9, 2019. https://ihsmarkit.com/research-analysis/plastics-sustainabil ity-risks-and-strategy-implications.html

7. Gardiner, "The Plastics Pipeline."

Chapter 8

1. M. Adams, V. Burrows, and S. Richardson, "Bringing Embodied Carbon Upfront," World Green Building Council, 2019. https://www.worldgbc.org/sites/default/files/WorldGBC _Bringing_Embodied_Carbon_Upfront.pdf

2. *LETI Embodied Carbon Primer*, London Energy Transformation Initiative, 2020. https:// www.leti.london/ecp

3. M. Aragonès et al., "Zero Emission Construction Sites, Status 2019," Bellona, 2019. https://bellona.org/publication/zero-emission-construction-sites-status-2019

4. Ibid.

5. Suncar, "Advantages of Electric Excavators." https://www.suncar-hk.com/en/electric-exca vators/advantages

6. "The Burden of Occupational Cancer in Great Britain," Imperial College London, the Institute of Environment and Health, the Health and Safety Laboratory, and the Institute of Occupational Medicine for the Health and Safety Executive, 2010. https://www.hse.gov.uk /research/rrpdf/rr800.pdf

7. Aragonès et al., "Zero Emission Construction Sites, Status 2019."

8. Charlynn Burd, Michael Burrows, and Brian McKenzie, "Travel Time to Work in the United States: 2019," American Community Survey Reports, 2021. https://www.census.gov /content/dam/Census/library/publications/2021/acs/acs-47.pdf

9. "2019 Permanent Modular Construction Report," Modular Building Institute, 2019. http://www.modular.org/HtmlPage.aspx?name=analysis

Chapter 9

1. Kate Stephenson, "Breaking Down Gender Bias in the Construction Industry," Green Building Advisor, 2017. https://www.greenbuildingadvisor.com/article/breaking-down-gender -bias-in-the-construction-industry

Chapter 10

1. Martin Geissdoerfer, Paulo Savaget, Nancy M. P. Bocken, and Erik Jan Hultink, "The Circular Economy—A New Sustainability Paradigm?," *Journal of Cleaner Production* 143 (2017): 757–68. doi:10.1016/j.jclepro.2016.12.048

2. Carla Candeias, Paula Ávila, Patrícia Coelho, and João P. Teixeira, "Mining Activities: Health Impacts," in *Encyclopedia of Environmental Health*, 2nd ed. (Amsterdam: Elsevier, 2019), 415–35. doi:10.1016/B978-0-12-409548-9.11056-5

Chapter 11

1. Jerry Brown and Stewart Brand, "The Origins of 'Planetary Realism' and 'Whole Earth' Thinking," *Noema*, February 9, 2021. https://www.noemamag.com/the-origins-of-planetary-realism-and-whole-earth-thinking/

2. Susan Sontag, *At the Same Time: Essays and Speeches*, ed. Paolo Dilonardo and Anne Jump (New York: Farrar, Straus and Giroux, 2007).

3. Alvin Toffler, *Power Shift* (New York: Bantam Books, 1990). (Note the pre-internet date, yet the comment still holds true!)

4. World Bank, "State and Trends of Carbon Pricing 2020," May 2020, World Bank, Washington, DC. https://openknowledge.worldbank.org/bitstream/handle/10986/33809/9781464815867.pdf?sequence=4&isAllowed=y

5. Climate Leadership Council, a collection of U.S. businesspeople and former Republican federal officials including James Baker III, Martin Feldstein, Henry Paulson Jr., George Shultz, Thomas Stephenson, and Rob Walton, 2017. https://www.clcouncil.org/wp-content/uploads/2017/02/TheConservativeCaseforCarbonDividends.pdf

6. For a comprehensive look at carbon retrieval pathways, see Paul Hawken (Ed.), *Drawdown: The Most Comprehensive Plan Ever Proposed to Reverse Global Warming* (New York: Penguin Books, 2017).

7. Adam Baylin-Stern and Niels Berghout, "Is Carbon Capture Too Expensive?," International Energy Agency. https://www.iea.org/commentaries/is-carbon-capture-too-expensive

8. Richard Conniff, "Why Green Groups Are Split on Subsidizing Carbon Capture Technology," *Yale Environment 360*, April 9, 2018. https://e360.yale.edu/features/why-green-groups-are-split-on-subsidizing-carbon-capture-technology

9. David Sandalow, Roger Aines, Julio Friedmann, Colin McCormick, and Sean McCoy, "Carbon Dioxide Utilization ICEF Roadmap 1.0," November 2017.

10. "A Roadmap for the Global Implementation of Carbon Utilization Technologies," The Global CO_2 Initiative (GCI) and CO_2 Sciences, November 2016.

11. Mike Scott, "Here's How Hydrogen Could Clean Up the World's Dirtiest Industries," *Forbes*, April 6, 2020. www.forbes.com/sites/mikescott/2020/04/06/hydrogen-could-be-the-clean-fuel-of-the-future-for-the-dirtiest-industries/?sh=784d7404988d

12. John Parnell, "2020: The Year of Green Hydrogen in 10 Stories," Greentech Media, December 29, 2020. www.greentechmedia.com/articles/read/2020-the-year-of-green-hydrogen-in-10 stories?utm_medium=email&utm_source=Daily&utm_campaign=GTMDaily

13. Patrick Molloy, "Run on Less with Hydrogen Fuel Cells," Rocky Mountain Institute, October 2, 2019. rmi.org/run-on-less-with-hydrogen-fuel-cells/

14. https://www.marincounty.org/-/media/files/departments/cd/planning/sustainability/low-carbon-concrete/12172019-update/low-carbon-concrete-code.pdf?la=en

15. Jennifer O'Connor and Matt Bowick, "Reducing Embodied Environmental Impacts of Buildings: Policy Options and Technical Infrastructure," Athena Sustainable Materials In-

stitute, December 2019. http://www.athenasmi.org/wp-content/uploads/2019/12/Policy_white _paper_December_2019.pdf

16. Brown and Brand, "The Origins of 'Planetary Realism.'"

Chapter 12

1. There are many variations on the definition for the precautionary principle. Here's a simple one: "Where there are threats of serious or irreversible damage, lack of full scientific certainty shall not be used as a reason for postponing cost-effective measures to prevent environmental degradation" (UNEP 1992). Engineers routinely apply the same concept in the design of buildings and call it Factor of Safety; the bigger the risk, the bigger the safety factor we use. If a few lives are at risk, we're careful; if hundreds or thousands of lives are at risk, we are very, very careful. Hard as it may be for us to grasp, in our climate emergency everybody is at risk.

2. Benjamin Franta, "On Its 100th Birthday in 1959, Edward Teller Warned the Oil Industry about Global Warming," *The Guardian*, January 1, 2018. https://www.theguardian.com/environment/climate-consensus-97-per-cent/2018/jan/01/on-its-hundredth-birthday-in-1959-edward-teller-warned-the-oil-industry-about-global-warming

3. Global Justice Now, "The Case for Climate Justice," 2020. https://www.globaljustice.org.uk/resource/case-climate-justice-illustrated-booklet/

4. D. J. Beale, A. V. Karpe, and W. Ahmed, "Beyond Metabolomics: A Review of Multi-Omics-Based Approaches," *Microbial Metabolomics*, ed. D. Beale, K. Kouremenos, and E. Palombo (Cham, Switzerland: Springer, 2016). https://doi.org/10.1007/978-3-319-46326-1_10

5. J. Curl, *For All the People* (Oakland, CA: PM Press, 2012).

6. The Truth and Reconciliation Commission of Canada, "Honouring the Truth, Reconciling for the Future: Summary of the Final Report of the Truth and Reconciliation Commission of Canada," 2015, p. 6. publications.gc.ca/pub?id=9.800288&sl=0

Chapter 13

1. Tim O'Reilly, "Climate Change Will Reshape Silicon Valley as We Know It," Wired, March 8, 2021. https://www.wired.com/story/climate-change-silicon-valley/

2. Architecture 2030, "The 2030 Challenge for Embodied Carbon." https://architecture2030.org/2030_challenges/embodied/

3. Structural Engineering Institute of the American Society of Civil Engineers. https://se2050.org

Chapter 14

1. Rebecca Solnit, "Dare We Hope? Here's My Cautious Case for Climate Optimism," *The Guardian*, May 1, 2021.

Contributors

Lola Ben-Alon is an assistant professor at Columbia Graduate School of Architecture, Planning and Preservation, where she directs the Building Science and Technology curriculum. She specializes in socially and environmentally sustainable building practices and natural building materials. Ben-Alon received her PhD from the School of Architecture at Carnegie Mellon University. She holds a BS in structural engineering and MS in construction management from the Technion, Israel Institute of Technology. At the Technion, Ben-Alon co-founded *art.espionage*, the Experimental Art and Architecture Lab. She also served as a curator and content developer at the Madatech, Israel National Museum of Science, Technology, and Space.

Pamela Conrad is a principal at CMG Landscape Architecture and founder of Climate Positive Design. Conrad focuses on climate mitigation and resilient design in the public realm. Her work is informed by a background in plant science and a passion for the environment rooted in growing up on a farm. She is an American Society of Landscape Architects Climate Action Committee member, 2018–2019 Landscape Architecture Foundation Fellow for Innovation and Leadership, and recipient of the 2019 NCRE Women of Influence Award. She has published numerous works and presented internationally for developing the landscape carbon calculator Pathfinder app and Climate Positive Design Challenge.

Gayatri Datar is the co-founder and CEO of EarthEnable, a social enterprise that aims to make living conditions healthier for the world's poor by using sustainable materials. Before founding EarthEnable, she worked or consulted for Dalberg Global Development Advisors, the World Bank, the Bill and Melinda Gates Foundation, the International Finance Corporation, and grassroots nongovernment organizations in India, Namibia, Nicaragua, Albania, and the United States. She holds a BA in economics, an MPA/ID from Harvard, and an MBA from Stanford, where she was an Arjay Miller Scholar. She is an Echoing Green Fellow and a Forbes 30 Under 30 recipient.

Ann Edminster is a California-based green building consultant with a national practice, laser-focused on decarbonizing homes and communities. Trained as an architect, she facilitates design teams, coaches, other building practitioners, works on applied research projects, teaches, develops education programs, and rabble-rouses in the climate space in her spare time. More than a quarter-century ago, she focused her master's thesis on embodied carbon (a wee bit ahead of the times), and a dozen years ago wrote the first book on zero energy homes—somewhat more timely, to be sure, but she's still waiting for the times to catch up.

Lisa Morey is owner and founder of Colorado Earth LLC based in Golden, Colorado. Colorado Earth manufactures both adobe bricks and compressed earth blocks, known as Ecoblox. The company also provides full design, engineering, and construction services that focus on high-performance buildings and materials. While living and practicing in New Zealand for 5 years, Lisa learned to appreciate the benefits of earthen mass walls, including fireproof, moldproof, energy-efficient, low-maintenance, and superior acoustic performance. Lisa is a professional engineer and architectural designer and is motivated to see earthen masonry become more used throughout the United States.

Wil V. Srubar III is an associate professor of architectural engineering and materials science at the University of Colorado Boulder, where he leads the Living Materials Laboratory. Dr. Srubar holds a PhD in structural engineering and materials science from Stanford University. His academic research integrates biology, polymer science, and cement chemistry to create low-carbon and carbon-storing biomimetic, living material technologies for the built environment and explores how buildings can be transformed into carbon sinks. He is also a co-founder of Minus Materials,

Prometheus Materials, and Aureus Earth. His work has been highlighted in the *Washington Post* and the *New York Times*.

Larry Strain is a founding principal of Siegel & Strain Architects in Emeryville, California, known for community projects and innovative sustainable design and research. Larry has served on the boards of the Northern California Chapter of the U.S. Green Building Council, the Ecological Building Network, and the Carbon Leadership Forum (CLF) and was on the research team for CLF's Embodied Carbon Benchmarking project. Larry has been writing and speaking on materials, carbon, and reusing buildings for more than 20 years, and for the last 10 years he has focused on reducing the total carbon footprint of the built environment.

Authors

Bruce King is the founder of the Ecological Building Network (EBNet) and a registered engineer with 35 years of worldwide experience in structural engineering and construction. He has organized three international conferences on ecological building and is the founder of BuildWell Source, a user-based collection of low-carbon materials knowledge, and of the BuildWell Symposia. He has published four previous books.

Chris Magwood is currently the executive director of The Endeavour Centre, a not-for-profit sustainable building school in Peterborough, Ontario. He has written seven books. He leads the Builders for Climate Action project, where he is helping create tools, research, and resources to support practitioners and policy makers in making zero carbon buildings.